The Bridge of Time

The Bridge of Time

A View of the Israeli People

James E. Myers

South Brunswick and New York: A. S. Barnes and Company
London: Thomas Yoseloff Ltd

© 1973 by James E. Myers

A. S. Barnes and Co., Inc.
Cranbury, New Jersey 08512

Thomas Yoseloff Ltd
108 New Bond Street
London W1Y OQX, England

Library of Congress Cataloging in Publication Data

Myers, James E.
    The bridge of time.
    1. Israel—Description and travel.   2. National characteristics, Israeli. I. Title.
DS107.4.M93   915.694'06'924   73-154
ISBN 0-498-01319-7

PRINTED IN THE UNITED STATES OF AMERICA

To Edith, my understanding wife.

The Bridge of Time

Introduction

After having written extensively of the 1967 Israel-Arab war, the so-called Six Day War, and after having lectured about that stunning fight and the people who fought it, the writer was astonished at how vague the knowledge of Americans was about the Israeli Jew, the common folk in that land. Few could locate in their minds just where and how distant the United States was from Israel itself! And most had the oddest stereotypical notions, mere fancies, really, of the people. They saw them as heroic soldiers fighting from tanks, or as indomitable infantrymen, or as sweating farmers and laborers draining swamps to grow oranges in reclaimed land, or as scarred and praying Jews perennially swaying at the Western Wall. And some there were who saw only prototype fascist Jews doing to Arabs what Nazis had done to them.

Such misconceptions were at most dangerous to knowledge and understanding, at the least, mischievous. It came to seem that an understanding of the ordinary Jew comprising the folk of Israel, his place in the Middle East, was critical if the Western world were to glimpse a direction its own world might in future be forced to take.

Just how could the life and thoughts of a mere two-and-a-half million Israeli Jews be all that important? Well, the kernel of the reality of the matter is that the Israelis, western-oriented, sit smack-dab in the middle of the oriental Arab world and form a strange foreign element in it. Yet the Arabs control the largest known reserves of oil in a time when the Western world desperately needs it to generate power for its industry and commerce. Power shortages linked to Middle East oil and the leverage that oil gives to the Arabs can be critical to the survival of the West's way of life. And so world peace, world war, even world survival can hinge on that greasy if necessary matter—oil. And Israel's survival quite possibly may come to depend on just how the Western world thinks of her in terms of its need of Arab-controlled oil. Will the West sacrifice Israel to get its oil? Only one thing is clear and that is that Israel has the strongest military force in that area today. She may have *the* nuclear weapon. And this time, as the Israeli people tell it, they will not die easily, leaving the world untouched by their final rite of passage, as they once did in Europe. Such thoughts engender visions of Armageddon.

Aside from such portentous matters, the Israeli Jew now controls a land that is dear to Christians, too. Forty-five percent of Israel's tourists are not Jews. And Jerusalem is part of the iconography of Islam, figuring in its genesis since Muhammad knew it and The Rock where Abraham and Isaac encountered God in that decisive confrontation. The Arabs, too, are by Abraham, out of Hagar whose son, Ishmael, they trace themselves to.

It should by now be apparent that who and what the Israeli is has deep significance for the Western world.

But there is more. Consider that romantic, almost quixotic notion that for generations has sustained Jews in grinding exile, that hope sung in Psalm 137 of once again returning to Israel from which Jews had first been evicted by Babylonia, then Rome. Both these conquerors are no more and their languages are dead; but Israel and the Hebrew language live. Odd, strange, fateful, perhaps redemptive, the people who are the subject of it all ought to be listened to.

On a most somber note, the two most important events, for Jews, during the last two thousand years have been the holocaustic destruction of six-million Jews—two out of five then living—and the subsequent restoration to the remnant of the State of Israel. These Noachian events somehow touch the nerve of the heart of the soul of men and nudge them toward a consideration of not only the ancient People of the Book but their modern counterparts.

Finally, readers accustomed to being told exactly how things work, how states and peoples are structured, didactical things, such readers will be puzzled by the method used in *The Bridge of Time*. But if they will read through the book, allowing their own minds, instincts, experience, common sense, sensibilities, and sensitivities to play upon the work, they will be rewarded with a firm feeling about the people of Israel, some sense of how it is with them.

Chapter 1

If you sail from America, crossing the 6,600 miles of Atlantic Ocean, then continue on the entire length of the umbilical Mediterranean Sea, you run onto the forbiddingly barren coastline that forms the skinny western edge of the Fertile Crescent. The Crescent arcs north and rounds gracefully eastward to where there are such rich soils so generously watered by the Tigris and Euphrates rivers that the junction of them provides the mythic locus of the Garden of Eden.

But that skinny western edge, that easternmost border of the Mediterranean Sea, provided a land bridge up and down and across which marched rapacious armies of Assyrians, Egyptians, Babylonians, Greeks, Romans, Arabs, Crusaders, Ottoman Turks, in millennial processions.

Oddly enough, it is that throughway for conquerors that has managed in some mysterious way to provide a lush ambience for shockingly innovative, aggressive religions, and for terrible scorching prophetic visions. To it, Abraham came; and in it, Isaac and Jacob died. Moses opened its door to the Jews. Prophets there created a life style and literature, still very much with us. It was the home and death place of Jesus Christ and most of his apostles. Mohammed rode his great horse Al-Burah from Mecca to Jerusalem and from there moved through seven heavens into the presence of God.

A gifted people, the Jews once lived and created there a surviving Testament to their lives. These Jews were by Romans dispossessed and flung throughout the world, yet they clung to the notion of one day returning. That two-thousand-year-old fierce urge to survive, to physically regain the land and its ways, kept the Jews ethnically different, apart, persecuted—perhaps the essential quid pro quo the trade for their survival. In 1948, with the help of the United Nations, good luck, and perhaps another Power, they made it back.

Well! Who did these Jews think they were, coming on so strong to establish a Jewish state after two thousand years? And in the midst of fifty million Moslems who certainly did not consider them God's chosen. And what kind of people were these Jews? What did they want? What was their mission? How did they look, work, talk, think, govern, fight, relax? How did they view themselves, their nation, the frowning world?

Well, I had come to find out.

Chapter 2

I had been going to and fro in the land, walking up and down in it (to paraphrase another viewer), riding buses, hitchhiking, hiking, bicycling, staying always among the common people, recording and noting their ideas and ways. It was a delightful and rewarding experience, for the Israelis respect writers, especially of books, and treat them with honor, an unaccustomed experience for an American. They seem to link somehow the Book and books.

I had been in Israel six weeks, was alive with it, delighted to see so much change since the jangled war days of June, 1967, when I had written of the war and its aftermath.

Then came a letter from a good friend. He is astute and an experienced writer. He agreed that the best way to reveal a people was to let them reveal themselves through their own words and actions. He thought the technique of random interview and observation most suitable in gaining an understanding of a polyglot nation. But then he wrote something that left me in despair: "I am a goy," he wrote, "and an Irishman who is revolted by the idea that he should wish to return to Ireland. I still don't know why Jews want to go to a difficult, arid, remote land in the Middle East that is utterly foreign to the tradition and habits of the land whence they came—England, Europe, America, South Africa. My origins are all English-Irish: language, law, art, religion. America is my country. Not even the southern states interest me as a place to return to. I'm not attempting to argue with the Israeli ideal. But I can't understand this emphasis upon place. It seems to me that contentment and fulfillment lie more within one than without, more in one's inner resources than in whatever land lies about him."

These words bore me down. If my erudite friend, a novelist, journalist, literary critic, perceptive student of human nature whose own ancestors had, in starved desperation, left Ireland generations ago—if he did not, after more than twenty-five years of Israeli statehood, know why Israel existed and why Jews went there, then could anyone understand the highly publicized present and the Israeli Jew in it?

Had Hitler, like Attila the Hun, faded to a mere incident leaving my friend unaware of the tiny remnant of Jews left with no sanctuary after V-Day, and after six million of them were murdered by Nazis in Russia and Europe? Was he altogether unaware that more than a million Jews in Israel came not from Europe and America but from Moslem lands in the Middle and Far East—from seventy and more nations scattered about the world? Was he uninformed that, as in Europe, Jews had been evicted penniless from Arab lands?

Russia lumps West Germany, the United States, *and* tiny Israel (*mirabile dictu*) as the three most dangerous "imperialist" nations. The Arabs are sworn to drive the Jews into the sea. Armageddon is scheduled to occur at Har Megiddo in Israel.

More! Genocide, an obscene word made banal by Nazis who used Jews to define its meaning graphically.

And yet my friend, humane and decent and talented, admits

to ignorance of the Land, the Jews, their present needs as related to their recent past.

My work had suddenly come to seem as purposeless as writing on water.

A bar is for some a tempting place to find release from disappointment. After reading my friend's letter and being overwhelmed by its implications for my work, I had sought a bar in Jerusalem, that place of churches, synagogues, reliquaries, but very few watering holes. Finally I found one; so bright and clean that it could have been a dairy bar. There, sipping mellow Israeli brandy, musing on my impossible task, I found that my discontent grew rather than diminished.

"Bad news?" the man next to me asked.

"Unpleasant thoughts," I replied.

"Drink up. Let the fruit of the vine crowd out unpleasantness and joy flow in." He twirled his empty glass meaningfully.

Several drinks later, I learned that he was Joseph (Yosi) Weiss, a graduate of Columbia University, third-generation Israeli, wise to its people and places, and possessed of a considerable knowledge of the theater of the Western world. He himself had failed as a playwright, he said, because of the popularity of theater from more sophisticated cultures. "We Israelis are certain we know how to fight, build, save abandoned Jews, but we are still unsure of our artists. We love them but we don't buy their work."

Yosi did not seem disheartened. He grinned, revealing broad, stained, horselike teeth set in a wide mouth. His thatch of hair was wildly disheveled. He was short, heavy-shouldered, barrel-chested, a field worker type whose coarseness was redeemed by an ascetically lean face, soft eyes, keen-edged nose. His easy way, his clownish appearance, his obvious concern for me elevated my spirits.

I mentioned that Israel already had one Nobel Prize winner.

"S. Y. Agnon is essentially European," Yosi replied. "Successful Israeli artists must carry a mystique of foreignness, usually European, to sell their work to Israelis. Didn't you Americans go through the same throes of snobbery, coveting European art? Even our government does not trust us. When they want a great piece of art to hang in the Knesset, our parliament, they turn to a Marc Chagall, a Jew, but a French citizen who treats not of Israeli themes but of the past, of European Jewish shtetl life. What have we to do with such themes? Tevye belongs to nostalgia and Broadway; *Fiddler on the Roof* to rootless American Jews, ignorant of the miseries of shtetl life under the Czars, the Kaisers, Polish nobility."

Yosi sighed. "In any case, they do not produce my work."

"So how do you live?"

"A tourist guide, part-time. When I need money I work at my trade—a bore, mostly, redeemed by good pay."

"But it must be interesting to observe the reactions of Germans, French, Italian, Americans as they visit here?"

"Ah-h-h. No! The French are docile and love every foot of the land. So do the British in a decorous, aloof way. You know how they are, 'Great show, here. Topping. The Mandate times put you on your way. Didn't we?' And the Germans are jovial and terribly interested. *Click! Click! Click!* They photograph everything. None were ever Nazis. Teachers, yes, and florists, merchants, doctors, lawyers, but never Nazis, they tell me. And those who come on tours are so old now, so docile that I believe them. Still, when they are so precise in following my orders, walk obediently in line, always on time, so orderly, I wonder about their past. I look at them, so eager to please me, and I wonder whose Jewish business they expropriated, what Jewish professor they undercut, what strange operation they performed on—on . . . what exotic fertilizer they spread on their gardens . . . bonemeal? Ash? Whose?"

With reluctance I asked about American tourists.

"We love them. And we hate them. Always in every group there inevitably is one insufferable couple for whom the rooms are wrong, the seats are wrong, the food is wrong, the weather is wrong, and they are sure to ask, when we show them the great things that United Jewish Appeal money has done here, or

Bonds for Israel money: 'Sure, we know what we have done for you, but what have you done for yourselves? Show us that, young man. Hmpf!'

"So I wait. And when we pass Jerusalem's military cemetery I stop the bus, take the microphone, address them by name. 'Mr. and Mrs. Grosspielsky. Look at those white tombstones. Thousands. They are our deposit slips, tallies of our fair-share contribution. Unfortunately, our contributions are not tax-deductible.' Still, it's impossible to insult them or keep them from the inspiration they need and come for. Unlike Lourdes, we seldom fail to cure them."

At ten-thirty the place closed. Yosi suggested that I join him for a few drinks at his apartment. "It's early. I like you and tonight it is not good for you to be alone."

Yosi probably meant that the drinks were free and to hell with the conversation. But he had guessed right about my loneliness. Ahead of me lay a writing task that had suddenly left me in a bog of despair.

The taxicab ride was a stunning trip through the rocky, storied Jerusalem hills. In the soft night the lights of seemingly random suburbs flickered on hilltops, pulsated around and down hillsides into dark valleys, like precious stones thrown upon jewelers' black velvet. Yosi pointed to the Israel Museum, brightly lit like a reclined New York glass skyscraper, tapered, flowing, conforming to the stepped hills.

The cab stopped outside a row of apartments built of stone, each like the other: banal.

A single lamp illuminated Yosi's place, which seemed nearly empty of furnishings. From the floor of the living room a hi-fi sloshed out a Vienna Waltz that here seemed too soft. Several men and women observed our arrival. A pretty girl stood and walked to Yosi, kissed him sweetly. His arm around her, Yosi introduced me to his sweetheart, Ruth; then to Gershom the bus driver; Steve, a director of plays; Naomi, a travel agent; Joel, a photographer. "I've brought an American writer," Yosi said, "he aims to fracture the myth that all of us are heroic tank drivers, hard-working farmers, rabbis, one-eyed generals. I told him that all he needs to say is that we are ordinary people with an extraordinary will to live. He wants more!"

Later, Steve informed me that I should feel complimented that Yosi took me in. "He doesn't like many Americans," Steve said. "But he likes you and that means you are O.K. with us. Here's a kind of urban kibbutz that we all support."

"Do directors of plays do all that well here?" I asked.

"Not really," Steve said lamely. "But when I do get a play to do, the money goes here."

"And travel agents?"

"Wel-l-l, no," Naomi admitted. "It's my father's business, really, but I get a sort of regular salary and share it."

"Bus drivers?"

"Good pay." Gershom said. "I've made as much as $350 a month, but I worked eighteen hours a day, seven days a week to do it. Generally, I earn about $225 a month."

"Is that considered good pay?"

"For a young Israeli like Gershom, that's damned good money," Steve said. "You've got to understand," he added, "that the dollar and the Israeli lira cannot be equated by numbers. When he says $225 he means three and four times that, in Israeli currency. This apartment rents for about $100. That's cheap by American standards but damned high by ours. Especially if a man has a family to clothe, feed, and educate. Luckily, Gershom isn't married."

"Are you all unmarried?"

"My wife's in New York," Steve replied. "She hates it here and won't stay. I love it and can't live anyplace else. She's getting the divorce, not me."

"And mine's in London," Joel volunteered. "She lived here eight years and then couldn't take it any longer. She deserted me. Like Steve, I can't live anyplace else. It's a free life here. It suits me. It didn't suit my wife." Joel did not seem sad.

Naomi remained quiet. Later I learned that she was Yosi's cousin and that her husband lived with Yosi's wife.

Chapter 3

There was an air of decay, material and human, about Yosi's place. Everyone except Gershom seemed to be a loser.

And how did tough Gershom fit into all this? After we became friends, Gershom talked about himself. Undoubtedly, among all these artists drenched in self-concern, Gershom had little chance to speak. I asked him how he liked living in Yosi's bohemia. He said he only helped support the place; he lived at home. Through his friendship with all of them, he met interesting people and nubile girls.

Gershom was twenty-six and had an easy, pleasant face. He was crew-cut and blond, rather phlegmatic, and exuded a sense of physical resourcefulness. He had that special kind of alert yet distant coolness that makes an excellent infantry platoon leader.

His father, a Polish soldier wounded in the German-Russian takeover of 1939, fled and somehow managed to make it to Russia, fell in love with a Russian Christian and married her.

Then I understood Gershom's presence here. He was a Christian in the eyes of the powerful religious political party. Born of a Christian mother, he was not, in Jewish law, a Jew. And so, in this decadent, obviously impious haven he found acceptance, sympathy.

Did any of his father's people get out of Poland? "All dead," he said tonelessly, "killed by the Nazis."

Because his father was a Polish national he was allowed to emigrate from Russia to Israel. Gershom was a year old then. When he was eighteen, he was "lured" to a kibbutz by an eloquent proselytizer but he merely "liked" communal life. "And you have to love it to live it," he said.

Although Gershom had been driving a bus for three years, he was still on temporary status. Permanent status was supposed to be granted after an apprenticeship of a year and a day. The bus cooperative always fired him just before that final day and rehired him the day after. He did not mind.

Gershom understood the tightly controlled bus cooperative's solicitude for members whose families got first chance at the limited openings for permanent drivers. "Protecksia," he called it. "Each group looks after its own: The old-timers look after each other, the Iraqis care for the Iraqis, the bus co-op protects its families, as does the Jewish Agency its people. It's a fact of Israeli life. Anyway, I'm not financially ready to join the cooperative. I'll need $10,000 to buy a share for membership. I haven't got $200."

"But if you have so little money after three years, how can you expect ever to have enough?"

Gershom shrugged. "I'm going with a girl whose father is an old member of the co-op. I may marry her. She's insufferably arrogant and spoiled but it's the simplest way to become an insider. I work six days a week, spend six weeks in the army. I'd be gone a lot . . ."

"What's your army rank?"

"Private. I don't want to go higher. So I'm a truck driver. Still, as a private, I'm a damned good one."

Gershom was disgusted with politics. In the last election he deposited a blank ballot to show his contempt. He was certain there could be no peace because, he said, "the Arabs are too primitive, uneducated to understand what a peace could mean to them."

He was astonished that the Russians, considered so clever, backed the Arabs. "With a little gentler attitude they could have had us," he said. "You know," he mused, "if they don't make peace I believe we should move west to Cairo and north through Iraq. Then we should shift populations, disconnect peoples. Put Syrians into Jordan, Iraqis into Egypt. That'll bring peace. Then, after peace comes, we'll give it all back to them and return the Arabs to their rightful homes."

It was two o'clock in the morning. Everyone else had gone to sleep. Gershom got me a mattress and blankets.

I heard Yosi talking quietly in the back bedroom and I occasionally heard brandy swishing in his glass. Of them all, only Yosi drank. He seemed to be that *rara avis*, an Israeli alcoholic. Poor Yosi. Was he a drunk because of his troubles, or the reverse?

Chapter 4

The morning was melancholy gray, wind slapping gusts against Yosi's apartment building. Tiny streaks of water marked the floor under ill-fitted balcony doors. It was a blue-funk dawn.

Outside, the rain drove hard and cold. I walked until a bus came charging down the street out of the gloom spewing plumes of water. I stepped into the street to stop it. "You're not allowed to do that," the ticket seller growled from inside his cage at the rear of the bus.

"So why stop?"

"You looked like a drowning dog huddled there. We rescued you." He grinned.

It was kind of them to make an unauthorized stop for a wet customer. I settled in the seat as we passed the Israel Museum. Last night it had seemed all silvered cubes bejeweled. In foggy daylight it was gray, sogged sugar cubes melting away.

Downtown, in Zion Square, clutching my transfer, I waited for the bus near where Roman legions had camped long ago, holding Jerusalem and its Temple under siege. They had finally taken and sacked it, leveled and plowed the very hallowed ground, wanting no tangible remnant of glory to further agitate the rebellious, troublesome Jews. After that devastation, sheep pastured here near the black tents of nomads; nothing more. Suddenly, the feel of erosion, of time's abrasiveness, of history leaking away, even gurgling down the drains, left me depressed. The famous Jerusalem pink building stone was here stained with streaks of gray mold. Sidewalks were too narrow. Cart-wide, cobbled streets writhed away from cobbled thoroughfares. Ugly modern advertising signs and uninteresting store fronts created a faded façade that added to the feeling of decay.

But the people relieved the depressing scene. They were on their way to work and seemed unaware of the commercial ugliness, were too busy creating their lives, their state. They pushed, jostled, surged ahead unmindful of the rain. Unsmiling, intense, rude, purposeful, their sheer intensity sparked the morning gloom and lightened it.

I watched their faces and gloom dissipated. Dynamic, purposeful, they are good when it comes to succoring refugees, the needy, the fatherless, the widowed. John Dewey said that manners were little morals, but he had never stood among such a people on such a morning or he might have added, "but not needed by all people at all times in all places."

The bus slithered to the curb. No use being deferent. I shoved with the others. No seats. I asked the driver to alert me at my stop. The bus smelled of wet wool, sweat, stale cigarette smoke, and the faint cloy of oriental foods. There were no smiles, no frowns. Only determination.

Finally the driver nodded to me and I began the push through the packed aisles toward the center exit door. The bus careened like a badly guided rocket down the street and I could progress only in violent fits, as the driver zoomed, braked, accelerated for no apparent purpose except, perhaps, to demonstrate his superb control of the vehicle.

He slammed on the brakes and I flew uncontrolled toward the exit, halted by a very fat, rocklike woman's body. She merely shrugged at my apology, as if to say, "So what?"

Once outside, I furiously thrust my middle finger at the bored driver. But he seemed not to see my tiny obscenity. Anyway, what Israeli had time for such pettiness?

Chapter 5

At my pension, I noted that we had a new desk clerk. He wanted to talk but I was wild with the need for a shower, clean clothes, rest, after that bizarre stay among Yosi's ménage.

The clerk would not let me pass. "My name is Arie," he said, "and I note on your registration card that you are a writer. I have been waiting to speak to you. Would this be of interest?"

He held a clipping from the *Jerusalem Post* dated September 20, 1961.

"About you?"

He smiled beatifically.

"I'll read it with care."

A tall, rugged, erect man with a shock of gray-blond hair, there was vigor about him, and a sense of controlled pain. He was perhaps sixty years old. "See here?" With a thick forefinger he pointed to a paragraph stating that, in 1961, Arie had been awarded the Cavaliere Al Merito Della Republica Italiana, by the president of Italy. In 1951 he had founded the Israel Dante Alighieri Society and maintained a keen interest in Italian culture.

"Why did you bother?"

"The Italians saved my life and the lives of many Yugoslavian Jews. The villagers and their priests were wonderful. Would you like to know more about it?"

Arie's eyebrows worked and his blue eyes anxiously smiled.

"Let me first get a bath, some lunch, and then we'll talk."

"There are others working here," he added quickly. "Moshe, Shmuel, Rena. You would interview them, of course. Yes?"

It occurred to me that no one had, like Arie, established in Israel the Teutonic equivalent of a Dante Alighieri Society for Germans or Austrians. Suddenly the idea of taping Arie's story seemed extraordinarily exciting. I told him we would do the story at once.

It was hard to know why men like Arie yearned to tell and retell their stories. Perhaps, in Israel, there were so many like him that no one would listen to what had begun to seem banal. Perhaps it was merely simple pride that he had had the luck and wit to make it through that valley of destruction that was Hitler's Europe. Perhaps, as psychiatrists say, there was a feeling of guilt at having survived when so many had not. Maybe Arie's escape from the Nazis signified to him ontological evidence that God's promise for Abraham's seed was in our time further manifest.

Arie was an artillery officer in the Yugoslavian army when the Nazis invaded. His guns commanded a 180-degree field of fire along a main stretch of road down which a Panzer division roared into Yugoslavia. He could have delayed the advance, but there came a sudden order to hold fire. He watched his executioners roll unchallenged toward the apocalyptic shattering of Yugoslavia. Arie could read German, had read the conqueror's newspapers. He knew what to expect of the Wehrmacht.

Suddenly he was alone. His crew had fled. Then he fled, hiding by day, traveling only by night toward Zagreb, his home. He switched clothes en route and was finished forever with the Yugoslav army.

In Zagreb, he cautiously approached his home. His wife and family were safe. Already, the Croatian Ustashi party had prepared death camps for Jews, Serbs, and political enemies. Arie knew that he must get his family out. But where could he take them? Palestine was hardly to be considered because the British were granting few permits for Jews to enter. No nation wanted Jews! But Arie knew the Italians and trusted them. His only chance was to flee to Italy. He was trapped, but not quite.

In Zagreb, a shoemaker he knew was doing a huge business forging papers for fleeing Jews.

"Why a shoemaker?"

Arie shrugged. "Why not? He had stolen a tiny press and learned to forge passports. Easier than shoemaking."

With the forged papers he and his wife (they were childless) and nine members of his family fled. At a checkpoint on the Dalmatian coast, they joined a long line of refugees. He knew some of the people and saw how they were refused entry when they gave as their reason for leaving Yugoslavia the wish to visit relatives, to vacation, to do business . . . any but the true reason, which was that they were Jews and must enter Italy or die. Arie watched the dejected faces of those refused entry as they walked back to Yugoslavia and death. . . .

At this point in his story Arie was pale, sweating, his speech fragmented and at times slurred. His was not a recollection but a reincarnation of things past. . . .

When Arie's turn came, he was asked why he was leaving. He took a deep breath and replied, *"Ebreo." "Venga!"* The Italian guard at once said. Arie passed the word. "Admit you are Jews," he told them, "if you want to enter." Then Arie's family passed to Italy and sanctuary.

They joined two hundred other Jews in Trieste. The Italians did not know what to do with them. . . .

Arie paused. "You must understand," he said, "that Tito had already organized the Partisans who had killed Italian soldiers. Still, the Italians did not retaliate against us and send us to the Germans or put us in camps. They refused to become animals, sought for solutions, remained human beings." Arie searched my face to see if I understood.

Arie's family and eight other souls ultimately went to Sossano, a small village near Florence. At first, the villagers were distant. They had never seen Jews, knew them only by New Testament reputation. Fortunately, the townspeople refused to take seriously the rantings of the few anti-Semites among them. Yet, there was uncertainty about the villagers' attitude and Arie, with his sensitive intuition, knew this was potentially dangerous. If they were not friends, likely they would become enemies. He must try more actively to win their friendship.

Christmas came a few months after the Jews' arrival. Arie went to the church, "to pay my respects, to build bridges." The worshipers saw him at once, Arie said. "And this intrusion of the Christ-killer at a worship of his victim's birth must have seemed to them absolutely blasphemous."

The disapproving murmurs became so loud that the village priest turned from his devotions. He quieted his congregants, told them that these few Jews were victims of persecution not unlike Christ himself. He explained that they were homeless and destitute and that, although Jews and not Catholics, all true Catholics must recognize that all men were Christians in the sense of being loving humans. It was their Christian duty to aid, love, and accept these abandoned Jews. "They are the favored of God," the priest told them.

"I cannot explain how firm yet sweet he was," Arie said. "The people quieted. A few heads nodded in agreement. Devotions were resumed. I stayed to the end. The worshipers left the church, noticing me no further."

Arie learned Italian in order to teach German in the village school. Others in his group worked in the fields or found jobs in town. Arie enjoyed one of the most idyllic periods he had ever known. Then the Italian government collapsed and the Germans initiated their murderous procedure to make Italy *judenrein.*

Ugly rumors of the Nazi occupation quickly reached the village. The fascists in Sossano suddenly became important, taking control. They warned that those who aided Jews would be treated as traitors.

Still, rumors of impending Allied victory were strong. Arie's group was split; some wanted to stay and some to flee. "But where could we go?" Arie asked it of me as if addressing a judge. He hunched his shoulders, tilted his head, turned up his palms in the time-honored gesture of Jews without answers. Arie peered past me into the distance toward the Judean hills whence cometh, occasionally, the help that saves, sometimes, His chosen, the Book says.

One day the village priest came to him and said, "Fly away! Go! Here it is no longer safe." He gave Arie some money and the address of another priest who lived on the Swiss border.

Most of the Jews, believing in Allied victory, would not leave. Arie argued with them. He sent for the priest, who repeated what he had told Arie. Still they would not leave. "Too tired, hopeless," Arie said.

At dawn Arie and his wife, now six months pregnant (he cursed himself for having thought they were safe enough to risk having a child) and six others departed Sossano.

The remainder?

Arie eloquently shook his head.

The Swiss border guards were difficult. They were quite correct, cold, legal, firm. That they were Jews was unfortunate, but the entire border was lined with refugees, Jews and others. That his wife was pregnant elicited merely a shrug. "They are chilled like their mountains," Arie said. "In Italy, a bambino means something. Tell them your wife is pregnant and the Italians melt. But the Swiss . . . like stones."

Arie found the priest whose name was handed him in Sossano. The priest added more money to the little that Arie had until the bribe was large enough to allow Arie's party to cross to Switzerland and life.

The long narration had jangled Arie. He glanced about, instinctively furtive. "We stayed in various Swiss camps until the war ended and the Red Cross returned us to Yugoslavia. "There were once seventy-five thousand Yugoslavian Jews," he said tonelessly. "Only ten thousand survived.

"In Yugoslavia we tried to rebuild our lives, but Zagreb, the dead, memories—all made it too painful and we decided to emigrate to the one place that offered us a chance to live as Jews without being afraid."

"And you never regretted coming here?"

"Never. *Baruch hashem,* we are alive, we are free, we have enough. And yet I once returned to Sossano. Because I established our Israel Dante Alleghieri Society, the Italian government invited me to Rome. One day, I slipped away to visit Sossano and, you know, they welcomed me like a brother. Church bells were rung. They organized a banquet. We celebrated all night. Oh, such a people!"

Arie suddenly was no longer a fugitive; his face held the secure joy of a trapped miner freshly emerged from the pit. "I hope you will say that our life is a gift from the Italian people and their priests."

I had only one more question and could hardly voice it. "Pope Pius XII," I finally said; "did you feel that Rolf Hochuth did him an injustice by portraying him as guilty of complicity in the death of Jews?"

Arie did not quickly answer. He lost his smile, seemed suddenly anguished. "I have seen *The Deputy* in Hebrew, English, and German," he said. "I—I—can only say that he had . . . enormous problems. Catholics to save. For him the Church came first. What were a few million Jews, radicals, communists, when weighed against the awful danger to the Church and its hundreds of millions?"

"But was he guilty?" I persisted, suddenly obsessed with the need to know what Arie truly thought. It was unfair of me. Arie was again sweating. His face was lined. He loved Italy, Italians, the clergy. But what did he think of the Prince?

"I think—I think . . ." Arie said slowly, laboring to voice his long-buried thoughts. "I think Hochuth was . . . one hundred percent right in his conclusion but wrong in his characterization. The Pope was not a simp or a fool. He was a mechanically correct ruler, therefore all the more guilty."

The luncheon hour was over but Haim, the gray, stooped waiter, managed to find some soup and bread. The good bread wadded in my mouth. The asparagus soup tasted phlegmy.

Haim was disturbed. "Perhaps a whiskey would help your appetite?" he asked, voicing the natural assumption that all American writers drink.

Unable to eat or drink, I walked to the stairs and climbed to my room. The bath beckoned but the bed was close and I stretched out on it. Random images of Yosi, Arie, Gershom, Naomi, Ruth all crowded upon me. Of them all, Arie seemed most fit for Israel. The others could live the same life in Greenwich Village or in communes anywhere—New York, Paris, London. Gershom could certainly make it in Detroit. But Arie? Where else could he find peace? Italy? Maybe. But if he could have found peace there he might have stayed. Perhaps Arie can find no peace except in his own land, among his own people, living and dying there, dependent on the sufferance of no man or nation.

Chapter 6

One evening the telephone rang and it was Yosi. "Today we all worked," he said, "and the icebox is full, the pantry is loaded. Come on over and we'll have a party just like in New York."

I told him I must go to Eilat in the morning, that I had to work to prepare for the coming week.

"Eilat? You want company? An interpreter, maybe? Your Hebrew is not all that good. Slight Yiddish. Halting German, no French, fair Spanish. How will you manage without me? I'll work for ten dollars a day and keep. I'm worth ten times that to you."

I explained that my plan of work did not include an interpreter.

"So make it seven-fifty," Yosi said. "Don't say no." There was a compelling edge to his plea. He needed the money, I supposed. Quickly I calculated the costs, figured the possible gain, and told him that we should try the scheme for a week and if then it did not work we would separate. He agreed. I told him to be at the bus station at six-thirty next morning.

Yosi did not arrive in time for the first bus to Beersheba!

I considered taking the next bus, but did not because I had begun to see how Yosi might fit into my work. Besides, something might have happened to him.

I called his apartment and Ruth answered, saying that Yosi had been ill, was just leaving, was sorry.

Soon Yosi arrived, walked carefully toward me, his head poised like an egg of tender shell. We went into the cafeteria and he sat beside me and groaned. I got him tea and he drank it gratefully.

Two more cups restored his cheeks to something of their normal pallor. The waitresses knew him and begged him to eat, offered him fried eggs, fried potatoes, bread, tomatoes, cucumbers, milk. Yosi closed his eyes in revulsion. I asked them to stop, but they insisted that food was his need. Bus drivers stopped to encourage him. Nobody smiled. They all knew him and seemed to understand. It was strange because in Israel an alcoholic is not understood and so is despised. Clearly, Yosi was respected.

In the bus, Yosi was subdued and rarely spoke as we moved south toward Beersheba. In a way, his silence was a blessing, for his foul breath was unbearable.

I told Yosi about my interview with Arie. "You must be careful," he warned, "not to become obsessed with such stories or your work will be too full of them. We have hundreds of thousands like Arie."

"I suppose the stories are embellished and grow more melancholy as the years pass."

"To the contrary," Yosi said. "We are beginning to lose the hard edge of anguish. History becomes rounder, easier, softer. Jews cannot seem to live with hate. Witness our memorials to the six million massacred; special days of remembrance; associations of survivors; holocaust history societies; all these efforts to memorialize the dead so that the young will learn the meaning of Jewishness in exile, so that we will not forget that Europe was once an abattoir for Jews. But the young are disinterested, cannot understand why their grandfathers were so docile. There is even a kind of frantic effort, almost contrived by the elders to bolster the feeling of outraged loss. As I said, they grow older and Jews tend not to hate their fellow man. We remember Haman with derision. Torquemada as a silly martinet. Chmielnicki as a puffed-up brigand—if they remember him at all. You've noticed that the Volkswagen is our most popular car. German goods are everywhere. German tourists are courted and made welcome. The wound is healing but the scar will remain, a tiny one, a fine, white line."

Undulating plains replaced the hills. I asked Yosi about the small villages we passed. He explained that they were moshavim and kibbutzim—two kinds of agricultural settlements. The purely cooperative ones, the moshavim, had clusters of small, plastered houses, each with a shed behind it for livestock. The kibbutzim were the purely communal settlements with large barns, large administration buildings, large apartment-like living quarters—everything needed for a collective, shared life. Thus, differentiated by the scale of their buildings, they were easily identifiable from the road.

There was something of the rejected, the inadequate and dilapidated, about these moshavim. One felt the same sense generated by cold, moldy buildings on Jaffa Road in rainy Jerusalem. But the kibbutzim effused a sense of busy success, good organization, contentment, purposefulness.

Gradually the hills leveled, growing undulant and treeless. One was reminded of vast silt loam soils of Illinois rolling on in near endless fertility. Here, too, soils were fertile, but needed irrigation water to make them arable. Yields of barley, corn, and sorghums often equaled those of Iowa and Illinois.

Large fields of green barley brightened the winter landscape. Chukar partridge abounded. Turtle doves were everywhere, their usual gray tinted slightly reddish. They were large, plump birds, and Yosi said nobody hunted them. "Why should they? Who wants to destroy such beauty?"

Bedouin flocks and herds added life to the quiet landscape.

The rich, fertilized, irrigated fields of the kibbutzim alternated with overgrazed, scruffy Bedouin pastures. Here one saw the enormous difference between a Western, intensive agriculture and an Eastern pastoral one.

"The Bedouin," Yosi remarked, "emphasize the clan, the tribe, and are often feuding with one another in a typical tribal society. Deuteronomic anathemas form a present reality for the Bedouin. 'And thine eye shall not pity; life for life; eye for eye, tooth for tooth, hand for hand, foot for foot.' It is a truth achieved by decorous and subtle modern man in his own obtuse legal way, but by the Bedouin forthrightly; with pristine, searing swiftness."

Yosi talked about the miracle of manna that saved the Israelites during their forty years of wandering. "The tamarisk bush is generally thought to have furnished food for their salvation. Several others could have done the job. One, a bush, is host to a sudsy cluster of insect eggs that are quite palatable, nutritious, even sweet. The Bedouin still use it when near 'The Mountain of the Wanderers' where the Israelites lost their way. It was, perhaps, the manna of the Israelites."

Unleavened bread, Red Sea parting, the voice of God in the wilderness, calf of gold, the Decalogue, manna—black goatskin tents, veiled women, camels, burros, flocks, and long-robed and kaffiyeh-wearing men. The Bedouin! Sprung also from Abraham and a living link to Israel's past, for the Jews once lived their ways and biblical prose is alive with references. Dispersion, persecution, adaptation have changed the Jews, made them modern, efficient, grooved to the twentieth century. As yet, the sons of Hagar, these Bedouin, had not paid the initiation fee, the cost to come into the modern world. They clung to the old ways of Abraham, of Ishmael, of Mohammed. It was a wondrous and yet pitiful thing to see these biblical relics, illiterate, disease-ridden, often hungry. Yosi told that in Israel the Bedouin were ending their long desert sojourn and were being settled on the land where schools, medical facilities, work could be given to them. The old ones resisted the change but the young welcomed it. Yosi's evidence lay in the distance: tiny tin houses built alongside traditional black tents. One could imagine the older Bedouin in his beloved goatskin tent saying to his son, "Abdul, you'll not get me in one of those newfangled square houses. What was good enough for father is good enough . . ."

Yosi complained of the dryness. He coughed frequently and finally took out his enormous syringe with a half-pint rubber bulb. Frequently, he sprayed his throat. Yosi said he was always freer of his affliction when near the sea and moist air. His delicate cough and steady use of the syringe worried me. Only later did I understand the true purpose of that syringe.

Chapter 7

It was late afternoon in Beersheba where we waited in line for the last bus to Eilat. Six Bedouin also waited, their wives isolated off to one side. Yosi knew one man. They greeted one another gravely and respectfully.

"How is life with you?" Yosi asked.

"Allah has been kind."

"Was he kind before you came to live with us?"

"Joseph, you always ask difficult questions. We did not have as much. But we lived with our brothers in Islam. Now . . ."

"But it is better now than before? More to eat? More work? Better pay?"

"Yes, yes."

"Then you are content?"

The Bedouin shrugged. Yosi was playing the propagandist to impress me. We all knew this. Finally the Bedouin replied, "I am Arab. I am Muslim. Islam is one. I prefer to have less among my own than to have more among Jews."

Yosi stared. The Bedouin stared. They exchanged cigarettes and then we walked away. "The son-of-a-bitch," Yosi muttered. "Respect them but suspect them. We are still Jews and they are Muslims of one true religion and destined to rule. The bastards, they'll never rule us again."

Among themselves the Bedouin relaxed. They smiled, laughed, seemed happy. A distinguished-looking older man arrived and they stood in deference.

"That man is a sheikh," Yosi said. "He is a usurer, takes more grain from them than is his due, is pitiless. Yet you see how they treat him. They respect only power. Nothing else matters in the desert. Beat a Bedouin and he respects you. Treat him as you would be treated and he thinks you do it from weakness. But what can Jews do? We have lost the simplistic ways of the desert."

]34[

There was the usual crush to get on the bus. A sensible seating arrangement was observed; last off, first seated. We got seats but were separated. Beside me stood a young man by appearance an American, carrying the *Jerusalem Post* and *Time* magazine. A soldier across from me rigged his canvas belt through the arm of his seat to mine, thus making a sling seat for the young American.

But it turned out that the young man was a Dutch Christian, spoke excellent English, was a lawyer, and lived in Eilat. In Israel three years, he considered becoming a citizen. Yet he did not really like the people. "The young are uncivilized," he said, "tough, crude, inconsiderate." He paused, perhaps remembering the kindness of the Israeli soldier next to him. "But once you make a friend of an Israeli kid, he's your friend for life."

The Dutchman said he liked the freedom of life in Israel. At first he had lived in the hills, with a colony of hippies. Life there was easy, cheap, carefree. "You just walk to the coffeehouse by the sea and a contractor comes along and says, 'Hey you! You want to work?' If you do, you go with him and work eight hours for ten dollars. After a while I got to know the contractor and one day he said: 'Klaus, get some men together and I'll give you work.' I did, and overnight I was a subcontractor. That's how things go in Eilat."

We talked a bit. Finally he declared that the Jews could not win. "They'll win every battle but the last one. It was that way in the Bible and it'll be that way again."

"Then why do you stay? You could get hurt."

He shrugged. "I like it," he said. "The Jews let me work, live my life. I feel good here."

We were deep in the Negev and the bus stopped frequently to let the Bedouin off. Their black-clad women walked respectfully behind the men into that dark night that once sheltered Hagar. They still obeyed a four-thousand-year code that frankly recognized the difference in woman, gave her a separate but assured status. She knew who and what she was. She did not ask why. Yosi said there must be implacable and stern rules in a nomadic society or else there could be neither stability nor security. "She is not a chattel. Hers is more the relationship of bishop to cardinal; a hierarchy of superiors, but a hierarchy nevertheless."

The bus was nearly empty and Yosi took the vacant aisle seat next to me. I offered the window seat but he adamantly refused it, was so vehement about it that I did not at first understand.

The sky was dusty with low clouds. The sun managed only a faint light so that desert and sky took on the same red-beige tone and seemed joined, endless, without horizon or perspective. To our right the lights of Mizpah Ramon burned sharp and clean as glass chips. This wilderness of Zin, trying place of Israelites, jarred complacency and I could not relate the stones, hills, sky, earth to anything known before. The town itself seemed to float mystically in a monochrome earth and sky. It seemed a mirage. Mizpah Ramon. A Jewish agricultural settlement, truly there, evidence that the desert was arable, viable because the Jews had returned.

The Bedouin in flowing blacks and whites, leaving the bus to return to the desert that Moses knew, affected me deeply. One could in the mind hear the tumult of the children of Israel striving with Moses, calling this place evil, desolate, demanding to know why he had brought them out of Egypt to where there is "No place for seed, or of figs or of pomegranates, neither is there water to drink." It seemed an absolutely beautiful and utterly sinister place this evening and my sympathies were suddenly with the children of Israel, not Moses and Aaron. A fearsome price Moses had exacted. And for what? Some far distant, uncertain deliverance promised by a God they did not really believe in. Certainly Egypt and slavery were easier than this spooky wilderness that only the likes of David Ben-Gurion could find enchanting.

Yosi began once more to talk about the Bedouin. He explained that the men who were once charged with the terrible duty of fighting and the care of their military camels had now only domestic camels. In a day of institutionalized, impersonal warfare, the Bedouins' warrior function was limited to petty feuds punishable in the law courts of Israel.

T. E. Lawrence said that nomadism is "that most deeply

biting of all social disciplines." But Lawrence did not know about huge tanks, tractors, atomic weapons, guided missiles, bacterial warfare . . . and three million Jews settled on the land.

"Still," Yosi said, "the ways of the desert are not soon lost. Strength is still worshiped. Let us become weak, lose one battle, and our Bedouin go *whoosh* to the other side. We know it. They know it. Only strength, conquest, victory count in the desert. So we are strong and strike hard. We respect them at all times . . . but we suspect them always."

"You said that once before."

"Remember it. It is vital to the understanding of all Arabs."

Our bus had two drivers; Yosi said this was for safety in case one of them was hit from ambush as we approached the Jordanian border. Two guards sat in full battle dress with automatic rifles. They looked wiry, tough, resourceful, and they wore the round black skullcap, the yarmulka, of the religious Jew, Israel's fighting priests. How incongruous to see them here, in their own land, defending themselves, fusing piety with strength as in David's time. Nobody paid them much attention. They were here as expected. So what! But suddenly it was clear why Yosi preferred the seat on the aisle; it was less vulnerable to a bullet than the window seat!

There was little conversation, smiling, amenity among the passengers. One felt that same stoic manner everywhere in Israel. They will do what must be done, take what must be taken, suffer what comes. In that bus on that dangerous night, moving through land that Abraham knew, now among his "seed," I felt the quality of endurance that brought them through forty years of impossible desert and four thousand years of perilous history to this moment in time, space, spirit.

Soldiers in yarmulkas, Edom's hills ahead, irreligious Yosi, religious guards, blood, desert, massacre, Bedouin—all blended in a dizzying, mind-blowing experience. I seemed capable of some marvelous insight, felt it near me, reached for it, lost it for no reason I could explain. A near-vision! It is a land for them.

Chapter 8

In Eilat, in the tiny hotel, Yosi unpacked his handbag: two pairs of socks, transistor radio, and three bottles of brandy. These were all he needed.

In the morning we dressed as warmly as we could against the unusual damp cold that blew upon this Miami Beach of Israel. Swathed in raincoats, using towels for scarves, we joined the other guests dressed in the same manner. Even the waitresses were armored against the unseasonable cold, against which few hotels in Eilat provided adequate heat. We ate the typical Israeli breakfast of several kinds of salt fish, yogurt, tomatoes, cucumbers, olives, salami, various cheeses, eggs, wonderful bread. The good breakfast put a tiny bloom on a blasted morning.

Outside, the wind blew from the north, vicious as driving sleet. Needing film, we entered a camera shop. An aging man in a heavy turtle-neck sweater, knit cap, and rubber apron turned and yelped at the sight of Yosi, rushed to embrace him. "It's Menachem," Yosi said, "a member of my infantry company. We took this town in 1948. Private Menachem, Serial Number 74 . . . whatever it was. I forget. But it ended in T. Are you still a T, a private?"

"I have neither talent nor stomach for leadership, Yosi. You know that. Yes, I'm the oldest private in the army. Only now I'm too old and in Civil Defense. To hell with business," Menachem suddenly said. "Let's go to the stockroom and talk."

There Yosi explained that he was helping me gather material about the people of Israel. Menachem was delighted. Of course he would tell us of his life. He said what most Israelis say: "I could fill your book."

Menachem was sixty-two years old, slim, tall, with delicate features heavily eroded. There were the pouched eyes, crevass-like facial lines etched by innumerable nights of too little sleep, the faintly hurt expression from too many bouts with alcohol, drugs, and orgy. Yet his eyes were merry, shrewd, and he moved quickly.

Menachem called up circular stairs and a beautiful young girl came gracefully down. He took her hand and introduced his wife. She looked to be about twenty-five, wearing slacks that showed long, young watermelon haunches taut from vigorous use. She was tall, full-blown, and ripe as a choice heifer. She moved about Menachem like a doting daughter, brimming with love for him.

Up front the door slammed. "See to them, Shoshana," he ordered. So business couldn't really wait! Menachem had not got that look of shrewdness by turning business away. Soon she was back and served us hot Turkish coffee in tiny cups. It was fragrant, sweet, delicious. She sat next to Menachem while he told us of his life.

He is the sixth generation of his family in Israel. His great-great-great-grandfather was a famous rabbi from Riga, who settled in Israel in the eighteenth century, in Safed, that holy Galilean city. After an earthquake destroyed Safed, the family moved to the more ecumenically religious Jerusalem. In time, his secular father left Jerusalem to help found a new city called Tel Aviv, and Menachem was the first baby born there.

Menachem talked about his early secular schooling and his days at the American University in Beirut. Many of today's Arab leaders were in school with him. One, the son of the then ruler of Bahrein, was interested only in women and swimming. "He bought himself a diploma in swimming and graduated with it. Unfortunately, they gave no diplomas in whoring although I was told he was indefatigable. Could he have got credit for sex, he'd have been a Ph.D."

Yosi laughed. "Sex is of enormous importance to an Arab," he added. "They are preoccupied with sexual prowess to the point of neurosis."

"Yes," Menachem agreed. "My Bahrein friend was not respected half so much for his swimming as for his sexual prowess."

Shoshana stirred, obviously finding the conversation offensive. She asked to be excused. She stalked up the spiral staircase with the purposeful grace of a fashion model.

"Our young dislike such talk," Menachem explained. "They are more puritanical than ever my great-grandfather was. With them, sex is not for joking. It is special, not to be made light of."

"They are freer with sex but more serious about it," Yosi added. "There is a kind of sacredness about it."

"Arabs regard their women in different ways than we do," Menachem said. "A woman for them is an obstacle to be surmounted and conquered in a sexual duel. Their women look upon it similarly, discuss sexual powers of their men at the wells, at gatherings. They brag and exaggerate as much as do the men.

"A pregnant wife is a man's virile badge of honor. Women and Jews are main topics of conversation among them—in that order—an adversarial relation."

"Honor is their strength and weakness," Yosi added. "That is why we cannot have peace. We have beaten them too often. It is a kind of sexual thing with them. They are less manly because of us, for we are numerically weak and they are fifty million strong; we are Jews and they Muslim; we are Western oriented and they are of the East. And we always whip them in such a humiliatingly short time! Each time we do it we diminish their manhood. They cannot forgive that."

Menachem nodded in agreement.

"Do either of you think there can be peace?" I asked.

"Never," Menachem said. "And we don't need it. Does America have peace? And when she gets it, how long does she keep it? And has Europe known peace? No, we must put up with war; perhaps forever."

The words of the Dutch boy in the bus came back. There has always been a final battle, he had said, and Israel loses it. Suddenly it seemed colder in the room.

"I know the Arabs," Menachem said reflectively. "In Egypt in World War II, I lived among them every chance I had. I speak Arabic as fluently as English . . . I know them as Moshe Dayan knows them and they do not call him 'The Arab' without reason. And I really respect them. At one time I wanted to be a physician and spend my life as an eye specialist ministering to them."

Menachem's father would not allow him to be a physician,

insisting that he enter the family bank. They put him at a desk to add up columns of figures, but he spent his time studying the faces of people as they withdrew their money; counting it. "The varieties of avarice," he labeled the experience.

Menachem was not a banker. Soon they made him a bank guard. He liked the new job because he had access to weapons and could sometimes steal for the underground movement. "Everyone took a little something," he said drily. "Then, after May 14, 1948, when we declared ourselves a state, I joined the Haganah to fight. I fell in love with Eilat and vowed one day to live here."

"But you lived in Tel Aviv for many years," Yosi prompted him.

"True, And Tiberius. And I studied photography in England and Italy. Remember *The Quiet One*, by Richard Bagley? I helped him make that film. Photography became my greatest passion. For a time I worked with Uri as a photographer for his scandalous newspaper. But he was too pro-Arab for me. And he forced me to do certain dishonest photography that disgusted me. I quit, set up my own shop in Tel Aviv, prospered, and then discovered Tiberius. Beside Lake Galilee there was a deserted Arab house going to ruin. Its Arab owner had fled in 1948. I took it over, fixed it up, spent so much time there that one day I decided not to return to my shop in Tel Aviv."

Another customer rattled the door. Menachem bellowed for Shoshana to come down and mind the trade. Yosi looked at me and we smiled. We saw again that Menachem did not at all disdain business. He merely affected to.

"This newspaperman? What about him?" I asked.

"He is brilliant," Menachem began, "a member of our legislature, with a small following of some ignorant and some avantgarde people. But like many Israelis of German background, he cannot refrain from worshipping those superior to him in power and population. The Arabs really are powerful and certainly numerous, only they don't know how to use what they've got. Uri would give back all that we have just so that they would tell him what a nice fellow he is. Of course, afterward they'd slit his throat."

"What kind of a newspaper does he run?"

"A combination of *Time, Playboy,* and your ugliest of pornographic sheets."

Menachem scowled and seemed upset. Yosi gently led him back to the subject of his house on Lake Galilee. "My third wife and I lived there in absolute peace," Menachem continued, "but we had so many people dropping in for free drinks that I decided to open a club and get paid for my hospitality. It worked. We prospered. I added motorboats and water skiing, the first in Israel.

"But I was no businessman. I spent it faster than it came in.

"We became so successful that we hurt other clubs in Tiberius. They struck back. One day two hired thugs came in and began to beat me. I had a gun under the bar, but restrained myself from using it. I could have killed them. One of them picked up an ashtray and hit me in the mouth with it."

He opened his mouth to show that half his teeth were false.

"After that I sold out to the first man with an offer. Then I came here and built the finest villa in Eilat, lived like a king. But it was too showy so I gave it up. Now we live upstairs. It's the simple life for us." But Menachem's eyes glowed with memories of those glorious affluent days. Yosi's look seemed to say: "You can take the artist out of the businessman but you can't take the businessman out of the artist."

Customers were waiting. Shoshana called. Menachem walked us to the door where he pointed outside and said, "What a small country and what a big desert."

We strolled toward a restaurant, passing two characters straight out of an ancient western movie. Rifles strapped across their backs, cartridge belts around their middles, they leaned against the wall of the post office as if guarding it. They were easy to talk to. "We're going for coffee," Yosi said, "care to join us?" The older man shrugged, looked at the younger, who nodded.

They were Frank and Harold, and they were waiting for the morning mail. "It is," said Frank, "the only exciting thing that happens here."

They were working as hired guards at a nearby desert kibbutz and were stationed atop its powerhouse.

Frank was a South African of twenty-five, powerfully built, blond, bearded, and handsome as a Norseman. Harold was English, wiry, stooped like a boxer, and he had about him the spongy, bewildered, pummeled look of the steady loser.

Their rifles were Enfields. Yosi asked how they could defend the powerhouse with such ancient weapons. Frank grinned, "Hell, we aren't even sure they'll shoot straight," he said, "but we are told to get off a warning shot or two if we see anything. Then the soldiers at the kibbutz are supposed to take over. Actually, we're merely an early-warning device. What we really worry about is a mortar attack."

"There is a culvert in the road about one hundred yards away," Harold suggested tonelessly.

"With mortars working at you, you'd never make it," Yosi said.

Frank laughed. "Let one mortar shell miss us and before the next one comes we'll be in that culvert. Bet on it."

"What brought you to Israel?" Yosi asked, adding hopefully that he supposed it was South African anti-Semitism.

"Life for Jews is fine there," Frank replied, "perhaps safer than any other place in the world. Once a few local Nazis decided to celebrate the anniversary of Hitler's birthday. It was in Johannesburg and a bunch of Jews raided the place, smashed everything. There was an enormous flap but the Prime Minister and the government sided with us."

"Then you admit there are Nazis and anti-Semitism there?" Yosi demanded fiercely, trying to salvage something of his original premise.

"Of course," Frank replied evenly. "Where isn't there? Don't we have it here?"

"Then why did you leave South Africa?" Yosi persisted.

"I've been here three years. Harold, four. My folks came to South Africa from Lithuania. They were Zionists and from them I knew I belonged here."

Yosi was pleased. He asked if Harold came for the same reason.

"No, I'm not so romantic. I ran away from my wife."

"But you could have gone to Canada, Australia, many places. Why Israel?"

"Honest to God, I don't know," Harold said. "I suppose I liked the idea of living in a Jewish state, but mainly I came because my wife hates the idea of Israel. She might follow me elsewhere but never here."

"And what do you do for women, out there on that rooftop?"

"Frank manages very well. He's blond, and Israeli brunettes are hungry for 'whites.' As for me, I enjoy celibacy."

Frank showed us a photograph of an exquisite girl, very dark, delicate. "My fiancée," he said proudly. "Moroccan."

Yosi studied the photograph. "What beautiful children you two will have," he said avuncularly.

"I have no money to marry. I earn $125 a month and live on $25. Harold and I eat only once a day just to save. Perhaps in time I'll have enough."

The mail arrived and the two men left us. We walked toward the port. "Can you imagine what Frank's kids will be like?" Yosi asked. "He, the product of centuries of closed, ghettoized breeding among Lithuanian Jews; she coming from the same restricted breeding, but in Morocco. Their kids—the progeny of two unique but inbred parents—will be superior to either of them. All around us it is happening, a people apart, dispersed for millenia, here suddenly come together and their matings produce an entirely new offspring, a unique amalgam." He paused, struck by the implications of his thought. "Yes," he went on slowly, "perhaps that's why our kids are so different, more daring and beautiful and wiser than their parents."

"Aren't you being racist?"

Yosi froze. "I did not say they will be superior to other people but to their parents." He paused. "Still," he went on, his stiffness softening, "it is a unique phenomenon we have here . . . never before has it happened; geneticists should be overjoyed at the laboratory for human genetics we offer. Well-l . . . we shall see what we shall see."

Chapter 9

The feel of the frontier permeated Eilat. There was vast space, clean air, careless dress, hope, bustle, and a quiet possible only where a wildness of desert and sea mingles.

Rich tourist hotels, grotesquely modern in this biblical setting, lined the sea between Eilat and Jordan's port city of Aqaba. Tourists came for a day or two to see King Solomon's copper mines at Timna, to bathe in the Red Sea, to wonder at the Exodus story nudging them here. They gazed at the mountains of Moab in Jordan and reflected on the Deuteronomic injunction: "Thou shalt not seek their peace nor their prosperity all thy days forever."

But, as Yosi had said on the bus, Jews today have forgotten the searing, implacable justice demanded of them while in the desert. Now they are softer. Now they seek the peace of Moab. The bazaars of Aqaba beckoned Jewish tourists and it seemed such a shame they could not go there.

We walked toward the port one morning, hoping to talk to the workers and managers there. But we were stopped by a guard. Yosi blandly told him that we were journalists and wished to talk to the director. But the director was busy. We were taken in hand by a foreman named Israel. He described in detail how the port worked, tonnages, security precautions, types of workers. He omitted no technical detail, and I tried to catch Yosi's eye to indicate that we were not interested in dull operational detail but people.

Yosi avoided me. He seemed fascinated. Finally Israel concluded and invited us for coffee in the mess hall. Yosi winked at me and then I knew it was necessary to listen to Israel, to gain his confidence so that, over coffee, casual conversation could emerge. Suddenly I was delighted that in Jerusalem I had waited for Yosi.

For a time, over coffee, Yosi and Israel discussed Eilat, its isolation, lack of cultural events, inadequate schools, and told us that the government gave much higher pay for those who would come to work here. Most came for a stint of duty; then, sated with the dull life, returned to richer lives in northern towns. Gradually, Yosi turned the conversation to Israel himself. Slowly, slowly he told of his life in Bucharest.

One day a troop of Nazis came to his home and took away his father and three older brothers. Forever. But he, only nine years old, was taken with his mother and sister to a freight yard and put in a cattle car headed for the Russian border. There, hundreds of Jews were assembled and marched northeast toward some unknown destination. Six Ukrainian civil guards accompanied them. "Only six! Six!" Israel repeated in wonderment.

Israel's mother had smuggled some jewels and traded them for food. Once, lame, she hired a wagon, paying in advance. They tried to climb aboard but the driver whipped up his horses, spilled them backward into the mud, and drove away.

During the march, they were rarely allowed to leave the road. Drinking water was scooped from ruts.

The sick and old were told to drop out of line to wait for wagons. Israel could hear shooting back there where the old people waited.

Once the guards themselves became so lame and bored that they herded the group into a ravine. They were about to massacre them when a Russian officer came riding past and stopped them, had the guards whipped, sent them away and replaced them with Russian soldiers, one of whom gave Israel a bonbon, and said, weeping, "I, too, have little children."

In the permanent concentration camp, they once again had Ukrainian civil guards. That winter his mother starved to death. His sister was poisoned with botulism and paralyzed. She crawled on all fours. Bodies were hauled off and dumped in the snow. Starved dogs fought over them.

Israel talked compulsively, describing an arm, a head, smaller parts left gnawed on the frozen snow. But he was really not talking to us. He was reliving the past as had Arie. Yosi, too, was lost in it. His theatrical sense of the horrible was aroused and he was overwhelmed by the steady, quiet flow of history so terrible it ought never to be uttered; so human it ought never to go unmentioned.

The murdered have their rights! Israel talked to us because he did not want his family's agony to go unrecorded. God willing, it would not.

I was grateful for the science of communication that created the tape recorder. My hands shook so that I could not write. I did not want to listen. Yosi was pale. Compulsively, he sprayed his throat with his syringe. In the still and quiet of the dry air, the odor of the spray reached me, sweet and oddly familiar. . . .

In camp there was no heat except that generated by the hundred and twenty human bodies. Wood for cooking was stolen in forages through the countryside. While foraging, Israel and three boys were caught by a civil guard armed with a single-shot shotgun. He ordered them to blindfold themselves. They refused. As soon as he fired one shell, killing one boy, the others ran away, as they had planned, escaping before the guard could reload.

"Three out of four saved," Israel murmured.

"A normal score, Jewishly speaking," Yosi added.

In the spring, they were forced to dig with their hands for sugar beets not rotted in the fields. It was heavy work for weakened bodies and many died. Yet one of the two Ukrainian supervisors was kind to Israel, took him to his house, fed him, gave him extra food. "Even though I was filthy and covered with lice, he took me into his home. And there was the camp bookkeeper who had a son who helped me with food and other things. His mother was an anti-Semite and beat the boy when she learned of our friendship. But the father defended us."

In summer, only Israel and forty others lived.

"A miracle," Yosi whispered.

"It was no miracle," Israel said flatly. "I just did not get sick. If you got sick you died."

"And the gentiles? Do you hate them?"

"No, I do not hate. They are merely gentiles; they are people, good and bad ones. The Russian captain. The bookkeeper. Others.

Once a guard hit mother with a rifle butt and I kicked him hard on the shin. A gentile crowd had gathered and these passed me among them. While the guard howled and hugged his leg, one of the people hid me in his house."

There was a moment of deep stillness between Yosi and me, a kind of prayerful silence at the puzzling quality which gave men like Israel the grace to retain not only their dignity in the face of unmentionable indignities, but grace to believe in mankind's innate decency. Israel, all unknowing, was like another Abraham, who had so cleverly bargained God down to spare Sodom for the sake of only ten righteous persons in a city of wicked thousands.

At the end of the war, a Zionist youth organization spirited Israel from an orphanage and sent him to Palestine. He was thirteen years old.

Off Haifa, six British warships steamed around the tiny leaking ark bearing Noah's children. The refugee ship's captain signaled that steering cables were cut, boat out of control. The British knew he was lying and sent a destroyer to cut across his bow to force him to turn about. But the captain managed to ram the destroyer, seriously damaging it. Then the British tried to board the ship, used tear gas, but were repulsed by barbed-wire barricades and showers of bottles, crockery, ballast rocks. Finally the British threatened to shell the ship and send any survivors to distant Mauritius unless surrender came at once. They did surrender, after promises of sanctuary on Cyprus, which was comfortingly near Israel.

They were carried to Cyprus like captives to Babylon.

In 1948, Israel finally made it to a kibbutz near Jerusalem. Almost at once, he was involved in the War of Independence, fought well, and had served in the infantry reserve ever since.

Did he think much about the past?

"Only about what fools we were not to fight. We could have escaped or killed the six guards. But everyone advised caution. My mother put her hand over my mouth when I suggested escape."

Yosi asked if Israel had become religious because of his experience.

"No. I take my three sons to synagogue once a year so that they can see how it once was with their grandfather."

Israel paused. "Once at the kibbutz, on Sabbath, I rode out to check the irrigation pumps. An old Hassid walked up to me, took me aside, explained so sweetly about the meaning of Sabbath, the need of animals for rest, my own responsibility to keep the day holy, that I wanted to bury myself. I loosed the horse, returned on foot. Now if our religious leaders talked to me as did that Hassidic Jew . . . I feel the need. There must be a reason for Jewish existence. But our religious leaders compel us to observe the Sabbath. I will not submit."

Israel was angrier at the rabbis than he seemed to have been at his Ukrainian captors.

I asked Israel why he had come to Eilat.

"Here I make more than a mechanical engineer in Jerusalem; and in school I never got past grade ten. It's dull . . . but not so-o-o dull. And there is a tax allowance for frontier service."

"Will there be peace with the Arabs?"

"Not in my lifetime."

"And your children's?"

"Perhaps. More likely my grandchildren's."

"Can the state last that long?"

"With the help of our friends, yes. After all, what's a couple of generations?"

A short, dark, mustached man entered the mess hall. Israel called to him, introduced him as Chaim. Chaim invited us to visit his office.

Israel would not permit an outside photograph, for security reasons. He stood in the doorway and I photographed him there. The man had strength together with serenity, and he gave out an essence of indestructibility. He smiled, revealing gold-capped teeth that glittered in the light. Blue-eyed, with cropped blond hair, he was fleshy but not soft. Capability marked him. A family man. A good man. I hoped to capture something of all this in the photograph, but failed. He appeared as just another Israeli. There are times when the word says far more than a thousand pictures.

Chaim took us to his office. He had hardly started to talk when he was called away. But he invited us to his home that night.

We strolled to the hippie colony in the hills. With grave hostility they turned their backs to us who were so obviously straight. Their concerted rebuff was disquieting, and we walked back to the sea.

On the beach there was a stranded fishing boat. To the lee of it in a sleeping bag was an American boy, recently arrived, quite lonely. "They don't know if I'm a spy," he told us. "Eventually I suppose they'll accept me." He told us it took time to gain their confidence, that if we wanted to talk with them we must be slow, easy—"cool." He suggested that we be seen at the coffeehouse, buy a few coffees, make ourselves friendly. "There have been too many scurrilous articles about us in Turkey, Greece, Europe. Fakey scenes of sex and drugs have caused them to be expelled from too many places. It's free land here, for them, and they don't want it loused up by yellow journalism."

"Let's make a beginning with you," Yosi said, his voice gritty with a hard edge of contempt. "So what brought you to this paradise?"

The boy looked at him, blinked, turned away, shut us out. I restrained Yosi.

"Why bother with them?" Yosi asked, furious at the boy's cool rebuff. "They are rude, dirty, and utterly useless to our society. And there are few Israelis among them. What can you possibly learn about us from Europeans and Americans?"

I shrugged but did not answer because I was not certain that he was wrong.

We went to the coffeehouse, an open shed fronted with shabby tables and chairs. But it was well populated with freaks on their way to and from the post office. Their language was English and French, and their concern was money; who got some and how much.

We picked up the tab for a table of six. They nodded their thanks and raised empty cups. We had them refilled. They were slender, wan types and seemed very gentle. One of them, a frazzled but beautiful blonde, smiled at my stocky friend, tried to catch his eye, finally came over and introduced herself as Maria. She was delighted to learn that Yosi was Israeli. We told her what we were doing and that we wanted to talk with the hippies. She quickly told us to address them as freaks, a term they preferred. She agreed to show us around, introduce us to the leaders. She thought that Yosi could ease the way if he were seen with her, especially since he was a dramatist.

"But," Yosi said, "my friend here wants the interviews, not I. I just don't care at all. Take both of us."

But she would not hear of it, insisting that only Yosi could pave the way, saying she knew best, and pulled him away. Together they walked toward the beach. Yosi did not seem too reluctant. Maria made an odd figure, dressed in sandals, a man's carcoat, her hair swirling in the wind. The five who were left at her table did not seem to notice. They sat and looked searchingly at their coffee, seeming beyond surprise.

At dusk, Yosi returned to the hotel room.

"How did it go?" I asked.

"A drain. She is insatiable. In that silly, see-through polyethylene tent, we balled all afternoon." Yosi was spread on the bed, his face lined, his limbs flaccid. He poured himself half a glass of brandy. The room was warm from the electric heater borrowed from the manager. Yosi began to scratch. Soon he was wild with frantic slapping and scratching and rushed to the bathroom and the shower. There he found himself covered with fleas. I too began to itch. Finally, in agony, Yosi went to the manager and got a can of insecticide. We sprayed ourselves, the room, the bedding. At last we were free of them and Yosi fell asleep.

He awakened two hours later. "You and your goddam freaks," he groaned. He snapped on the radio. The evening news broadcast had started. It came every hour, like a nationwide priestly chanting, heard with religious concern.

Everything stilled during the six measured heraldic bleeps that preceded the chant of the news itself. Then the announcer-as-high-priest came on. So many infiltrators and Israelis killed . . . the United Nations frowned on Israeli air strikes . . . Abba Eban pronounced . . . Golda Meir soothed . . . a bus was blown up . . . a narcotics ring was captured. . . . There seemed never to be a happy note. Always the broadcast dealt with the undeclared war and the state's problems. Yet it was the time of daily unity shared by atheists, agnostics, believers, dullards, socialists, capitalists, thieves, housewives. All Israel. Was it good for Israel? Such was the question in everyone's eyes. No answers, only questions. Still, the quiet during the regular broadcasts was a moment of national communion. Short of sharing real war, when it has come there seemed no other moment so generally, poignantly shared.

After dinner we hiked up the steep hills to Chaim's house. Inside, the heat was from a kerosene stove that gave comfort against the chill night only to those very close to it. Gita, Chaim's wife, kept a tidy apartment, decorated with things of the area—desert plants, driftwood, coral fans, gourds, seashells. Along one side of the living room ran shelving filled with much-used books. All was spare. All was adequate.

Both Chaim and Gita were born in Israel. Gita, who was reared in a kibbutz by parents liberated from concentration camps, tried to comport herself as a kibbutznik should; with simplicity of dress, direct speech, sobriety, indifference to money and what it buys. Gita said that she would return to her kibbutz but that Chaim did not care for the life. "I like privacy," Chaim said. "I need it and I want to educate my children as I see fit and not as a kibbutz committee directs me to do."

Gita said that the kibbutz people were different. "For a week we had two vacationing girls from my kibbutz. They did not help with the housework, cooking, anything. Chaim did not understand it. But in a kibbutz each must do his assigned job. My job is to keep house. Theirs was to have a vacation in Eilat, after which they would return to their work in the kitchen, laundry, fields, children's house or wherever assigned."

"Couldn't they have at least volunteered?" Chaim demanded.

"The idea never occurred to them. Even in the army we are different," Gita went on. "We are clannish. Others get packages from home and share it with all. But a kibbutznik will call only kibbutz kids for sharing."

Chaim looked at me and raised his eyebrows as if to say, You see what provincials they are?

"Don't complain, Chaim," Gita snapped. "What they lack in social graces they make up in fighting ability and leadership."

An older couple entered without knocking; Shmuel and Rivka—best friends of Chaim and Gita—had been invited to meet us.

Rivka was a cultivated Alexandrian Jew who taught English and French in the public schools of Eilat. She did not like life in Eilat. "I do not like to see enemies across the bay every time I look up," she said.

She was very proud of Israel's public schools, "We have television to teach mathematics and English. And almost a hundred percent of our five-year-olds are in kindergarten. Only two percent of our kids from six to fourteen are not in school." She went on with statistics.

Finally Shmuel interrupted her. "Some will disagree, Rivka. But, after all, Jews have always been specialists in education."

"It is especially necessary for us to have the best," Rivka added, "because sixty percent of our children have illiterate parents, from Moslem countries where they were second-class citizens, living as in the Middle Ages. In one generation or sooner, we must erase the time gap of many generations, and education is the eraser."

And what about the generation gap between those parents and their children?

She sighed, "We can't do much for them."

"They'll die off," Chaim said. "Didn't Moses have the same problem? Didn't he have to wander forty years until the old died off and the young warriors came on fresh, unspoiled by recollections of Egypt's fleshpots? So it is with us."

"And we, too, feel a generation gap, Rivka and I," Shmuel said. "My children don't understand our ways and even less the ways of their grandparents. How could they? They haven't been where we've been."

Yosi drew from Shmuel that he was an expert in explosives,

working for the Timna copper mines. He had learned his trade working as a sapper for British Intelligence in Greece, during the Second World War. When the Germans invaded, he blew up the canal at Corinth and escaped, with six British and French helpers, to a fishing trawler, their hideout for a year. From it they mounted sorties into occupied Greece.

But Shmuel seemed such a quiet, unobtrusive man. He was rather short and a bit fleshy, nearly bald, with a pleasant, mild, but shrewd face. But the skin of his hands was tough as stretched cowhide. Otherwise, he could have passed for a myopic Jew whose most explosive experience was revelation in Talmud. It was difficult to imagine him in his greatest achievement as a saboteur of a German infantry division headquarters.

Shmuel told about that adventure, when he drove a stolen German staff car to the division's encampment. Smartly they returned the sentries' salute. At division headquarters, a Frenchman handed the German guards three dispatch cases stuffed with explosives synchronized to blow up simultaneously when one case was opened or within three minutes. "From GHQ. Take them to the officer at once. Immediate action required," the Frenchman ordered, in perfect German. Shmuel returned the Nazi salute and the staff car roared out of the compound. Shortly thereafter, they heard the explosion, ditched the car and uniforms, and, fading into the streets of Salonika, they made their way safely back to their fishing vessel.

Near the end of the war, Shmuel was sent to Alexandria. There he met Rivka, whose people were proud Sephardic Jews who had lived for centuries in Alexandria. It took some doing for Shmuel to overcome their prejudice against his Polish background.

Rivka described the hauteur and dignity of her family. She told of her great-aunt who, when Hitler seemed invincible at El Alamein, was approached by a friendly Catholic priest who begged her to convert to Christianity to save her life. She refused, saying, "I didn't choose to be a Jew, but since God made me one, I think He wants me to remain one."

Chaim, too, was in Greece. He was in an operation that tried to rescue and send to Israel the few Greek Jews who remained after eighty thousand had been murdered by the Nazis. It was there he acquired a contempt for politicians that had never left him. In his group were two men sent by the Jewish Agency. They were neither qualified nor dedicated but simply political men of the dominant party. Quickly they became immersed in black market operations and brought an evil name to the rescue project, endangering it. After many requests and telegrams demanding the recall of the two men, Chaim received a wire from the Jewish Agency quoting the Bible: "Thou shalt not muzzle the ox when he treadeth out the corn." Chaim raised his hands in resignation.

"And it's still like that," Chaim said. "We have no real vote for candidates for office. We have to vote for a full slate or none at all, and this means that the old boys, fat with power and long in the job, simply perpetuate themselves in government. So I don't vote. To hell with it."

Shmuel nodded agreement. "The army is not like that. And that's one reason why it is so successful. Leadership rotates. Young officers and noncoms are brought in. A man retires early to make a place for the young. But our politicians never retire. They play musical chairs."

"Is that what is called *proteksia?*" I innocently asked.

They smiled. "So you've heard of our national disease," Chaim said.

"It's not so bad as they make out," Gita told me. "For if we could come so far in twenty-five years, then how could it be so bad?"

We left these two tough-tender couples and walked through the absolutely stunning black night to the *pension* where the manager informed us that a young lady had been to see Yosi several times. "Heepee," he said, holding his nose.

"Next time spray her with that can of insecticide and tell her I've gone to America," Yosi ordered.

Yosi flopped on his bed. "You've seen a typical evening in Eilat," he told me. "Coffee, cake, fruit, brandy, and endless conversation. Lots of gripes. But Eilat is the outback of Israel."

I did not dispute it. But Eilat seemed to have more character than any Israeli city except Jerusalem.

In the morning, Yosi begged off visiting the freaks. "Just ask for Maria," he said. "She expects to help you, and I paid the last full measure of devotion to arrange it."

But back in the hills no one would direct me to Maria's. They were furtive, seemed to be protecting her.

One older man who called himself Wesley had the decency to ask me what I wanted of her, and I told him. He was squatting over a small fire, making tea. He circumspectly checked me as if I were a bacterium, probably malign. Then he offered tea. We sat silently for a long time under the gray sky, shivering against the cold. The hot tea, laced with condensed milk and loaded with sugar, was the best I had ever tasted. Complemented, Wesley merely grunted through his grayish-white beard.

"You're wasting your time," Wesley finally said. "Here we have few Jews. There's Joel, a pusher. Danny is a police plant. Ephraim and Moshe could pass for freaks, I suppose, but they're too long in this straight country and don't quite measure up. Most of us are Western; Europeans, Canadians, Americans, Australians."

He sipped his tea and stared at the fire. I felt no special urge to move on. Wesley was not hostile. Squatting across from him, I had a sense of time-in-limbo, and I felt as close to the Midianites and Edomites as to this squatted British bum.

Wesley raised his head and stared at me as if to question why I stayed to scratch at his silence. Then he grinned, showing good teeth and a mouth that seemed used to laughter. "Why don't you ask me some questions?" he demanded.

"Where is Maria?"

"Leave her alone. She is a lost soul. Dead. Leave her to her agony."

Informed of Yosi's afternoon with her, he relented and sighed. "Just so you don't muck it up, I suppose you should know the truth," he said. "But if you ever use her real name, I'll hunt you to hell and back."

I promised him her anonymity. He then told the story disjointedly, pausing to sup tea, or to scratch or just to stare toward Jordan.

Maria was of an ancient and honored Prussian Junker family. Approaching puberty, she learned from the taunts of her schoolmates that her father had been a close assistant to Heinrich Himmler, creator of that genocidal obscenity, the destruction of all Jews. The Nazi Final Solution.

Haunted, tortured with knowledge of her father's Faustian culpability, she eventually broke under the strain of surrogate guilt. For a few years she passed from sanitarium to sanitarium. She eventually escaped to Israel, entering illegally. With no skills, altogether unstable, inevitably she found Eilat and the freaks, where she kept a semblance of sanity. Here she worked as a chambermaid at tourist hotels, or as a worker in a laundry. But always she must sleep with an Israeli Jew. Hers was a selective, compulsive sex.

Suddenly he broke off and brusquely asked, "Do you believe me?"

"Sure."

"You don't think I'm covering up for a whore?"

He seemed reassured, went on with the story. "She simply has a driving need for sex that is not pleasure or flagellation or masochism but a kind of insatiable penitence. It's as if the semen spilled into her could, somehow, generate a Jewish child; bring her peace.

"But she cannot become pregnant." He sighed. "All of us watch for this rather perverse but poetically immaculate conception. The poor thing may be sterile. Or God may have 'sealed her womb,' in punishment for the sins of her father . . . isn't it until the tenth generation? And what compounds the sadness is that she seems to have lost her attractiveness to men. She has taken a job as a go-go girl and works for almost nothing, hoping to attract lovers. But nothing happens. I cannot understand it because she's attractive, so willing, so gentle."

Fleas, I told him. Such vicious fleas as have not been seen in Israel since Tiberius was said to hold the king of them.

He seemed shocked. Then he smiled, began to chuckle, broke into a cosmic roar of absolutely joyous laughter. " 'The flea, though he kill none, he does all the harm he can,' " he yelled. He began a sort of Irish jig. "Oh, it's so simple. We can fix it. Thank God." His huge laughter affected me, too, and I felt good, jumped up to join him, jigging crazily on the hillside. Others joined. The circle widened.

It was no small thing to dance joyously and sing tunelessly at noon of a gloomy day.

Wes asked two dollars of me, then rushed toward town. He returned with a can of insecticide. He nodded to me, and we walked to one of the polyethylene tents. Wes passed unceremoniously inside, pointed the can into the double sleeping bag. Maria's voice wailed and was joined by a man's. Heads emerged, then bodies. Wes told them to remain five minutes cloaked in the fog of spray. He whispered in Maria's ear. She kissed his cheek. Wes emerged, sprayed himself, playfully spurted a jet or two at me and we returned to the fire.

He put his arm over my shoulder and now introduced me as his friend. "You'll be welcome," he told me. "They'll all talk to you." And so it was.

But the interviews were depressingly dull The pusher, Joel, was disjointed in his speech and views. He did not at all favor a separate Israel; thought Jews and Arabs should live together in a common territory and did not much care under whom they lived. "They are our brothers," he said softly. "We should live at peace with them."

"But do the Arabs know that they are your brothers?"

"Of course. Hit a dog and he'll snap at you. Pet him and he'll be your faithful friend. It is we who start things, not the Arabs. If we didn't they'd be our friends," he said wistfully, his voice drooping on an ending, hopeless note. Poor Joel, the pusher. His idea might one day get him a slit throat, but until then he had a good head for business.

Wesley introduced me to Maurice, an Algerian Jew. He was twenty-one, lithe, dark, handsome as Omar Sharif, and had been a sergeant in the French army, court-martialed for striking an officer. In the Israeli army he had not risen above private and nursed that insult.

But Maurice seemed a malcontent in most things, and the impression grew as the conversation continued. He hated Israel, considered the country "one huge kibbutz." He had lived in a real kibbutz, could not stand it, thought it too regimented a way of life. There, he felt like a machine.

"Kibbutz girls have no style," he declared, "lumpy, plain, boorish. The kibbutz life makes them machines. Ugly city girls go there to get husbands because in the kibbutz they seem beautiful—by contrast."

Then Maurice said a thing that revealed the sadness of his condition. He said that he would go to Mexico and continue his family profession of masonry. When he was told that Mexico has its own shriveling poverty, rigorous castes, and plenty of masons, he said: "Then I will move on. I am like a part of a puzzle. I will go from one country to another until I find one where the part that I am exactly fits the space there awaiting me."

The few Jews on the beach, in the hills, were misfits in the dynamic, optimistic, and somewhat mystical Israeli society. Maurice knew that he was out of place. The others did not. They had dropped out of the vigorous life to the north but they knew no better place to go. In the vastness of American space, such peculiar ones are absorbed without a tremor.

Once again I reflected how curious it was that Israel allowed them sanctuary.

That night we went to Maria's night club to watch her perform. At first Yosi refused to go, but then I explained Maria's illness. His eyes grew luminous and he could not speak.

She was there in a cage, trying hard to writhe seductively, but managing only spastic, gauche contortions, like a stick woman caught in high wind. "And she is as determined and awkward in a sleeping bag," Yosi whispered. "But she has one lucky feature; she is a blonde in a country of brunettes."

Maria's breasts were covered with a scant and dirty strip of cloth. Her g-string had a too-small patch that allowed golden pubic hairs to peep around it. Her bony face, lean but very sweet, had the hungry expression of a concentration camp child. "Feed me," it seemed to beg. "Feed me with love and I shall be saved, cured; if you will only love me."

The band was unpracticed, the drinks were weak, the crowd disinterested. Maria neither saw us enter nor leave.

Back in our room Yosi said, "We are not the only ones to suffer." He screwed the nozzle from his rubber syringe and poured its contents down his throat. He exhaled an enormous sigh that filled the room with the reek of brandy. It was then I learned why he kept the syringe and why he sprayed his throat so often. He turned away and fell asleep.

Chapter 10

Something was wrong with the tape recorder. We were given the address of a good electrician and walked up the hills toward his shop.

A vigorous man working on a television set stood and took my tape recorder to a workbench. In a few minutes he returned and said, "It was nothing. A little looseness." He refused pay, saying, "An insignificance."

He was from Argentina; tall, proud, intelligent. He came as a Zionist, married a Yemenite, and had lived in Eilat for six years. His father approached us. "It is not often that we see writers and playwrights in Eilat," he said.

The father had a clipped white beard and a fine, drooping mustache in a pure, aesthetic face. He could have been a Goya aristocrat—except for the period-like distinction atop his head, the black yarmulka identifying the pious Jew.

"I did not want my father to come to Israel; least of all to Eilat," the son told us. "He is very learned in Torah and is a fine violinist. I was afraid he would be too lonely here, but he insisted. He has found a few Talmidei chachamim, wise men of the Torah, and he has also started a string ensemble—there is an army officer, a postal clerk, fisherman, and the like. Music attracts musicians as Israel attracts Jews. And so he is happy."

"Do you give concerts?" Yosi asked the old man.

"Not yet," he replied. "In a few years we will be ready."

Yosi looked at me. "In a few years," the old man had said. He had not enough life for such patient waiting. Still, perhaps it is true what is said about trees, that only old men have enough life to plant them.

We talked about Arabs and chances for peace. Neither thought there would be peace in his lifetime. Neither man had talked with more than half a dozen Arabs. "We just never come in contact with them," the son said.

Yosi asked why Eilat was chosen as the town in which to do business. The old man answered. "He wanted to be near where it all began; near that desert in which Moses wandered for forty years and where he received the Law."

The son accompanied us to the door. "That's what he believes," he softly told us. "The truth is that they needed electricians here and there was an opportunity for a shop. So I came."

Yosi needed a shoe repairman and the son pointed to a shop about a block away.

"How strange it is," Yosi said, as we walked away, "that the scion of fifty generations of European scholars is attracted to and marries a Jew from Yemen, whose culture is Arabic, and whose people lived there as artisans and craftsmen for hundreds of years."

"Still, both her parents and his must have been pious."

"That is their single shared characteristic. But did you notice that the son does not wear a yarmulka? And that he assured us that he did not come here for mystical reasons? The young abandon the mumbo-jumbo of diaspora Jews. Whether of East or West, here they live as Jews and need no artificial symbols to identify them."

"But diaspora Jews, too, live as Jews."

Yosi did not agree. "I studied in America. I saw how ignorant and unlearned the Jews were. Americans they will be, but not Jews."

"And here you are so Jewish? You yourself have never been

in a Sabbath school, a cheder, or had much religious instruction. And you are no different from most Israelis."

"We study the Bible in public school," he replied heatedly. "It is a part of our life. We live a Jewish life. Like the Germans live a German life and the French a French one. How can we not be Jews when we are surrounded by the dust of Noah, Abraham, Lot, Isaac, Jacob, Moses, Solomon, and all the rest?"

In the shoe shop we met the Greek proprietor, his Hungarian wife, and their adult son. Brought together by a peregrinating matchmaker, they were married in Athens and had had a few good years before the Germans came. She and her child were taken to Auschwitz. The husband, too, was in a concentration camp. They would not discuss the miracle of their survival or life under German terror. She held up her arm with vividly tattooed numbers on it and said, "It is enough."

She spoke Yiddish and a fair Hebrew, but the father and son spoke only Greek. Clearly, the woman dominated the shop.

Yosi sat in stocking feet waiting for his new heels to be hammered on by the silent, gnomelike husband. The shoes were soon mended. Yosi wanted to spend more time so I decided to have a shoulder strap put on my leather camera case.

Eventually, Yosi led the wife into personal conversation.

"We are happy here," she told him. "Only it is damned expensive. This shop is about twelve feet square and costs us $150 a month in rent. And it's a bargain! Down the street there's one even smaller that rents for $200. We need a larger apartment but a three-room apartment sells for $18,000. We live in two."

"But the poor," Yosi prompted. "they pay less, of course."

"That's different," she said. "A man from Tunis, a porter, earns in a month what we pay here for rent. Eight children. So he pays only $15 a month rent. The government pays the difference."

"Does the unequal rent anger you?"

She shrugged: "I am glad for it even though I do not like its causes. After all, when we came here we had special help to get started. And if we want Jews here, new citizens to help build the country, then we must be prepared to help them start a new life. We don't complain. Only it's so damned expensive."

"Do you have any help in the shop?"

"Shoemakers are not to be found. We pay two dollars an hour for help when we can get it and then they can't even hold an awl. So we do it alone, as a family, and we do quite well."

She said that her neighborhood had mostly Rumanians, Hungarians, Moroccans, and, since only she could speak Yiddish, they had few friends. They worked a twelve-hour day. Movies eased their loneliness. Too, they had the dogs and cats.

The son was forming a child's shoe on a wooden last, his mother constantly directing. The husband struggled to fit a strap on my camera case, his wife pointing out the way to go about it. Both men accepted her orders unquestioningly.

Yosi asked her how they could watch movies when the two men did not understand either the English language or the Hebrew subtitles.

"They understand," she told us. "We see the same movie three-four times; they understand. And I explain. And if not there, then where? Should they stay home every night?"

"Were they Zionists in Greece?" I asked.

"No," she replied. "We came here because it is better for us to live here than in Greece or Hungary or any other place. Nothing more than that. But, blessed be the Name, we are just glad to be here."

She was a short, fat, unkempt, driving blob of a woman and she had seen the worst that man could do to man. When she told us that she was "just glad to be here," I felt such a well of emotion that it almost choked me. Yet Yosi seemed unmoved. Daily, hourly, all of his life he had lived with souls snatched from extinction. As we left the shop, he remarked, "Incredible! An apartment here costs as much as in Tel Aviv." Now *that* impressed Yosi.

Chapter 11

Yosi waited for the last bus for Jerusalem before Sabbath eve.
"It'll be nice for you to spend Sabbath eve with Ruth," I said.
"It's not so much that," Yosi said, "as that I must enter Jerusalem before Sabbath or the bus can't enter at all. The zealots stone a public vehicle entering Jerusalem during Sabbath."
"The zealots?"
"The ultra-religious."
"And so how do people travel on the Sabbath?"
"They don't unless they are rich, own cars, and so can drive on Sabbath. The rich are favored!"
"The people must want it that way or they could change it."
"No!" Yosi said violently. "If an individual vote were taken on whether or not the buses should run on Sabbath, eighty percent would vote to let them run."
"You're a democratic country. So change things," I said.
Yosi looked at me with all the pity and condescension of a music teacher correcting the squawky errors of a ten-year-old clarinetist. "The parties run the country; not the people. And the labor party needs the religious party's backing to stay in power. So they make concessions. A disgrace!

"You should hear Naomi tell about the time she stopped her car to let one of those extreme religious types cross the street. You've seen them. Long black silk coats. Broad-brim round fur hats. Pants legs tucked into long white sox. Dressed like eighteenth-century Polish aristocrats. This one was caught in midstreet and couldn't decide to cross over or go back. Confused, he shuffled backward and forward, fluttering like some white-footed black moth. Traffic stalled. Naomi shifted into gear and shot straight at him, jamming the brake at the last moment. The fool spun around like a top and then fainted. Of course everybody came around to help revive him. It was very amusing. I almost wish she had hit the bastard."

"You don't mean that," I said.

"Look! I know that such stubborn clinging to tradition kept us alive for thousands of years. But they don't have to make it so difficult for the rest of us. If they want to dress like that and walk on Sabbath, pray all day, fine! Let them observe all 613 commandments. But they have no right to keep my buses from running on Sabbath. That's coercion."

"There must be a good reason."

Yosi ran to catch the bus. He stuck his head out the window and yelled, "Good reason? Insane reason! They are crazy with God."

Chapter 12

It was time to move north. I waited for the bus in the early cold morning, clear and cloudless. The eastern mountains held a soft-edged nimbus penciled by the almost risen sun. At the foot of Edom's mountains Aqaba nestled in misty darkness not yet touched by morning light. But above where I waited, to the west and high, the concrete buildings of Eilat had caught the first light and returned opalescent hues of pale green, shadowy gray, faded ivory. Back of me the desert gave off such dark, loamy colors as to seem fertile prairie. It was a magic moment soon interrupted by trucks roaring up and down, people walking briskly, everything bouncy without frivolity, serious without melancholy, hopeful without exaltation. A vigorous people.

Misty Aqaba seemed a living fossil. Eilat seemed a lucky mutation in life. It had been a murderous international generation that Israel, Chaim, Shmuel, Menachem had all bucked tenaciously so as to make Umm Rashrash into Eilat. Or had a hundred generations behind them silently built the city?

I was surprised to see Wes, my bearded, aged hippie friend.

He was swathed in a blanket and wore the same tattered blue knit cap. Inside the bus, he seemed taller and leaner, his beard whiter, eyes bluer, face more gaunt and wasted. He sat next to me and his odor was not so much unpleasant as unnerving, compounded as it was of wood smoke, the faintly alfalfa-like fragrance of hashish, difficult and strange sex, and the excretions of secret fears and hysterias. But he was good as a traveling companion. He told me he had begun to feel Christ-like, that life in the magic hills had done it, with its sharing and contempt for worldly possessions. "Didn't Jesus say to give all you had and follow Him?" Wes asked.

"Sure. But you told me you were a Jew."

Wes stirred uncomfortably. "Don't believe everything I tell you. I did become a Jew. But I never really left off being a Christian. After all, Jesus was both, wasn't he?"

At Grofit, Wes got off and stood among the freaks waiting for the contractor's truck. They stood in their rags looking like some hobo group out of America's thirties. I was reminded of Yosi's story about the two hungry, cold German Jews watching the lavish funeral cortège of a nineteenth-century Rothschild. When the opulent hearse, all gold and silver, passed, one of the poor Jews peered closely at it, sighed enviously and said, "Now that's what I call living."

At Grofit an elderly kibbutznik got on the bus and sat next to me. A naturalist, to him the desert was a fertile thing waiting only for the seminal blessing of water. He pointed out spots of cultivated green among desert kibbutzim to prove that with water the desert could flower. "And we get the highest prices for our produce," he told me. "When the rest of Israel is in winter, we are in our prime growing season. Sometimes they pay us double for our vegetables. Sometimes we fly them to Europe for even greater profit."

Carefully smiling, I said that I thought the kibbutzim were contemptuous of money.

He did not return the smile. "We are not contemptuous of money," he said slowly, "only of how some people covet it, collect it, use it. We must have the means to buy food, clothing, fuel, tractors, equip our army, build housing. We need money. *I* don't need it. *We* need it."

Chapter 13

In Beersheba, at the tourist center where Yosi was to meet me, all was bright and inviting. But its restaurant had the look of an American fly-blown small-town coffee shop.

Behind me I heard a regular shrilling like that of crickets, but it was only the waiter's heavy boots squeaking. He seemed so disappointed that I wanted only coffee that I ordered a sandwich as well. He brightened and squeaked away toward the kitchen. It was such a loud squeak that I wondered how he could put up with it all day. Since it was now noon and I was the only customer, I wondered also how he could stay in business.

He returned, presenting the sandwich with extra motion and flourish as if it were a rare wine. I told him the food was good, the coffee remarkable, and he beamed, stood by, waiting patiently until I invited him to sit and share the bottle of wine.

"I am the proprietor. It is not proper."

"But unless you share wine with me I do not want it."

He shrugged, then sat.

His name was Laci and he had been in the Hungarian Air Force as a pilot until 1938 and the Anschluss. Then he fled to Italy to seek a ship for Palestine.

Italy! Not only Arie and the Jews of Yugoslavia had found there a temporary haven. . . .

Laci took a tiny ship flying the flag of Panama which had been chartered for refugees by Israel's firebrand revolutionary soul and poet, Vladimir Jabotinsky, who got the money for the job from the Jewish Agency. Six hundred people had come in panic from all over eastern Europe.

At Rhodes they took on an additional two hundred Jews. The ship was built for 150 passengers. Laci smiled slightly, still bewildered at the awesome condition of his escape. The ship sailed four months trying unsuccessfully to find a haven. No country would take the impoverished Jews, least of all British Palestine. Finally, anchored off Haifa for the third time, near dawn, Laci slipped off his clothes, jumped ship, swam to a wharf and hid under it all day. That evening, chilled and near exhaustion, he climbed to the wharf and ran to hide in a cement mixer. A policeman watched him run but made no move.

Soon, Laci heard a cart rumble up. "Get out," a voice whispered, but Laci was afraid to move. He was stupid with cold, hunger, hopelessness. Then the voice called louder, this time in Yiddish. Laci stiffly climbed to the top of the mixer where he was grabbed by gentle hands, wrapped in blankets, thrust into a barrel which was then hoisted onto a cart loaded with other barrels. The cart swayed and jounced away.

He was taken to a private home where he was fed and clothed. In a few days he was sent to work in the cement factory in Haifa. The rescuers could give him only a start. There were other ships, other Jews.

The depression of the thirties was still a heavy curse on Palestine and Laci could get only periodic work. He did odd jobs, slept in the parks on warm nights, and on cold nights he slept in sheltering doorways.

On New Year's Eve he went to Tiberius to work in the pipe factory. There he was caught in another cement mixer—the Arab riots of 1939. He managed to stop a bullet with his foot. Infection set in and the British took him to Rothschild Hospital in Haifa where his foot was saved but he was left with that limp.

He could find no work. "I would have gone mad if my friends had not helped me," Laci said quietly. He told his story in the strangest way, as if he were talking about the experiences of a friend and not of himself. There was no self-pity to the story, no blame or recriminations, only wonder.

Arie Stern had not talked this way, nor had Israel. But men have many lives, each so episodic, chaptered as to seem a retrospective dream. For men who have suffered deeply it is a blessed condition without which life might not be bearable.

"I can't believe it all happened," Laci affirmed, revealing a truth and a kind of divine psychic therapy.

Laci drifted to Tel Aviv where he worked as a night watchman in a restaurant on Allenby Street. He liked the quiet work, the warm stove, regular meals. But one night the fuel supply tank exploded, burning both Laci and his boss. Laci showed the scars on his arm and chest. His boss was severely burned, recovered, but could no longer operate the restaurant and sold it.

Laci again was out of a job. He joined a labor battalion in the British army.

"Would they take a man with a crippled foot?" I asked.

"They needed bodies. I was strong as an ox, even with that foot. I served in Egypt and that's where I met my wife, Marlene, the light of my life."

After the war, Laci had a number of restaurants, all failures, until he opened one in the northern part, in Nahariya, peopled by German Jews who loved the rich foods that Laci offered.

But Marlene developed asthma and they had to close the only successful restaurant they had ever had and move to the desert, to Beersheba, to this obviously failing restaurant. Poor Laci.

"I hate it here," he gritted. "The people are oriental Jews who live and eat like Arabs. I'm not used to them. I want to move away."

"Where will you go?"

"Someplace free of this *dreck* from Morocco, Tunis, Iran." He gestured in contempt. "Still, if I had a little money I could fix this place up and do well here. Maybe I'd create a rathskeller. Or maybe a night club—it's terribly dead in Beersheba at night. Or maybe a cafeteria. If I had a little money—"

"How much is a little?"

"Oh, say—ten thousand dollars."

"My, that's a lot."

"You think so? Well then. Hm-m-m, $7,500 might do it."

I whistled at the steep figure.

"Well, I could make many changes with five thousand."

"Who has such money?"

"I thought maybe—maybe—you might know of some Jewish investor. All American Jews are rich. They come in here on tour and I see them."

"I am only a writer."

"But you live from it?"

"Yes."

"Well, even a thousand or two could make an enormous difference."

Together we burst out laughing. He was tipsy now. He raised his glass. "Maybe not partners but friends, yes. . .?"

"Sure."

"But if you hear of anyone who wants to invest in a fine restaurant. . ." He fell to laughing again. The cook came out. People appeared at the door, astonished at the loud laughter, rare in Israel. And there was in his laughter that hint of hysteria that hooks the curious.

I asked Laci about a good hotel. He recommended one owned by Rumanian friends. I asked him to divert Yosi to me there, if he came.

In the tourist center the receptionist confirmed that the hotel was cheap, small, clean. She made a reservation for me and then we talked.

She had come to Israel, a child from the Mellahs of Morocco. She remembered only that life there was "not so bad. We managed. We weren't first-class citizens, but as long as we did not compete with Moslems, we were safe. My father had close friends among them. He was a shoemaker, very religious. Suddenly there was Israel. We came."

"And you are religious?" I asked.

"Yes, but not like my father. My husband is a sabra—born here, and is observant only on Sabbath eve when we light candles, say a blessing."

"And will you raise your children to be religious Jews?"

She shrugged. "Let them choose. If it is important to them, fine. If not, also fine."

"Will peace come?"

"I do not like to talk politics. I am only a woman. But my father says, only after a very long time. We lived among Arabs for centuries. He says generations must pass."

"Generations?"

"We took their land."

"But Jews have always lived here. And three hundred thousand Israeli Arabs live here now."

"These Arabs are not to be trusted, most of them. Why should we? How have they proved themselves? Many harbor terrorists. Many resent us and all the good we did them. We took the land and did it such good as they never dreamt of. But my father says they cannot soon forgive us the taking."

Suddenly she reverted to the job of advising tourists and would say no more about herself. She showed a map of Beersheba as it was planned originally to be. A verdant desert city that linked housing and business districts with green belts, parks, flowering lawns, open space.

I remarked that the reality of Beersheba was not at all like the planning of it.

She agreed, explaining that the utopian planners had not reckoned on the great pull of desert agriculture on the limited water supply. And so the planned green parks, green links, green open spaces meant to join the sections of the city were now brown desert making a series of separate villages—exactly what the planners had *not* wanted. She chuckled. "But I like it this way," she said. "I admire Arab villages, the smallness, the earthiness to them, of earth taken and shaped into buildings that almost at once begin to melt down to earth again. Beersheba begins to feel like that, a bit decayed, nomadic, mysterious, and more charming than if it had been successful as a European-style city."

Chapter 14

The receptionist had suggested I spend some time at the new University of the Negev, nearby. I bused there and moved from person to person in a ricochet movement which ended exactly where it would have done in the United States—the Public Relations Department. There, Daniel, an English Jew, directed University propaganda intended for visiting philanthropists, journalists, others for whom the administration and teachers had no patience.

Daniel ("Call me Dani") at once gave me the standard lecture given all those who come for information on the University; the mad influx of pupils, inadequate dormitory facilities, classroom shortage, teacher load, and the great work being done in spite of all the shortages. Of course, he said, money was the answer, but all the other universities vied with this newest one for limited money. He gave me a sheaf of informative literature nearly two inches thick. "Read this," he assured me, "then you can really understand our problems."

I listened, nodded, encouraged, and very soon had Dani talking about himself. Yosi had taught me the ways!

In England, Dani's father had been both single-mindedly socialist and militantly antireligious. "But," Dani said, grinning, "he saw me a bar mitzvah."

"And are you now observant?"

"I have two children. We light candles on Friday night, try to keep something of the tradition. But my son has discovered the Bible! How strange are the ways. He reads it and the commentaries. He is only twelve but has an adult's knowledge of the Book."

"Is this an example of religious revival brought on by the Six Day War?"

"I suppose the boy's interest to be more literary than religious.

But in Israel something mystical stirs, perhaps fleetingly. But, I'm way past all that mythic nonsense. Yet the people search for something."

Dani paused. "They tell the story," he went on, "of the prime minister's addressing troops to thank them for winning the war. 'What about thanks to God!' the chief rabbi of the armed services demanded of him. 'God doesn't need my recognition,' the prime minister said. 'Ah, but you are not allowed to pervert the facts,' the rabbi replied."

Dani laughed. "That's the trouble with the religious. Facts become miraculous dogma and vice versa; like military regulations."

Dani was folding, twisting, forming odd figures out of paper. He perspired slightly so that his pale, aesthetic face gleamed. Flighty, he seemed about to run away. A novelist himself, he was used to listening, observing, and seemed not to relish the reversal of roles.

"And why did you desert England and become an Israeli citizen?" I asked, knowing that *aliya,* or Going Up to Israel, is almost always a pleasant, prideful topic to those who had made the leap.

"During World War II, with Nazis bowling over all of Europe, my folks were not so sure they would not capture England. So they put my brother and me in a Christian private school where only the headmaster knew who we were. If worst came to worst, they figured we'd be safe there.

"We were welcome there. But we did not feel welcome. Still, we came away from it with a fine *classical* education. Later, I joined Habonim, a Jewish youth group devoted to Zionism. There I felt welcome. There I got my *humanist* education. Most of us came to Israel and joined one kibbutz or another. Then I married and we left the kibbutz because my wife did not like communal rearing of our kids.

"We tried a radical *moshav shitufi,* but it was too doctrinaire. They wouldn't take my advice, oddly enough, and bend to meet changing times. So we left. And here I am." He smiled, still nervous—a gentle, troubled man.

Daniel was a P.R.man by necessity. He was a fictionist by choice and revealed shyly that his historical novel had been published by the Jewish Publication Society of Philadelphia. He told how the idea for the story evolved. One night with his son, he read the story of those feisty Jews, the Maccabeans, who challenged their powerful Greek conquerors in the second century. Dani had long known the story. "But this night," he said, "I was suddenly seized with the notion of the grandeur of their religious drive, the shock wave of fervor that enveloped them, sealing off common sense, compelling them to be so nutty as to attack the undefeated Greeks. Their intoxication with God and with Israel shook me. Disturbed me. I could not sleep that night. The mood and motivation of the Maccabees became almost an obsession with me.

"I wrote the novel under a terrific compulsion to capture them in the incredible, desperate, religious exaltation that drove them." Dani sighed. "European and English publishers all rejected the manuscript, dejected me. Finally, Chaim Potok, then editor of the Jewish Publication Society, thought it worthy and sent me a contract."

Dani was very diffident about it all.

"In its own publishing field, Jewish books, it is excellent," I said. Of course he knew this. But his reserve seemed to dissipate in the great joy of hearing another say it.

We were interruped by Lauro, a student. He had come for help from Dani to organize a club for Western students who, he said, were in need of companionship, fellowship, a sense of belonging here in Israel. In a rush he said that Israeli students kept within their close-knit society into which Western students were rarely invited.

Dani sat, listened, seemed to have receded back into his shell. But Lauro persisted. "The foreign kids are a heterogeneous young group, the Israelis are homogeneous, older, have served and still serve in the army. They resent the special help given these inexperienced American and British kids; Dani will you help?" Lauro asked.

Dani fluttered his hands, stood, nervously paced the room.

"Time," Dani said, "give them time. A club will only create a ghetto for Western immigrants. I don't like it."

"They leave Israel," Lauro persisted. "More will leave. We had a hundred Western kids and now forty have left."

"A club is not right," Dani snapped. He was tense at this revealing dialogue, aired before a stranger. "Time. It takes time. Maybe . . . a pruning process is good. Maybe it should be that way."

"No!" Lauro shot back. "It is not right."

Dani stood and then moved toward the door. He was white with anxiety, beside himself with indecisiveness. He was a creative artist. What did he have to do with the sociology of foreign students? He sang their praises publicly but did not have to nurse them, make them happy. "I have an appointment with the dean," he told me in a tiny voice. "I'll be back very soon." Then he was gone.

Lauro sighed. "He'll come around. We must not let these kids return home ambassadors of discontent. Dani must help. I'll keep after him."

"It is not his way, his strength."

"I know. These socialists talk and write interminably but they cannot manage practical matters."

"They built the State of Israel."

"True. But it is today not the state they planned. Their socialism held the seed of its own disintegration. Here, you have a mechanical engineer making only ten percent more than a common laborer, thus you invite the rot that destroys. Israel will eventually be a hybrid state. We'll cross state ownership with private enterprise. The profit motive is the best yet to generate successful management."

"What about your underpaid soldiers? That's successful socialism."

"That's different. That's survival."

Lauro was born in America where his father, a rabbi, once supervised kosher slaughter in a Dubuque, Iowa, packing house. But the mother was dissatisfied with the Jewish schools there and so the arrangement was terminated in favor of a post in

Caracas, Venezuela, where the father had been accepted as rabbi for fourteen very old, rich, respected families who had fled Spain during the Inquisition 450 years ago. They had their own Sephardic synagogue.

But Caracas did not satisfy the militantly Jewish Lauro. He saw the process of assimilation at work on the Jews of Caracas and he feared it would affect him, his family. He forced the family to move to Israel by threatening to go there without them. Least of all his mother wished to go, for she had lost all her family in the Polish holocaust and feared another "final solution" at Arab hands. "She wants roots, now," Lauro said, "set deep. She is tired of running. It broke my heart to see her once again having to move from one place to another. But Israel is . . . well, Israel. She is contented here although still frightened."

I thought of Arie, in the *pension* in Jerusalem, and his friends left behind in Sossano, his friends who were too tired, too discouraged to flee farther, to Switzerland, who wanted to set down roots in Sossano and who were never given the chance.

"Do all of you remain observant Jews?" I asked.

Lauro hesitated. "It is harder to be an Orthodox Jew in Israel than any place in the world. Israel itself is the block; just being here seems enough. Does a fish need swimming lessons? I doubt that ten percent of our students are religious in the Orthodox sense."

"And your father?"

Lauro shrugged. "Who needs rabbis or kosher butchers in Israel? Here they are as numerous as stones in Jerusalem. He now manages a hotel near Tel Aviv."

"But all of you are glad you came?"

Suddenly his cheeks flushed, his face became merry, even joyous, and he grinned hugely, pressed his yarmulka flat to his head and said, "Yes, all Jews must come here. There is so much self-confidence here, enough to strengthen Jews everywhere. And there is such power and drive in the people. They sit here like the rocks and hills and none can move them.

"Yesterday I talked to a little man who runs a candy stand. He was once a great merchant in Poland. Now he makes only enough for his wife and himself to live scantily. I asked him if business was good and he replied with a so-so gesture. 'But we are contented,' he said and smiled such a beautiful smile. 'Thank God we are here.' He kept nodding as I turned away. I looked back and he was still nodding, still smiling."

Lauro was selling, being the missionary. Both of us understood this. It seemed certain that he would get his club. He seemed as assured as Dani's Maccabeeans—Dani would follow him because Lauro seemed tougher, more rocklike. Still, Dani had worked harder and longer than Lauro to make a life in Israel. There was metal in both. Only the degree of case-hardening differed.

Chapter 15

The bus dropped me near the hotel in the wild west downtown of old Beersheba. Bedouins instead of Indians walked the streets. Some Israelis wore traditional north African robes, others dressed in mufti as farmers, and yet others were slick-fashioned, conspicuous. There were camels, donkeys, horses, carts, trucks, little cars and big ones, a mélange of types and props, and it could have been a production lot of an American movie company simultaneously shooting ten different scenes for six different movies.

The place had a bouncy, tense feel about it like a cranked-up motor that could backfire and break your arm. A bank here was recently robbed and a teller was shot to death. Strolling soldiers, weapons slung over shoulders, were a comfort but their immediate concern was popping the meat out of sunflower seeds. They spat out the hulls and the sidewalks were strewn with them.

The hotel had thirty rooms and served only breakfast to the working clientele that stayed there. I started to type when an old man burst wild-eyed into my room. "My sweater. My sweater. I left it," he said. His eyes searched the room and then he started to leave.

"Search a bit," I told him, "it may be hidden. Take a look."

But he would not. He closed the door. A search of the room revealed nothing but a fine mist of dust over everything. The room had scarcely been used. Its walls were the ubiquitous yellow of all but the newest hotels. One Matisse print hung angularly on the wall. The bed had a marvelous double satin quilt but under the quilt was a mattress of iron. The bathroom was about thirty inches wide and six feet long and held a basin, toilet, lipless shower stall that flooded the floor. But the room cost only five dollars a day, including breakfast.

Later I asked the manager if the old man had found his sweater. "Sweater? What sweater?"

"He was an old man. He seemed to speak with a German accent. He came unceremoniously into my room looking for a lost sweater."

"Ah—Miron." The manager sighed. "He is frightened. He sees spies everywhere. He heard you typing and thought you must be sending messages to the Arabs, to France, to some place unfriendly. Please forgive him. He has been blighted forever by Bergen-Belsen."

I needed cassettes for my tape recorder, and the manager directed me to a shop. But there were none. A customer obligingly offered to take me to other shops. He was Moishe, of German parents but a sabra. He looked to be something less than affluent.

Asked if peace would soon come, he said, "Perhaps something comes soon; but not peace, more a respite. I have many Arab friends. They can sit and watch you for years and then unexpectedly make their move. They tell the story of a long-standing, smoldering feud between two Arab families. Suddenly open warfare broke out and we had to stop it. The heads of those families and one intermediary were brought before our authorities and asked the reason for the feud.

" 'A son of his family violated a daughter of ours.'

" 'When?' the Israeli officer asked.

" 'Forty years ago,' the second chief replied.

" 'Why were you so hasty?' the Arab intermediary asked."

That evening, the streets were crowded. There were movies. There was television. Still, people want to be with people and the street is the place for that companionship. In an arcade, several men and a boy clustered around glossy prints of lesbian scenes from a coming French movie; beautiful girls were posed in frankly libidinous postures. In this beleagured, puritanical land where sodomists were once stoned to death, following Levitical injunction—the display and interest in pictured homosexuality was shocking. Religious Jews averted their yarmulka-topped heads. Soldiers looked briefly, seemed puzzled, then turned away, more interested in sunflower seeds and conversation. But one boy, perhaps ten years old, frail, pale, briefcase clutched firmly, gazed with something more than wonder at the odd scenes. He wore the beanie-like black yarmulka of the religious Jew. His eyes were clamped on the glossies and he seemed to center on one that displayed two beautiful nude blond girls. A few passersby nudged him on but he always sidled back. Across the hall the proprietor of a soft-drink stand watched the spellbound child. At last the boy stood alone. Slowly his hand stole into his deep pocket.

The standkeeper admitted that pornography was on the increase in Israel. "It is everywhere on the rise. Some crime, some perversion are proofs that we are once again truly a state."

"Why was it so late in coming?" I asked.

"The kibbutzim are stern moralists. And the religious groups fight against it. . ."

"But that little boy—he is of the religious—"

"True. But he is first a little boy and then he is religious. When he is older and understands, he will turn away his eyes as is proper. Hey!" the standkeeper called. "Go. Shame. I shall tell your father."

The little boy spun around as if suddenly hurt. He blinked his way back to reality, then scurried off.

Every morning at breakfast I was greeted by an itinerant window trimmer, named Baruch. He was so thin as to seem emaciated, wore a turtleneck sweater, khaki pants, and sandals. His receding chin, prominent teeth, sparse hair, and big ears gave him the appearance of an anthropomorphized Bugs Bunny. Baruch was a gentle man who at once responded to my question as to how life in Israel seemed to him. He plucked at his sweater, his trousers, then spread both hands in explication. "We are clothed. We help one another. It is enough."

Baruch was born in Russia but had lived in Israel for thirty years. He had been trained as a chocolate maker here and had risen to become a finisher of bonbons, one who puts the clever, artful images atop each piece of candy. He decorated each piece as mood directed. But his boss wanted to standardize the operation; so many of this style, so many of that, and all done uniformly so that customers could distinguish by its decoration, the flavor in the creamy center. Faced with such commonsensical efficiency, Baruch rebelled and was fired.

"Nobody would hire me," he said. "Who wanted a sixty-one-year-old bonbon decorator? And even if they did, not one would hire me. I was too artistic, too individualistic for our bourgeois manufacturers. In Tel Aviv I ran into an old friend, an executive in Hamashbir, a cooperative department store run by the trade union movement. 'Come to work for us,' he said. 'But I'm too old,' I said. He said, 'We need a window trimmer and you're hired.'"

Store decoration, I suggested, was a more suitable genre for an artist than bonbon decorating.

"Not at all," he shot back. "I was known everywhere for my marvelously wrought figures, clever arabesques, imaginative Purim motifs, Pesach designs. Let me assure you, mine was no small art."

"Baruch," laughed another diner, "you could make a fine art of reaming a sewer. The owner had to compete and you were inefficient. Now your stores are inefficient. Tell this American how many people you need to decorate the Hamashbir store here."

"Isaac," Baruch answered softly, "you know. You tell."

"Twelve," Isaac sneered. "Twelve lousy workers to do a job that in America would be done by two men in half the time."

"And who are you to talk?" Baruch, now stung, shot back. "You who lived in a kibbutz, wasteful of manpower. Is that why you left? Inefficiency?"

"It is not inefficient. We worked for the common good and nothing could be more efficient than that."

"So? Then why did you leave?"

"My wife did not like the life."

"It is always the wife's fault. I have yet to meet a former kibbutznik who did not blame his wife."

"No," Isaac said, but without conviction, "I'll go back one day."

"You're too old, Isaac. They don't need you."

Asked how he now earned his living, Isaac replied, "I sell cotton-processing equipment for an American manufacturer."

"Good pay?" I asked.

"Sure. About $400 a month."

"And what is the nature of the consulting work you do?"

"Plant layout. Systems engineering."

"Efficiency," Baruch burst out. "That's the bane of Israel. It is people who count, not efficiency."

"I should expect you to say that," Isaac laughed. "A chocolate decorator and too slow about it."

Slender, tiny Baruch, sixty-one years old, seemed ready to leap at Isaac. Hastily, I asked Isaac if he had been to America. "Yes," he replied. "Several times. I like the Americans and the British. They have drive, efficiency, guts. But I don't like American Jews," Isaac went on. "Too flat. Uninteresting. I would rather read about Eskimos. It's the Jewish diet, all processed bread, antibotics in the food, additives, preservatives, colors. Fake. It's not natural. It's why they are so big, soft, fat, and have so many mental diseases."

"But Jews hardly vary from other Americans in their dietary habits, illnesses," I said.

"Look! I've been there. I've seen them. Flabby, garrulous, loud," Isaac persisted.

Baruch turned in fury, "You'd have no Israel, no kibbutz, no cotton mills to sell to if the American Jews had not given the money and support to keep us going."

Both men glared. Then Isaac stood and walked to my table, turning his back on Baruch. "Here is my card," he said. "I live near Tel Aviv. If you want to see how I grow vegetables organically, without chemical fertilizers or pesticides, the natural way, earthworms and all, come to visit. That's why I'm so strong. Here, feel this—" He crooked his arm and steeled his biceps. It was very hard, broad, deep. "That's what properly grown vegetables did for me," he said, turning to glare at Baruch. "That's what's wrong with American Jews, and some Israelis— they don't eat right." Certain as Moses, he strode out the door.

"Still," Baruch said slowly, after Isaac had gone, "he was a hero in the War of Independence. There is no room in him for doubt, and that may be why he was a fine commander. Still, he is crazy. What Isaac will not understand is that I, too, could dress these windows with two men in half a week. But we have unemployables, social welfare cases, men with criminal records, war-damaged kids. We give them honest work."

"And Isaac? How could he disapprove of that?"

"He does not believe in mixing business with social welfare. We often talk of it. He thinks we must take care of such people but that to use business to do it invites inefficiency."

"Does it?"

Baruch shrugged. "Who knows?" he said. "We are a cooperative with a captive clientele. So what if we are not so efficient?

"Consider Ezekiel, shell-shocked in the Six Day war. He sits at breakfast and stares at his plate. His mind is damaged and he cannot get it off battle. I tell him, 'Hey, Ezekiel, why don't you eat something?' Surprised, he says, 'Oh!' looks around, sees where he is, then begins to eat. We go to work and I help him. Others help. My friend once helped me. We help each other, and one day perhaps Ezekiel can help someone. But Isaac would reduce the overhead, increase the profit by putting Ezekiel in an institution, on a dole." Baruch shrugged, lit a cigarette, and stared moodily ahead.

"Do you have children?" I asked.

"Two. A daughter in Tivon and a son in a kibbutz. He could have been a great sculptor but he is a mechanic, drives tractors

]*82*[

and such. I visit him sometimes. Greasy fingers, nails chipped, knuckles scarred. Once in despair I shouted at him that he was wasting his talents, his eyes, hands, heart. 'Why do you do this dirty work?' I demanded. He looked at me and said, oh so gently, 'Father, someone has to work with the dirt.' " Baruch's face held the shadow of a smile.

Needing a shirt, I asked Baruch if Hamashbir had good ones. "Excellent," he said. "Let me take you." We strolled down the street to Hamashbir, Beersheba's leading department store.

The store windows were still trimmed with winter clothing. I asked Baruch if spring and summer things ought rather to be on display. "Yes, I suppose so," he said. "But people have sense enough to know it will soon be spring. We are not rich enough to buy in anticipation of the season. So what's the hurry?"

I was struck by the preponderance of blond hair on the dummies.

"In Sweden they like best brunettes," Baruch remarked with a grin. "Here we are mostly brunettes, so. . ."

Inside, Baruch introduced me to Zoltan, a Czechoslovakian who had lived twenty years in Beersheba. He wore a small mustache, had sparse hair, a lean look, and the bent stance that in all lands typifies harassed lower management. He was evasive about store operations or revealing trade secrets to strangers.

Baruch drew him out, and we learned that the store markup was twenty to twenty-five percent, nearly half that in America. There was a regular annual rebate of five percent to members, and the store showed a net profit of two to three percent. I told the assistant manager that his profit was remarkable on such a low mark-up. He replied that it could be even lower. "In order not to drive the small shopkeeper out of business we do not sell as cheap as we might."

Asked about shoplifting, he said the loss ran one-half percent of volume, and he thought it scandalously high. He knew that American losses ran two to ten percent and shook his head, "And the young never think about it. Where there is enough for everybody, why steal?"

Baruch winked at me. Later he explained that shoplifting is

increasingly a problem with the older people and the poor from Arab lands. "It is true the young do not think of stealing. Sometimes—the children from large Oriental families . . . deprived . . . sometimes . . . you understand?"

In the men's department, a pleasant salesgirl measured my neck and arms for a shirt. Shirts were priced at $10 but were on sale for $8, and I bought a boxed one that looked as if it had been pressed by a bulldozer and boxed by a monkey. Baruch apologized. "We are not yet skilled at packaging. But wait till you put it on. You will see the excellent make, fine material."

We stopped in the carpet department to talk to a tall, heavyset man, very dark of skin and wearing a mustache exactly like Nasser's. He was Eliezer, in Israel eight years. In Egypt he had sold rugs. In Beersheba he sold rugs. "What else do you expect of an Egyptian?" Baruch remarked and laughed.

Eliezer had been thrown out of Egypt without compensation for his home, automobile, business inventory. He arrived penniless.

"What happened to all that you left behind?"

Eliezer only shrugged, but Baruch said, "The party faithful sequester and get what the Jews leave."

"But Jews live in houses left by Arabs when they left Palestine in 1947," I said.

"Not I," Eliezer replied. "Some do, but not I. For me it was a total loss of everything except my family."

"Do your children still speak Arabic?"

"Yes. We keep it up. One day there will be an accommodation with the Arabs. Then we will need Arabic."

At ten-thirty we walked back to the hotel. The cab stand had closed, the town's discotheque had shut down, a few tiny restaurants were still open, but most folk of Beersheba were asleep. "You see how quiet it is? How safe?" Baruch said. "Walk where you please, nothing will happen."

Chapter 16

The last evening in Beersheba was spent with Judith and Ephraim. It had been a quiet, pleasant evening in their tiny, book-filled home decorated with art from Nigeria, where both had taught school for children of Israeli technicians and diplomats.

Ephraim now sought an advanced degree in Old Testament studies from the University of the Negev. "It is a great history book," he said.

"Not holy? God's word? Only history?" I asked.

"Only that!"

"Then how do you account for the return of the Jews?"

"The logic of history brought us here," he replied.

Judith's salary as a teacher in Beersheba supported the family. She taught first grade and could detect a difference between the attitudes of Oriental kids and those from Western lands. "In the Esther story, Haman, the Persian Hitler of 2,500 years ago, was discredited and hanged. We tell the story, hang a puppet Haman. Reaction? 'How awful,' the kids from the West say. But the kids from Oriental homes—Iraq, Iran, Turkey, North Africa—invariably shout and clap their hands."

"Perhaps the Oriental children recall the atrocities their parents suffered in the homeland, with modern Hamans?" Ephraim volunteered.

Judith looked at him. "And do you think the European children grow up ignorant of the holocaust and Hitler?" she replied. "The Orientals grow up to become the best fighters in our army," she said. "No small contribution."

"At least they are most relentless," Ephraim admitted.

Ephraim walked me home. On the way, he told me that his father, a Polish lawyer, enormously erudite, had abhorred religion. Ephraim grew up altogether secular.

But shortly after arriving in Israel, his father died and his mother took him to a kibbutz, the only place where she could manage to rear him. "As the years passed," Ephraim said, "my mother became more religious, until today she is Orthodox. I think she superstitiously sees my father's early death as a punishment from God for neglecting Him."

"But you do not believe this?"

"I believe only in the inexorable logic of history."

"Yet you have chosen Torah as a lifetime study."

"As history only," he replied, his voice faintly sharp.

"But you could have studied a thousand histories. Why Jewish history?"

We were standing before the hotel entrance. Ephraim would not come in. He seemed nervous and eager to leave. I repeated the question.

"The subject interests me only as history," he replied. "That alone. And goodnight," he said testily.

We shook hands and I watched him hurry into the night.

One wonders about the Ephraims, the Danis and their sons. They are too vehement in their denial of the religious experience and of deity brooding over this land. One wants always to ask: Is He working through you, Ephraim, Dani, who reject him much too vehemently?

Chapter *17*

The land between Beersheba and Arad was, in the soft light of early sun, oddly feminine with long moundings, declivities, and promising rounds. What ought to have evoked strong, implacable, masculine images did rather conjure a sense of the feminine that was equally strong and implacable. Odd. Perhaps it was that the green barley, trying desperately to grow, and failing, drooped twisted in the relentless drought. The yeasty fields near Jerusalem had had all those blessed rains denied Arad-Beersheba. Galilee flooded while the Negev thirsted. It hurt a farming man to see the spent passion of those juiceless fields.

"What will the Bedouins do for livestock feed?" I asked Yosi, who had belatedly, inexplicably joined me the last day in Beersheba, and had been forgiven.

"We will provide it," Yosi said. "As you see, they must pasture off the green plant, for it cannot mature a seed crop. So we 'lend them grain and hay. It is our way. But they would manage even without us, as they always have."

"How?"

"Smuggling."

"What?"

"Hashish."

Chapter 18

At first glance, Arad seemed a fortress. Its cast-concrete outbuildings were cubes set beside and upon one another. Yet there was about the buildings a curious, comforting indigenous style suggesting Arab villages, those earthen cubes built around and on top of each other: stacked extrusions of the hills themselves, presenting a sense of defense.

Arad, Yosi said, was styled for defense, with all the amenities —stores, schools, walks, playgrounds—inside the ring of stockade-style dwellings.

We debouched onto an Arad street and marched up heroically wide, rough-cut stone steps to the hilltop hotel. Everything seemed atop hills. Yosi explained that whoever controlled the hills controlled Israel, now as it was four thousand years ago. "Of course,"

Yosi went on, "there were other considerations such as air circulation, drainage, and the mystical need of Muslims and Jews to soar above things. " 'Arise! Arise! Get ye up,' " Yosi quoted. "Look up! Think up. Reach up! We share a sense of place, of airiness and soaring and freedom. You'll recall that Bishop Pike was irresistibly drawn to wander these hills but met his death in a valley. No shadow of the valley of death—but a merciless valley of death."

Yosi was quiet for a time. "But for safety a man is advised to follow King David's 121st Psalm: 'I will lift up mine eyes unto the mountains,' not the twenty-third Psalm."

Arad was established in this outback in order to claim and defend it. Mere ownership of Israel is not truly a possessing of it. The Jews lust for the land, the taking of it to themselves is a protective custody, both physical and spiritual. Once settled, possession is theirs and all the law they need. Arad is, perhaps, the prototype of Israeli possession techniques; first, build the town, move people there, *then* find some way for them to earn a living and be happy. To hell with logic, logistics. Facts! Make facts! Successful guerrilla armies function that way; and tycoons, and all passionate peoples, especially Americans.

Yosi explained that the Arab fiercely loved his *own* village, family, clan, fields. But the Jew fiercely loved all the land of Israel, not for his village, or family, or clan, but for his entire people. Everything subserved to possession of the land so as to ingather the exiles.

To Christians this land is holy in a sweetly distant way. Since the Crusades, its meaning has been in the nature of a sacrament. To Arabs, Israel has strong political and ethnic meaning but less religious meaning since Islam ranks Jerusalem after Mecca and Medina as a holy city. But for Jews, all Israel has consummate religious and ethnic value, bringing both survival and sanctuary in time, space, spirit.

Yosi did not believe in the concept of the Chosen People. But he admitted that other Jews believed that they were part of a Chosen People, indelibly branded by God so as to live a purer life. For such Jews it was impossible to conceive of a viable existence outside the purview of Israel. The Land was a kind of protein without which the muscle of Judaism atrophied.

We stashed bags in our dingy hotel room and strolled to a street lined with wood huts once used by the city's builders. There, in a restaurant, we ordered lunch. It was Friday.

A slender, wiry, red-haired truck driver staggered into the restaurant lugging a huge tray of challah, traditional Sabbath bread.

Yosi knew the driver, whose name was Ilan, and I did not learn until later that he had been brought, as an eight-month-old orphan, by the Red Cross to Israel.

Ilan's springy torso was covered with a tattered T-shirt. But his eyes were bright and fierce, barely missing a hard, flat look of cruelty. He sported a huge red mustache that matched his bushy hair. Yosi finally got him to sit long enough to drink a glass of lemonade. "Ilan fought in the Golan Heights," Yosi told me. "A paratrooper."

"Rugged terrain," I remarked. "I saw it shortly after the Israeli Defense Forces took it."

Ilan softened upon learning that I had seen the gouged trenches and dugouts, the obscene pox of concrete fortresses in hills themselves varicose with skeins of barbed wire, altogether futile.

"Wicked country," I suggested.

"When isn't war wicked? Many of us died out there. But we saved our people in the valley below. We just outfought the bastards."

"You don't like Arabs?"

"I hate them. They killed my brother-in-law in the Six Day War. I've just begun to carry a pistol. Like this morning. I started at four A.M. so as to finish delivering bread before sundown; Sabbath. Lonely road. Ambush. Things are happening. I mean to be armed."

"But Ilan," Yosi said gently, "your brother-in-law was killed winning the War in 1967. Why carry hate into peacetime?"

"Peacetime! You call this peace? It's all the same with Arabs.

I remember before 1967. I had an Arab friend in Jerusalem. We were buddies. We went swimming together, played cards, were close. I pick up the paper one day and read that he was a ringleader of a group caught planting grenades in a Jerusalem restaurant. He would have smiled while killing me."

"But you have got somehow to learn to live beside them," I suggested.

"I'll tell you how to live with them. Lock them up at dusk each night for a year. Then, if they have behaved, let them out for an hour. A year after that let them out for two hours, but only if they prove themselves. Moshe Dayan is crazy. He thinks he knows Arabs. Hell, I drive these roads alone, not he. No grenade can get him, only me."

"Still, there haven't been many incidents among the West Bank Arabs," Yosi reminded him.

Ilan smiled pityingly. "Yosi," he said, "you are a writer of plays; I am a trucker. Dayan is Defense Minister. Before you talk, drive my truck from dawn until after dusk. Listen to Arab talk. See Arab faces. Do business with them. After that, you can judge, you and Dayan. I tell you they will kill us all if they can."

Ilan's English was quite American. A period of wanderlust had once taken him to France where he had worked for the American army. He was fond of Americans. "But the American soldier is lazy," Ilan said. "My God, but they are easygoing. Such—how do you say it—blocks . . . stones. . .?"

I spoke the word.

"Goldbricks. Yes. But very kind." Ilan stood to leave.

I begged a moment more of him, and asked: "Feeling as you do about Arabs, can Israel ever have peace?"

"I am not a fool to think we'll have an Israeli ambassador in Cairo within ten years. We'll never have peace. And we don't need it."

"But as Yosi said, you live in comparative quiet with three hundred thousand Israeli Arabs now. Why can't you, in time, live in peace with all Arabs?"

"No!" Ilan said. He did not sit down but leaned on the table, emphasizing his words with body english. "They seem—primitive.

Not like us. Even in Israel. Their food-handling shops are filthy. Their bids for public works are rigged to help their friends. That's the Arab mentality."

"A moment more," I begged, as Ilan turned away; "do you believe in the biblical boundaries from the Euphrates to the Nile?"

"More land? Only for defense. If we need it for that, we'll take it. But only for defense."

"And if the Russians intervene to stop you?"

"So much the worse for Russia," Ilan said, and grinned as if he meant it for a joke. But there was about his posture, his grin, his hard eyes, no look of frivolity.

We shook hands and Ilan rushed off.

"So now you know how deep runs the animus of some Israelis for Arabs," Yosi said. "And Ilan is more reasonable than some others. Take our soldiers, the sons of parents who had to flee Arab countries. Some of them had to be restrained from shooting Arab soldiers who only wanted to surrender. Actually, I agree with Ilan, as you know. They should all emigrate. There are plenty of Arab countries for them to go to."

Nearly everyone in the restaurant had been listening to the discussion. A slender young man seated at the next table spoke up: "He is a fool to hate Arabs. We are meant to live together. You cannot sensibly hate fifty million Arabs just because one Arab friend turned sour, or someone in your family was killed. That's crazy. We must live with them."

"Ah," Yosi said menacingly, "you know the Arabs?"

"Some. From contacts at the Hebrew University. Unfortunately, we learned nothing about them in school."

"Then how can you be sure that Ilan is so wrong?"

"I know that Arabs are human beings first and then Arabs. They must want peace. Sometimes I think it is we who hold back, clinging to things as they are."

Yosi rose so rapidly he rocked the table. "We would be dead and buried ruled by your sweet reasonableness!" he shouted, and stalked out of the restaurant.

I apologized for Yosi's harshness. "There are very many like him," the young man said, "but more like me." He extended his hand. "I am Shimshon and this is my wife, Efrat." He nodded toward her.

Shimshon was slender, blond, delicate of bone and feature. Dressed in flannels and a pullover, he could have graced an English after-tennis party. But Efrat was reared a farmer's daughter in a coastal moshav and she knew the meaning of work. Her thick, tough hands, splayed feet, broad hips, bovine breasts made her seem like a Diego Rivera peon.

Shimshon was in Arad earning money to put himself through the School of Social Work at Hebrew University. Earning $150 a month as a laborer at the Dead Sea, he was able to save $100. His room cost him $12 a month. His food was carefully bought and prepared by his lumpish wife. In two years he would earn enough to study. His ambition was to work among Arabs, devote his life to them.

"But how can you advise a people about whom you know so little?" I asked.

"All people are alike. We need to bring them our Western ways, techniques, systems. Social work is the way to it."

In Eilat there had been Menachem, who had once wanted to devote his life to curing Arab eyes. Here in Arad was Shimshon who wanted to help cure their hurt psyches, their "primitiveness." And Ilan had just left after declaring that he hated Arabs, would pen them until tamed, and who carried a pistol with which to kill them should he need to defend himself. Contrasts. Diversities. A stiff-necked people.

Near the hotel, in a little shop, I found Yosi admiring a piece of magnificent batik. He chose it for his Ruth. Impressed with the artistry, I asked the storekeeper if it was Israeli.

"Oh, yes," he replied. "And from here."

"Perhaps you could tell me the artist's name so that I might chat with him."

"He is a she. A superb artist. I'll write the number for you. Just ask for Efrat, wife of Shimshon. Everyone knows them."

Chapter 19

Quite by accident I met Colonel Itzhak, the man most responsible for founding Arad. I literally bumped into him in a grocery store. He was a thickset man of great vigor and when we accidentally collided, my supplies and I sailed in several directions. He was kind and helpful and we soon had things resacked, dignity restored. That started our acquaintance.

As a kind of final apology, Itzhak invited me to his home for tea. He lived in a simple wood cottage, "for weekends only," he told me. "My work forces me to live elsewhere but we come here for the peace of the place and because Arad is our love. The soil suits our roots."

He spoke excellent English, having taken an advance degree in business administration at the Harvard School of Business.

In 1933 Itzhak had come as a boy to Israel from Poland. Two brothers came with him, the only members of a huge family to survive the Nazi and Polish holocaust.

As he told it, Colonel Itzhak's face loosened for the briefest moment to register a distant grief. Then the mask returned. "I've spent my life in the army," he said, "a professional soldier in the armored corps. Then I was for a time our Ambassador to Tanzania. But now I'm trying to manage Arabs in our newly acquired territories."

I suggested that he must know the Arabs very well to hold such a job.

"I try to know them," he said, smiling a bit ruefully. "But it is not easy. Many Israelis call them primitive but that is for us a stupid oversimplification. They are not primitive. They have many wonderful people, a few well-educated. But their masses are largely uneducated, deprived, exploited. And they are Moslem in culture. Not Christian. Not Jew. Even Christian Arabs are Moslem in culture. That is the root of knowledge necessary to understand Arabs."

"Then do you believe they should be a separate nation, for Palestinians, in the West Bank and Gaza?"

"I doubt there should be a Palestinian state. There has never been an independent Arab state in Palestine. And if nations like Syria, Jordan, Egypt, Iraq fail at trying to be nations, how much worse for Palestinians who do not truly covet statehood?"

"Then what is all the shooting about?"

"I think they want us out of here. After that they will decide what to do. Then comes the peace they promise. Jordan will get a piece, Egypt a piece, Syria a piece." The Colonel chuckled at this old and now tired joke, usually told in reverse by Arabs about the Israeli wish for a peace; a piece. . . .

"Then what is the solution?"

"They can live with us, or emigrate to their brothers in Arab lands. Arabs have always moved about and among one another. It would be an easier transition than when Germans fled to East and West Germany or Indians to Pakistan. Meantime, we need laborers; and try to get Gaza Arabs to move close to job sources, to Arab cities like Nablus, Kalkilya, Tulkarm, where there is much work. But they are afraid."

The Colonel handed me a broadside printed in Arabic with Hebrew and English translations:

> In the name of the Revolution, we caution you to avoid registering your names in the Zionist labour exchange and to avoid journeying to the West Bank. The Revolution will strike with an iron hand any man who tries to abandon his fatherland.
>
> We warn you against the new imperialist plan, which means nothing but emigration, departure from your homeland, families and children.
>
> We must not become victims of Zionist propaganda to the effect that there is work in the West Bank and a shortage of hands there. This is lies and deceit.
>
> Boycott the labour exchange, and do not leave the Gaza Strip. This is to inform you that we shall open fire on any workers who journey to the West Bank, and who thus show their agreement to emigrate.

"They lie," the Colonel said. "There is too much work. The people neither believe us nor their fellow Arabs. They sit tight.

Perhaps one day they will realize that we are not like Arabs nor the British nor the Turks; that we are benign and only want what is best for Israel."

"But it is true, isn't it, that Arabs have lived in Gaza for generations? It is their homeland? For them to move would be to smother traditional rights and roots?"

"It is not true," Colonel Itzhak said grimly. "They lived in squalor, filled with disease and ignorance. Is that a homeland? Americans did not think it so when they fled Europe for a better life! English people did not sever less firm ties when they settled Australia. The Arabs in Gaza could only improve their lot. It is the politicians and the intellectuals who delude them."

"But they want you out," I repeated. "They say that if they cooperate with Arab terrorists you destroy their houses, but if they cooperate with you they will be assassinated."

"We have not killed a single captured terrorist or collaborator. It is the Arab who kills. Wouldn't you rather be on the side of humane people than of killers? We offer a choice. They must choose."

"Or emigrate?"

"Yes."

"They say that is what you want them to do."

He shrugged. "They destroyed this land. It took three generations of Jews to bring it again to life. Arabs had hoped to let us reclaim it and then take it from us. They figured wrong because they do not understand us, nor try to."

I asked why Jews and Arabs together could not live in peace as we in America from many lands had done.

"It is difficult to make people understand," Colonel Itzhak said patiently. "When I was in Tanzania, its Prime Minister laughed like hell when I told him that we wanted only to be a model nation of Jews; a nation that all other new nations could use as a model. He believed we were a Zionist conspiracy to subjugate the world. Imagine! Little Israel. The Protocols of the Elders of Zion all over again. No matter how hard I tried to tell him his ideas were wrong, that The Protocols were a forgery done by vicious anti-semites, he still did not believe me.

"But we knew this mentality in Poland. There my mother kept a homemade elixer of strawberries on the kitchen shelf. 'For Emergency Only,' it was labeled. For emergency! That's one of Israel's purposes; a place for hounded Jews to find sanctuary, in an emergency. It is selfish but also altruistic because we show the world that turned its back on damaged peoples . . . East Pakistanis, Biafrans, South Sudanese, that it is wrong! And we show it even though they do not want to see how to be human, decent. We are a Jewish state. A humanitarian state. Others are welcome. Arabs are welcome. But we must be a Jewish state. For the world's sake."

Colonel Itzhak paused, smiling faintly, his mind moving back to some recollection. Then he spoke, "In 1953 I was sent to France to General Staff School. One night the general in charge of the school started to talk about politics. 'You know who will be our next Premier?' he snarled. 'That dirty dog of a Jew, Pierre Mendes-France.' Nobody uttered a word. The next morning I reported to him and resigned from the school. 'Why?' he asked. I told him that he had insulted my people. 'But you are not a Jew, you are Israeli,' he said. Then he said a clever thing that left me defenseless. 'But there were three French Jews sitting with the group last night. They said nothing. There are ten Jews altogether in your class. Why should you alone feel insulted?'

"What could I do? Degrade those French Jews? I stayed. But at no time during the course did one single Jewish officer identify himself to me as a Jew. They wanted to be known as Frenchmen!"

Itzhak's eyes were soft with the wonder of that distant time when he learned that French Jews who were officers hid their identity from him. For a moment he revealed the innocent surprise of the wandering Jew faced with puzzling, relentless hostility. "But," he said, "when these French officers, Jews, are one day expelled from France, only we will take them!"

Itzhak shook his head. "The Jewish mind is terribly complex," he said. "It works in strange ways." Suddenly he grinned. "Only this afternoon I stopped at a service station to get a slow leak fixed. I told the young man there to fix the tire. He asked if I had a spare. I said I did but that it was beyond repair and that he should fix the one on the car.

" 'I want to see the spare,' the youngster said.

" 'Fix the tire on the car,' I ordered him. 'The spare can't be repaired.'

" 'I want to see it.'

"So the boy took the spare from the trunk compartment, examined it carefully, then said, 'It's beyond repair. I'll fix the tire on the car.' Now that is the Israeli mentality. Stubborn and balky. An American would have fixed the tire without question, sold me a spare, filled the car with gas, washed the glass, and sent me on my way. An Arab would have unquestioningly fixed the tire on the car, as ordered, and that's all. But an Israeli boy wants to know, takes nothing for granted, must prove to himself what it is he has to do. How can we make that clear to the world?"

Back at the hotel I told Yosi about the interview with Itzhak. Yosi snorted, saying, "Itzhak has the messianic complex. He thinks all Israelis are geniuses. But we are not. We are Yosis and Ruths and Ilans and Itzhaks and lots more. Here," he went on, tossing the newspaper to me, "read this if you want to know how primitive some Jews are.

"WIZARD" BILKS JILTED GIRL

A magician and fortune teller was yesterday sentenced in the Magistrate's Court to a one-year suspended jail term for defrauding a young woman client. Judge Shlomo Yifrah also ordered the accused to return the money he had taken from her.

The 23-year-old woman, from Kiryat Ekron, was desolate after her boyfriend left her, about six months ago. Friends persuaded her to turn to a local magician known as "Rabbi Maimon," 72, who has worked in his profession for 56 years. After consulting a book called *Raziel the Angel*, he told the woman he could bring her boyfriend back for her for $35. After haggling, she agreed to pay him $17.

After a few days with no sign of him, the woman returned to Rabbi Maimon, who gave her seven pieces of paper and told her to burn one each day. This didn't help either. He then asked her to bring a rooster and a hen, weighing four kilograms each, and to undress before him. Finally, Rabbi Maimon instructed the woman to have sexual relations with an Arab, and to bring him his semen. This time, she refused. Rabbi Maimon then told her he could get her the semen for $15.

She paid him, and received from him a small cloth bag containing a note which carried a request to the angels and the four winds of heaven to assist her. She was instructed to wear the bag around her neck. Only then did she suspect that the magician was not going to come through, and she went to the police.

"So you see," Yosi said. "All the primitive people are not Arabs. Ilan and Itzhak choose to overlook the simple, superstitious, primitive Jews among us."

A suspended sentence and return of the money seems a light sentence for that bastardly "wizard," I suggested.

"And what would you have done to a 72-year-old man?" Yosi asked. "Let him rot in jail? No. *Caveat emptor*. Such a fool girl deserved to lose. I'd have given the girl a suspended sentence and let the old man keep the money. We have thousands of Jews like that girl. It's the old shell game. There is a sucker born every minute, even in Israel."

Chapter 20

Fronting the hotel was a tiny plaza surrounded with shops and rented offices, all quite small. But the smallest was a curio shop for tourists and it, like its owner, Beni, was slightly off course, since tourists stayed in newer, more modern hotels. The workers in Arad stayed at ours and bought few souvenirs.

Beni was a huge, stooped, bushy-haired, doe-eyed, pipe-smoking prototype of the abstracted American scientist. He had an enormous, drooping and untrimmed mustache that held bits of his last meal.

The morning we met, Yosi whispered that I should buy something, that Beni needed money. I mulled over the oddly shaped Eilat stones, coppery minerals, polished to a high degree. Another customer walked in and at once Yosi deserted me. She was an American girl, perhaps eighteen, blonde, fubsy, but there was about her an air of sexual generosity. She accepted Yosi's attention as if she were offered Coke but wasn't thirsty.

She was, she told us, from the immigrant absorption center, where Western immigrants learned Hebrew and Israel's history. But she did not like life here. "What, dear girl, is wrong?" Yosi asked in soft, disarming tones.

"I just don't want to live here," she answered him. "My father insisted, left me no choice. But I don't have to like this barbarity."

"You poor kid," Yosi said, "but we're not so bad once you know us."

"It's so dead," she said, as if she had not heard Yosi. "Los Angeles is alive with swingers. The ocean. Groovy resorts. People who are with it. Israel is Nothingville. And Arad is even less—Zeroville."

"Let me entertain you," Yosi chanted.

She grinned. A very sweet, appealing smile. Then she came over and we helped her select a dozen stones to send home. Beni seemed happier.

The girl did not want to return to the Center. "I tried to get a group to go down to the Dead Sea and swim but they're all so damned responsible," she said. "Hey! I got a car. Close up shop and we'll all go."

"No-o-o," Beni replied gravely. "Four busloads of tourists are due. I must stay to serve them."

"Ah-h-h, Beni," Yosi said. "They'll all go to the other hotels. You won't miss any business."

Beni demurred. So did I. "You'll learn a lot about Western immigration from her," Yosi scolded me, but his voice held no firm insistence.

"Such stories I'll bring you," Yosi whispered. "Great additions to your book. She must know a mint of tales about life in this absorption center." Yosi sprayed his throat thoroughly and then left with his young prize.

Beni and I sat for a time outside his shop on the patio, in the sunlight that wrapped us in warmth and brought rare ease. The high sun was benign though in a cold, sharp blue sky. A steady hum, a silky sound, came off the desert.

Beni began to talk. He was among the first settlers in Arad, coming here from Eilat because his wife hated that town, the climate, the isolation. Beni had most wanted to be a sculptor. He had found a talented Israeli artist to teach him but the man died suddenly before Beni had learned much. Needing money, loving the desert, both he and his wife had accepted an invitation to come with the first cadre of settlers to Arad. Here he did photography, some tour guiding, worked at the Dead Sea, and with his wife minded the tiny curio shop. Altogether, he managed a living. "My big hope here," he said, "is to build a museum for the town. We'll charge admission and I'll get a share of the receipts. From that we can live. The museum will be my art, my sculpture, and I have devoted the last six months to assembling the collections for it. With my bare hands I am building it." He held up his hands for me to see how huge they were, and how strong and symmetrical. His face was hairy as Esau's but the hands were Jacob's.

A group of about twenty-five tourists had entered the hotel across from us. They were elderly, middle-class, tired. I suggested that the group would make meager pickings for Beni's shop but he replied, "Who could guess from the bee's drab dress what marvels of pollen are hidden?"

I wandered over to the hotel and found that the visitors were Canadian Jews come for coffee and to hear an acceptance speech for a $25,000 gift of theirs to furnish a nursery in Arad. An American Israeli addressed them. He was tall, suave, blond, young—Arad's Public Relations Department. There was a flick of malice in his frequent mention of the "small but vital gift." The elderly Jews did not notice. They hung on every sweet word and tasted no sourness. There was the aura of agape about their open, generous faces. The P.R. man veered his approach to suggest that $25,000 was good but more was better.

To him, Jews must have seemed a bottomless cornucopia. And these seemed such lovely Jews, all adoring of this young man, seeing something in him that they had missed in the sinks and terrors, the inhumanities and incarcerations of Poland, Russia, Germany—all Europe whence they had found their way to Canada.

There are a few American Jews who give a quarter of a million dollars annually to Israel and look to be a little bored with it all; another "thank you" from the Prime Minister; another plaque in the rumpus room; another "God bless you," from the president of some university. It must seem like a boring tax, nothing more.

But these older, poorer Canadian Jews come to Arad would get for public recognition only a tiny announcement buried in the *Jerusalem Post,* near the bottom of a middle page.

Never mind! Their little gift had been made from small, monthly savings, and offered out of a noble, sacrificial spirit that had also compelled them to come and see what they had done.

Never mind! Their gift was an unguent, a poultice to heal their own past hurts, and their faces showed that the cure had worked.

The speaker finally trudged away, seeming to be aware that what he said was superfluous. For, after all, everyone there knew that the gift was a contribution to a two-thousand-year-old floating, portable synagogue that happened, just then, to have beached itself, become determinedly anchored and then wrapped itself in the garments of a nation.

Chapter 21

Of course, Yosi did not return to Arad. Doubtless his research was strenuous. Beni put his wife in charge of the shop and came along to help me.

The patio outside his shop was like a plaza in Mexico in that it was close to Beni's shop and the people who crossed it were his good friends and business neighbors. One of these, an accountant named Ascher, stopped to chat. He wore a tweed suit, brogues, white shirt and dark tie—the image of the British businessman in Mandate times. He was dangerously fat, one of the few obese Israelis I had seen.

"Ascher was one of our earliest settlers in Arad and is our accountant. Tell us, Ascher, how you happened to come to Israel?" Beni asked.

Ascher seated himself carefully, wanting no wrinkles. "My father did not want us to live in Hungary," he said. "He feared the army and its overt anti-Semitism. I was scheduled for America, but a billiard hustler, a friend of father's, had just returned from Palestine and advised my father to send me here. They discussed it, argued, decided that whoever won two out of three games of pool, that person would decide. Father lost."

"Then I presume you were not Zionists?"

"We were loyal Hungarians, only they did not want us."

"Have you ever wished that your father had won the game?"

"At first. I arrived a month before World War II. No work. I hauled bread in daytime and was a night watchman. From both jobs I earned about four dollars a day, yet I could get work only two or three days a week. I tried to join the British army but they rejected me because I came from Hungary, enemy territory. Then I really cursed that billiard shark. Finally, by a ruse, I enlisted and was sent to North Africa and fought up through Italy.

"Right after the war I made an illegal visit to Hungary to

search for my family. They had been murdered—or so I thought, until I found the janitor of our family's box factory. He took me to his cottage and there I found one brother alive. He had been hidden for years in the basement. That simple janitor had risked his life to give him sanctuary, had even managed to salvage some of the family's jewels. I gave him half the jewels and used the other half to bribe our way out of Hungary, and to buy sixteen machines to manufacture steel barrels. All of it was the result of the saintliness and heroism of that simple Christian Hungarian.

"I started a barrel factory but went busted in 1953. Again we started. Busted in 1959."

"Perhaps you should have kept all of the jewels," Beni said.

"Then I should not have lasted half so long," Ascher said cryptically. "anyhow, now I am an accountant, managing others' money," he chuckled.

"Tell him of your plan for the Arabs," Beni prompted.

"First you should know that I like the Arabs. I like their style, close family relationships, religious piety. We could learn much from them. But we can never be at peace with them. And we should recognize that. Let us here in Israel set up a system of cantons, like the Swiss have, and arrange for each canton to have a proportion of two Jews to one Arab. We are three million, they are one and a half million. Let elected representatives then be sent to a legislature such as yours in America. It would work very well for all of us."

"And why not a separate state for the Arabs?" a new voice asked. Ascher and Beni smiled deferentially. It was Ami, a short, blue-eyed, bandy-legged, heavily mustached, graying, very capable-looking owner of a tour agency that provided guided expeditions through the Sinai Desert.

"They wouldn't know what to do with a separate state," Ascher said.

"Well, let them try," Ami replied gently. "It would keep them busy and give them something to think about other than how awful we are."

"They'd be just another enemy state for us to fight," Ascher argued.

"The more Arab states, the more fragmented their opposition to us," Ami replied.

"I'd just rather have them where I could control them, educate them to accept us," Ascher said.

"You delude yourself, Ascher, if you think you can educate them to love you. They are Moslem, Arab, primitive. When you most need them they will not be with you. Who can build on that? Let them have a state. They will become so involved they'll have no time to interfere with us. We don't control Jordan, Syria, Lebanon, Egypt, and yet we manage to live alongside them."

Ascher left, shaking his head at the younger man's ideas. "Ascher is used to the European system of controls," Ami said. "He does not understand the enormous cultural and religious difference between the frightened, demon-ridden, dangerous, ordinary European Christian peasant he used to know, and the intelligent, decent, but primitive Arab Muslim peasant."

"Then I can presume that you would take no more land?"

"Correct. We need peace, not land. Don't you agree, Beni?"

Beni nodded gravely. Ami continued, "Real estate gives no security. We could take everything from the Euphrates to the Nile. Easy. But we would be further from peace. Why should we be afraid? It is a great thing we have done here. Does such a people have to feel fear?"

Ami had had only nine years of schooling but was a captain in the armored corps, a scout for tanks, operating by jeep dangerously far ahead of supporting fire. "It is a phenomenon of the Israeli armed forces," Beni explained, "that they use men according to their ability, not education or background."

"Ami, how do you explain the extraordinary quality of the Israeli soldier?" I asked.

"We're good soldiers because—well—we're good soldiers." He shrugged. "Perhaps we have learned, from centuries of defeat, that we must stand up, in our own land, depend on ourselves alone, and refuse to go gentle to the Arab knife."

"Does it bother you that Jewish seminarians are excused from the draft?"

"No. Those religious Jews who want to leave the seminary to

take a term of military duty can do so. Many do. They make good soldiers. But what does bother me is the influence of the Orthodox rabbis. They are not good for Israel. They are part of European culture, not Israeli. Here they inhibit our solutions to problems, limit our choices. Sure! American Jews take comfort knowing that in Israel there are Jews carrying on grandfather's tradition. But it doesn't comfort us. Our kids know the Bible, study it daily in school, think religiously without even being conscious of it. Rabbinic influence we don't need."

"Do you feel the same way about your trade unions?"

"I don't especially like their bureaucratic ways. And their mini-buses are my competition for fares to tour the Sinai. Still, we must have them. They are a safety valve between military men and the politicians. A buffer, they keep the two from getting together and maybe, just maybe, making us into a fascist state. If the Arab states had our trade union tradition, they would not have military dictators running their governments."

In World War II, Ami fought for the British in the Jewish Brigade. He fought up through Italy and into Germany, staying on to rescue survivors of concentration camps and secretly funnel them to Israel. "We used every ruse in the book and invented a thousand more to get those poor half-dead Jews safely out of Europe and into Palestine. It was the most important work of my life."

Chapter 22

One morning Beni borrowed a car and took me to Masada. Just below Arad, we gave a lift to Stefan, a middle-aged, handsome, bearded French Jew of Czechoslovakian origin. He was impeccably dressed in smart trousers, shirt and tie, and a beautiful suede coat that he refused to take off, even though the day was hot. Stefan was an artist who, as a boy, had escaped the Nazis in his native land, fled to France to join the underground. There he created posters, slogans of resistance, to embolden the cowed French.

But Stefan had rarely seen a Nazi. He had never killed a man and was proud of this. He was now visiting Israel because his family no longer felt comfortable in France. "We are welcome there," he said, "but we not feel welcome. You understand? *Feel*. Things changed since Israel's birth. The Frenchman, he have streak of anti-Semitism. Jews from Algeria come, it get worse. So I here. To see. How we be welcome here?"

"Yes," Beni said. "You will be welcome. It is a place for all Jews."

"Can I make living?"

"For an artist it is not easy. But there is good work for every man. You can paint and also do other work. We live. So can you."

"Ah," Stefan laughed, "words of youth. Of daring. But I am not youth. I have family. I feel unsure."

"Never mind," Beni said. "I shall assure you."

The great rock holding Masada loomed above us. It seemed an altar atop which were great ruins rejected by deity. "It was once Herod's winter palace and his fortress of last resort," Beni told us.

We climbed the mountain-like earthen ramp the Roman legions had built to reach the 960 men, women, children besieged on top. Three years the people withstood Roman siege and finally, doomed, they drew lots to destroy themselves rather than endure capture and certain slavery. The stark landscape, hot dry sun, absence of birds, trees, grass, all lent to the bitter tragedy. We seemed a planet away from the lush Levantine trappings of Tel Aviv and the soft shores of the Mediterranean.

On top of this sheer-walled fortress-altar, Beni pointed out the throne room, baths, cisterns, courtroom, ingenious water system. Finally I told him to quit his tourist presentation and let us silently savor the austere reality.

We wandered about the surprisingly large mountaintop. Groups of teenagers sat and listened desultorily as their teachers related the heroism of Masada's defenders; one felt these kids had had all this too many times before. And tourists roamed hurriedly, anxious to get out of the direct, punishing sunlight. Hurry, hurry. The guides urged them on. Poor tourists. Wanting so much and getting it in eye-dropper dollops hastily let into them but most of it wasted at the fast pace they kept. Only a mood could remain. Perhaps this quick brush with ancient tragedy was enough in the light of their own enormity, of six million dead. They, too, a kind of suicide.

Soldiers strolled, preparing for a swearing-in ceremony. Beni explained that they came here because Masada was to them a Thermopylae and Corregidor rolled into one. "In Second Chronicles and First Samuel it tells how David and his men got them up into the stronghold to evade the pursuit of King Saul. They were . . . 'Men of might and men of war fit for the battle, that could handle shield and spear, whose faces were like the faces of lions and they were swift as roes upon the mountain!'

"There was a Jew named Flavius Josephus," Beni continued. "An apostate who deserted to the Romans. We owe to him our history of that time. The tragedy of it was that after surviving Assyria, Babylonia, Egypt, Greece, and lots more, we lost the land finally to Rome in 73 C.E. They dispersed us all over the world. But we're back now, three millenniums after King David." Beni looked at Stefan as if to say, "Join the ageless parade."

The uniformed, armed soldiers seemed pensive, determined, assured. "They steel themselves. They ask, 'Can I do?'" Stefan murmured, taken out of himself by Masada's mass suicide, the proximity of real death, even today, just over the Dead Sea in quite visible Jordan.

"Sometimes I think we are foolish to do all this archeology," Beni said. "Still, these digs do give us evidence that we are not a dream, nor foolishly quixotic."

But it was dreamlike to wander about, to stare down on the desolate eastern plain that Lot knew. Somewhere down there was the pillar of salt that once was his too-curious wife. If she were once salted, then salted she remained in this undecayed, utterly dry place drenched with antiseptic sunshine thirteen hundred feet below sea level.

How difficult it was to feel these stories in this place where dissolution and decay stood still, fixed like a deserted movie set once intended for a 1930 spectacular so outrageously bizarre, bloody, weird that the producer had finally scrapped the whole notion as being too ridiculous for even the most gullible public.

Musing on the difficulty in relating to all this ancient history, we started down the earthen ramp. Halfway, Beni stopped to point at ends of wood ties laid by Roman soldiers to stabilize the steep ramp's soil. The ends of these ties protruded as if recently hewn and placed there, perhaps cut in Lebanon, of cedar, very long-lived, visible links to long-dead legionnaires and the Jews they had trapped. The wood in harsh light seemed to have a sappiness to it. One felt that if a glass were put to the ties, Roman fingerprints would stand revealed. Two thousand years fell away. Eliezer and the Jewish Sicarii, their women and children, lay silent suicides in blood above. Romans, awed by the sudden quiet, like tourists had started up the earthen ramp. And the wood, the tie, was the touchstone to contemporaneity and the present reality of Masada. Organic wood, still here, made it all as current as a death in the family.

Stefan picked up a handful of siege dirt and let it drift slowly through his fingers leaving a film of beige dust on him that was like a layer of skin.

Beyond Masada at Ein Gedi, we hiked beside the marvelous cool stream of spring water, up through tropical greenery and on to pools and waterfalls. On either side the barren wilderness rose to reveal ancient caves set in sheer rock surfaces. Hereabouts David hid from murderous Saul, who correctly saw in him the only threat to his throne. Here today was the source of fresh water for Jews once again farming the arid land below. Here Stefan, a wanderer, had come seeking reassurance . . . home.

It was all grist for Shakespeare's pen and yet when he had the chance he could only view a Shylock and explain him as a hopeless, docile, yet brave victim of an ineradicable condition.

But Beni, Ami, Yosi, the Israeli had seized the day and reconstituted Shylock. They required no soliloquies or explanations, nor sly gestures. Resignations. Pleas. No. They *made* solutions. And Stefan a wanderer, seeking sanctuary, seemed to want to join them.

We hiked upward seeking the spring-source of the stream. After an hour we realized that we were lost. High up we came upon two youngsters giggling as they scanned the shore through binoculars. We asked the way and they pointed it out.

"What's so funny?" Beni asked.

"Down there," one of them managed to say before collapsing with laughter.

Beni took the glasses and fixed on a spot the youngsters pointed out. Beni stared a long time, then handed back the glasses and told the kids to move on. They argued. "On—on—" Beni shouted, shoving them on their way.

"What was it?" Stefan asked. "Nothing," Beni said, then whispered to me that he had seen the blonde American girl's car parked on the Dead Sea shore and behind it, screened from the road but not from the binoculars' view above, was Yosi stretched out naked beside his naked American girl.

It was a relief. After all the mildewed tragedy, the Dead Sea, the wilderness, the awful sense of the fragility of man in nature's hammermill, after all this to hear that Yosi was deep in elementary, joyous, comic sex, well, thank God I had found Yosi. He was the bent and bruised reed that sustained.

But we were lost again. Paths criss-crossed and led on to nowhere. At last we heard a voice from behind a rock. "The spring is the other way."

"How far?" Beni asked.

"An hour's hike," a young man said, stepping from behind a boulder. He wore the kibbutznik's matched blue uniform and cloche-like hat. He had camera equipment strung all over him and he had been waiting since dawn for a chance to photograph a rare gazelle, now almost extinct. "Perhaps this evening one will come," he said. "Best take some water before you go on," he added, handing us his canteen. Stefan trembled with craving as he took it. His suede jacket was black with sweat, but he clung to it. The kibbutznik gave us two oranges and an apple. "But you keep," Stefan urged. "You be here until dark." The young man only walked away.

The evening brought softness to harsh colors. Stefan exclaimed at the beauty. When we got down to the stream, we came upon a shallow blue pool wherein naked children splashed about. "Gauguin," Stefan murmured, and would not move. Finally, like a man in a dream, he walked on ahead toward the car.

We stopped for food at a wayside stand. The waiter was surly toward Beni, offering only lemon soda and cheese sandwiches. Then Stefan spoke to him in their shared Czech language and the waiter smiled, sat down. Stefan must have poured out his soul. Gradually, as Stefan talked, the waiter's arm moved up the back of the chair to rest comfortably on Stefan's shoulders. He nodded and murmured as Stefan hysterically poured out his anguish. Then the waiter talked to Stefan and in quiet, gentle tones comforted him. Stefan nodded like a little boy, smiled sweetly, murmured little phrases and words that seemed to be expressions of gratitude. It was a touch of grace to see this rude, rugged, potbellied, mustached, fierce and sullen waiter turn gentle and compassionate, like a rabbinical confessor-adviser, to a deeply troubled man. He was like the sweet waters of Ein Gedi walled in by harsh and unrelenting hills.

We arrived after dark at Arad. Since Yosi had not returned, Stefan napped in his bed. Stefan, neither young nor strong, had been sweated near exhaustion in that beautiful suede coat that must have been for him a totem, fetish, armor protecting him against the searing exposure to Israel.

At supper we sat with a large group of men, construction workers at the Dead Sea works. There remained one seat, across from us, and soon a slight, smooth-skinned young man took it. The workmen greeted him cheerfully but their manner was slightly forced. It was something like the attitude that comes over a group at an American private club when a bona fide member, a Negro, joins them for lunch. Or a Jew.

He was an Arab from Nazareth and a Maronite Christian. When the others had left, we stayed to talk. His shyness lifted when he discovered we were a writer and painter, both foreigners. But he still seemed cautious. "Everything is fine with us," he said. "We are three hundred thousand Arabs, citizens of Israel; fifty thousand Christians; the rest, Moslems. They treat us well. Everyone has work. We hope for peace but can't say when it will come." Yes, he felt quite at home here, had no wish to emigrate. No, he did not serve in the army but that was to obviate the anguish of fighting fellow Arabs. Yes, all had equal opportunity to work, as we could plainly see, since he himself worked as an accountant for a construction company at the Dead Sea. Yes. All right. Of course. And always the young man held that gentle, restrained smile, like a female playing a studied part on the stage. Finally he stood, shook hands, bowed, and turned to leave. "In the morning, we see you?" Stefan called after him. "Perhaps," the young man said, but we did not see him again.

After breakfast, Stefan and I aimlessly strolled down the highway, waiting for eleven o'clock when the bus for Tel Aviv would depart. Stefan had made up his mind. He would leave that night for Paris to prepare his family for emigration.

A Volkswagen tore past, then stopped and reversed. In it were Yosi and the blonde. "We've looked everywhere for you," he said. "We have to get back to Jerusalem. Myrna will take us. Hop in."

I introduced Stefan and told them he was moving with his family to Israel. "You've blown your mind, man," Myrna said.

"Be quiet, my roe, my dove," Yosi told her. "You too will one day come."

But Stefan would not enter the car, said he would ride the bus.

We all remonstrated with him but Stefan simply would not enter the car. "I cannot, I cannot," he declared, his face twisted in embarrassment.

"Look, man," Myrna said, "it's Israel's most popular car. German Jews who can afford it drive one. German cars have taken over and you'd just as well get with it."

Stefan walked away. "I cannot," he muttered. "I am unable."

Myrna drove alongside Stefan as he walked on. "I've got a friend with a Peugot," she said. "I'll trade him and we'll be by the hotel to pick you up in half an hour." It was a gentle command and Stefan smiled assent.

In the hotel room Yosi said, "What a story I've got for you. Fantastic. I've worked like a dog for vignettes and hers alone is worth the trip. Would you guess that her father sent her here to keep her from marrying an Italian-American boy, a Roman Catholic? Well, that's just part of the story. Wait'll I tell you the whole of it. I pumped her good."

"I'm certain of it," I said.

In the Peugot we rode from Arad to Hebron. Flocks of black goats possessed the barren hillsides. The Arab women and little-girl shepherds in traditional, seemly black were tall and short exclamation points emphasizing goatly ownership of the rocks. At every turning the flocks speckled the hills where eroded soil was trapped; tiny valleys of families worked using primitive hoes to chop weeds. Not even the primitive reaper known to Cyrus McCormick had come to these hills; they used scythes, then tied and stacked bundles and sheaves by hand.

There was no irrigation. This was Asia; the agriculture, Abraham's. But Stefan loved it. His hands moved as he arranged scenes on his mind's canvas. And the afternoon bathed objects in strange light that mystically limned them, adding unexpected dimensions, strange perspectives. Pale. Floating. Unreal. A light fit for prophets. Prophecies.

Approaching Hebron, we passed many vineyards. Yosi explained that the finest grapes came from here even as they had when Moses sent twelve spies to search out the promised land and report back of its promise, its people.

"In the Cave of Machpelah, Hebron, Abraham is buried," Yosi went on. "Arabs claim descent through him by Hagar, his abandoned wife, who birthed Abraham's son Ishmael. Abraham is holy to Moslems. We respect their right to pray at the Cave but they did not respect ours until we took Hebron by force in 1967."

"Who wants the smelly old place?" Myrna said. "I'd bulldoze it down and run a superhighway across it. That would settle the problem and stop all arguments. I'd do the same with every lousy relic that has cost so many barrels of blood. It's just rock and dirt and misery after misery. Who needs it?"

"I do," Stefan said softly.

Yosi drew a slow, deep breath.

Myrna drove faster.

Chapter 23

The sun shone low in our eyes as we entered Jerusalem. The golden dome of the great Mosque of Omar caught the sunlight and seemed a huge candle that cast a golden patina over Jerusalem's stone. It was a different city from that rain-drenched one I had left weeks ago. Transformed. Angels' abode. All that Jews, Christians, Moslems had ever prayed for. Jerusalem the Golden.

Sabbath eve. Sparse traffic. A peculiar, expectant stillness. To the east, one star brilliant and lonely and cold. To the west, a few early lights in homes. The air, mostly mute twilight.

It was as if the world had stopped whirling. A soul-job. Even Myrna was quiet, subdued, touched by a timorous reverence.

We put Stefan in a taxi bound for Tel Aviv and returned to park beside ancient walls erected by Suleiman the Magnificent, who could never have imagined that Jews would one day possess his walls and park a clutch of motorized camels and donkeys beneath his crenellations.

"Stupid walls that do no good," Myrna said. "I'd bulldoze them, too. The whole shmeer, including the western wall. It was no part of the Temple. Herod built it nineteen hundred years ago and we Jews have paid with a million lives for thinking it the Temple Wall. And we still pay. To hell with it."

"The breadth of your ass is exceeded only by the width of your mouth," Yosi snarled at her.

"Up yours too!" she retorted.

The Sabbath had begun.

We stood before the western wall and watched the crowd swell. "No pictures," Yosi warned. "Echoes of graven images. They'll break your camera."

A long line of young men in white shirts, black pants, black skullcaps came down the esplanade behind us singing in time to a quick, simple, rhythmic step. A black-hatted, black-coated, black-bearded rabbi led them to form a circle, and they began to chant Psalms as they circled in ecstatic movement to the lovely words of Sabbath joy, voiding with poetic song the week's repressions, anxieties, inadequacies. Voicing faith. Everywhere group prayer.

Dressed singularly were some who represented sectarian origins in a Europe they could never again know. A high-voiced Yemenite chanted in piercing tones his evening prayers. His voice rose, fluttered, fell; strong with joy and hope.

There seemed a competition of prayer. Each ethnic group moved in its own fashion to praise God. It was something like a national political convention with group rights, geographical differences, chantings, marchings, caucuses. But together. All together in a symphony of masculine sound.

To the south, women prayed separated from men by a fence that seemed impenetrable as a stone wall.

Near us there was a scuffle and a crash as a bearded Jew, very strong, took and hurled to the ground the camera of a photo-greedy tourist. Above us, silhouetted on the luminous black sky, were soldiers guarding prayerful Jews. An American standing nearby suddenly left his wife and moved to join the group of dancing young Jews whose circle had now grown so large it had to meander around other groups. "Fool," his wife sneered. "He hasn't been in a synagogue in thirty years and now he feels he has to do this thing. It's ridiculous." But the American seemed happy in the circle as he struggled to mouth Hebrew with lips that hardly remembered.

"He'll have a heart attack," Myrna snapped.

"He'll live to be a hundred and twenty," Yosi said.

There seemed to be ten thousand Jews, many not praying, merely observing, somehow eased just by being physically present.

Soldiers against night sky. Women praying separately. Candles. Floodlights. Eighteenth-century dress beside twentieth-century fashion. To their backs the Mediterranean Sea, a watery trap. On either side and east, an ocean of Arabs held back by a spidery, tough line of fighting kids. "In the eye of the hurricane," an old man in Arad had described this interposition of Jews among Arabs. His words seemed graphically, terrifyingly right. And other words moved up from memory. "And I will give . . . all the land of Canaan." "If I forget thee, O Jerusalem. . ." "Remember the Sabbath day. . ." Decalogue. Insanities of millennial commitment now constricted within a national Endsville where three million lives swam all unknowing in gulfs of joys and agonies past, present, future. Too much. Too much for a seeker of arrangement, order, person, place . . . and words.

"Let's split," Myrna demanded.

"I don't mind," Yosi said.

We walked toward the west, away from Sabbath and mystery.

Sabbath with Yosi's friends was predictably extraordinary. Perhaps twenty people were assembled for the Sabbath meal. The kiddush wine was sanctified by a poet whose original prayer was a poem of six stanzas in praise of Jerusalem. Yosi broke the challah loaf and everybody salted his bit in the Orthodox manner.

"Why," I whispered to Yosi, "do you bother with the salt?"

"Why not?" he replied. "Is life less bitter now? Do we not need to remind ourselves of present bitterness?"

Naomi had prepared the traditional dinner of baked chicken,

bread dressing and gravy, salad followed by cheese, fruit, coffee. The meal ended almost without meaning to, gradually and informally as it had begun.

A young cellist from the Israel Symphony Orchestra played his own composition. Myrna liked it. In fact she liked the whole occasion. "I dig it," she told me. "Like the music is great and that dreamy poet . . . the shtick suits me."

"Do you really like serious music?"

"Sure. I dig all those composers. Like, what's his name? And all those others."

"And poets?"

"I dig that Israeli cat. He's it. Like . . . he said it all."

"Wordsworth, Baudelaire? Bialik? Dylan Thomas?"

"Dig them all, man. Far out. Every last one of them," she giggled.

Myrna was happy. Somehow, in a sudden and easy transition, Yosi had passed from lover to big brother. Gershom now held her hand. Her eyes were luminous. It was a certain loss for the Absorption Center but Israel seemed to have gained a new citizen. Myrna, through Yosi and Gershom, was home. And if she was as rich as Yosi thought, then Gershom would not have to worry about marrying that daughter of an influential member of the bus cooperative.

Yosi read part of a second act of his newest play. An air of piety prevailed, carrying with it an unmistakable feeling of sanctity, deference, kindness, and mutual esteem. By ten-thirty most had left as if from a synagogue.

In one corner Aharon, a young American lawyer, talked with Jonas, a middle-aged, bearded, pedantic professor of political science from Hebrew University. Aharon had the notion that the Israeli political system was vulnerable to totalitarian take-over since the members of the Knesset were mere pawns, did not legislate, voted as their party's leaders and ideologists ordered them to do. "It's an unsafe foundation on which to build a state," Aharon said.

"It is efficient and effective," Jonas replied. "It is best for a threatened society to be able to make quick decisions. We have no time for prolonged public debate. That way, cabinet members can move more quickly. Just suppose we had all hundred and twenty Jews arguing in the Knesset? The Arabs would be in Jerusalem before we could agree on the first sentence of a policy to repel them."

"But to whom can a citizen express his hopes, anxieties, opinions?" Aharon countered. "He can't write his congressman, as in America. For no official is directly responsible to him. It is like Mussolini's corporate state with all these bureaus, commissions, appointed officials."

"Nonsense. We have one of the most responsive governments in the world. Everywhere political scientists acknowledge our respect for individual rights."

"That is because the people now in government are still idealistic, and dedicated. But suppose in future years less noble persons take power. Avarice enters. Levantine indolence. Fatalism. Corruption. Are we so immune?"

Jonas was growing angry. "The citizen will always have his vote. He can vote the corrupt party out. Like that!" He snapped his fingers.

"Doubtful," Aharon insisted. "Given unscrupulous men, the party in power could simply bypass the Knesset as if the chairs were filled with manikins. Mussolini did it. Have we no Mussolinis?"

Jonas stood, white with anger. Suddenly he was no longer correct, proper, a pedant talking to a student. His anger burnt strong, revealing the Israeli. "Yes. We have Mussolinis. Do you think our extraordinarily humane kids would permit a government to become lax, Levantine; like an Arab dictatorship? And even if they did, do you think five and a half million American Jews, and the rest of our floating state, would sit meekly watching us become fascists? Ridiculous. The system works now. Twenty years from now we'll worry about twenty years from now." He turned and stalked toward Yosi and Ruth to say good night.

"Sabbath peace! Sabbath peace!" Yosi chided him. "Jonas, make peace with Aharon."

Jonas nodded, took Aharon's hand and manfully tried to say *Shabat Shalom,* but he stuttered and could not.

"These old-timers," Aharon said, "are themselves virtuous and think the new generation like them. But they are all socialists, dammit; poets, intellectuals, dialecticians, and they believe man is perfectible, once socialism comes to him. Such muddy minds! Hardly a lawyer among them. And they still run our goddam Knesset.

"Lawyers built the English system. And the American Constitution and nation. But we are stuck with socialists. Hell, no socialist could have written the Ten Commandments, I tell you, whose thou shalts and shalt nots frankly recognize that man is *not* perfectible. . ."

Aharon went on and on about the stupidity of socialist states run by muddling people with untrained minds. Finally Yosi said softly to him, "Aharon, dear friend, you Americans must earn your place, pay the initiation fee. Once that happens, you can take your place in our government. Meanwhile, let us muddle through with muddy brains. Somehow, we manage."

Chapter 24

One morning there was a provocative article by a Hebrew University professor on Arab terrorism and its probable effect. Professor H. stated that terrorism would get worse, that it ought to be as casually considered as traffic fatalities, and that Israel could not be destroyed by terrorists. The article said that terrorism drove the French out of Algeria because the French had France to return to. But Israelis had no refuge, no place to go. Further, Indochina was full of jungle giving sanctuarial hiding to guerrillas, while Israel was open, rocky, denuded of vegetation from centuries of overgrazing. Only caves here gave guerrillas sanctuary and the Israelis knew where most of these were. Too, Americans and others in Indochina had little love for the land. Few Frenchmen loved Algeria. But Israeli love for the land transcended life, he said.

But when I telephoned the professor, he was not eager to see me. "What can you learn about the Arab in an hour?" he said sharply. Hastily I added that I had talked to many Arabs, knew quite a bit about their culture, especially what they thought of Israel, Israelis. That got him! He suggested that I come to his apartment that afternoon.

"You touched him where he was most vulnerable," Yosi said, grinning when I told him of the unfair leverage I had used. "We are very concerned that the world think well of us. Professor H. is no exception. He'll want to counter Arab opinion of us. Very sly of you. . ."

The *sherut* (an oversized taxi) trip from Jerusalem to Tel Aviv was fast but grim; people en route seemed always to sit in dour silence, absolute strangers, for the hour-and-a-half trip, and I could never get used to their seeming unconcern, lack of interest in one another.

We passed the white gravemarks, these "tickets" in the military cemetery that Yosi made a point of mentioning to boorish tourists. The sherut passengers seemed as unaware of these white "canceled checks" as of the shrouded, upside-down clouds that boiled below us, misted the valley, hazed the stunning view.

Ahead of us the mist lifted and a perfect rainbow came through in four colors with countless intershadings. It leaped from the all-Arab village of Abu Ghosh to stricken, barren Jordan. The bow seemed an artery bringing Israel's promise of life for the arid eastern hills and a future verdancy.

Softly, harshly, in monotone, the driver chanted a passage from Genesis:

"And it shall come to pass when I bring clouds over the earth, and the bow is seen in the cloud, that I will. . ."

A second male voice joined, speaking the words, seeming unsure of the text, depending on the driver's confident voice:

". . . remember my commandments, which is between me and you and every living creature of all flesh; and the waters shall no more become a flood to destroy all flesh. And the bow shall be in the cloud. . ."

It was too much for the second voice. He could not recall; stilled. The driver chanted on:

"This is the token of the covenant which I have established between me and all flesh that is upon the earth."

All silent. One deep prolonged woman's sigh.

The driver snapped on the radio, at once swapping those three-thousand-year-old promises—secured by rainbows—for the day's news. Now the people came to life, suddenly seemed joined in a true community of interest by this hourly broadcast of the world and what it had done to them, to Israel. News over, the driver snapped off the radio and the community disintegrated again into each person's separate world.

Near Tel Aviv, a security check by police halted us. The policeman's swarthy face with enormous mustache seemed altogether Arab but was Jewish. Had he lived so long in Arab lands as to resemble them? Or was it the other way around? One cop scanned us carefully and then waved us on.

Beside the road were Arab cars and Arab passengers sprawled about them, quite at ease, chatting as if this were routine.

Oddly, the cars were all Mercedes-Benz. But the Israelis drove diminutive, cheap cars, like the Volkswagen. The driver explained the disparity by saying that Arab mechanical talent was lacking and that they needed a car requiring little maintenance: hence the Mercedes-Benz.

I was reminded of an experience at Sharm-el Sheikh, just after the Six Day War, in a captured Russian truck, seated beside its Israeli driver, who pointed to a door handle that dangled useless. The motor knocked at low speeds. The speedometer fluttered, its cable broken. Inside the glove compartment was the instruction manual—in Russian.

"But we'll fix it," the young driver said.

And Itzhak, in Arad, was confronted by the young Israeli gasoline station attendant who would not take Itzhak's word for the damaged tire; he had to see for himself.

It was a way of looking at things, a Western way, and these Arabs beside the road, in their maintenance-free cars, had not as yet mastered it.

In Tel Aviv the cab taking me to Professor H. was driven by a slight, blue-eyed, mustached fellow who hummed a faintly familiar tune.

"*Rigoletto?*"

"*Si señor*," he said.

"Are you from South America?"

"No. Bulgaria."

We spoke Spanish for a time but his language seemed strange until I realized that it was a dialect called Ladino, a patois of ancient Jews of Spain; a kind of Sephardic Yiddish that mixed Hebrew and Spanish and other languages from countries Spanish Jews had fled to in the fifteenth century.

The driver's ancestors had fled Spain, evicted by Isabella and Ferdinand who had declared Jews undesirable. "They burned Christian heretics," the driver volunteered. "Us they expelled." Somehow, they had settled in Bulgaria.

It was odd to have before me a direct descendant of that terrible time, 450 years ago; a Jewish cabbie who sang a tune from *Rigoletto* instead of the Psalms. And who sang without chains in language redolent of inquisition, dispersion, adaptation, endurance.

In 1968, Francisco Franco of Spain had at last given Jews the right to practice their religion. With that, the circle had run a full course of 450 years. And here, in Israel, driving the cab was another of those who had described an even fuller, wider circle and who had come full course after two thousand years of Spains, Moroccos, Germanies, Russias, *ad infinitum, ad nauseam*.

Bemused, awed, slightly dizzy with the Jewish omnipresence

in the history of the Western world, I asked the driver if he saw the hand of God in his own escape, survival, return to Israel. He seemed embarrassed. "It happened," he said, laughing. "We lived in Spain four hundred years. We lived in Bulgaria four hundred years. Now we live here. Why ask riddles? It just happened, that's all. I drive a cab. You ride in it. I sing a song. You recognize the melody. We are all somehow related."

"Jews and gentiles?"

"Of course. The same beginning. The same end."

He was at least fifty years old and so unusual a man that I thought to ask if he regularly attended one of the exotic Bulgarian synagogues.

"Tch! Tch! That's for the old," he replied.

He dropped me off near where Professor H. lived. *"Vaya con Dios,"* he said, adding, *"shalom u'bracha,"* for good measure.

The professor seemed startled to see me.

"But you invited me," I said.

"Yes, but you are a journalist and they often break appointments. I thought I had successfully discouraged you." His joke seemed to please him. He led me up four flights of stairs to a tiny penthouse room, with an open door leading onto the roof.

The tiny room put me in mind of a field tent. Perhaps he needed this austere study to let him write his cerebral books on Arab culture, and on nuclear war and nuclear peace.

"You are correct to try to understand Arabs if you write about Israeli Jews," he said. "A people does not develop in a vacuum but is conditioned by the physical and social forces that play upon it. European Occidentals shaped most of us at one time. Now we are hammered and shaped by Orientals, the Arabs."

"Will Israel be so hammered and shaped as to fit into the Levantine pattern?" I asked.

"If you mean can there be peace because we become like Arabs, I doubt it. And since they are mostly Muslims, they certainly cannot become like us. There is too much disparity for a common culture. Our people are dynamic, Western. We care for each other."

I mentioned the dour people in the limousine that had brought me to Tel Aviv, and said that they did not seem to care much for each other.

"Do not mistake reticence for unconcern," Professor H. said. "I know the situation you speak of. There is too much rocketing between peace and war, death and life, quiet and confusion, serenity and anguish. This withdrawal between emergencies into solitude is a way to maintain sanity. Our seeming indifference to one another is a way to store reserve energy."

"Are Arabs different from Jews in other ways?"

"You wrote of the June War of 1967. You know how charming Arabs are. They enjoy one another, happily talking, gambling, smoking. They are delightful companions. Until the pressure is on, such as a feud among themselves or a battle with us. Then they think only of themselves, their own security and safety. In 1967 whole armies disintegrated because officers did not trust one another and soldiers did not trust officers. But when the chips were down, you saw how we clung together."

"Why are Arabs that way?"

"The Muslim religion begets a kind of fatalism that considers all truth revealed and so there is not much real hope for change. We see it in brilliant Arab engineering students who return from American universities to their homeland, and are never heard from again. What they have learned is not practiced because it is new, different, innovational, and Arabs suspect change.

"Too, the long subservience under the corrupt Ottomans is a factor. Each Arab withdrew into himself, took a piece of the cake for himself. It was the only way to get along with the Ottoman Turks. Only the family was to be trusted. This outward friendliness but inner suspiciousness was encouraged by the Ottomans as a way to divide and rule the Arabs."

"Can they never change?"

"They can change. It is not a genetic quality. If they want, they can change."

"Is change likely?"

"Inevitable. But over a long time. But it could come quickly if a catastrophe hit them, something on the scale of the blast at Hiroshima that overnight brought the Japanese into this century."

"Have you any notion of the nature of such a catastrophe?"

"No. But it must shatter archaic ways of looking at life. The Arab thinks on two levels and Occidentals never grasp this peculiarity. One level is the real, obvious world that Westerners know.

"The second world is fantasy, Never-Never Land, holding dreams of conquest, of Saladin, glory, domination of the world as they did dominate it in the seventh century when they swept through Africa and Europe. Life would be unbearable without some fantasy. But too much of it is a curse so virulent as to be crippling.

"Consider those fantastic military reports in 1967. Arab high command thought Tel Aviv was in flames, their armies victorious, Jews driven into the sea. When reality hit, they blamed their defeat on American pilots, or British equipment, or faulty Russian advisers. They could not face the reality of Israeli power and devotion. To build your life on chimera, fantasy, invites the agonized pain in failure.

"It is otherwise with us. One of our colonels made a serious error at the Mitla Pass and lives were lost. He was interrogated, admitted his mistake, was immediately replaced, and we went on to victory. No Arab would admit such a mistake. No beautifully wrought report in elegant Arabic would ever mention it."

"But Nasser cashiered many officers."

"To relieve officers is not enough. You must first face the reasons for their errors so that repetition of them is avoided."

"What about the million Jews in Israel from Arab lands? Do they think like Arabs?"

"Some do. After centuries of contact with Arab culture, why not? But they were always second-class citizens in Arab lands, separate, thinking in terms of group survival. They remained hopeful and non-fatalistic because they clung to Judaism, which is not fatalistic.

"Still, we have trouble with some who act like Arabs. Multiple wives, enormous families—as many as thirty-seven children. But we move their children through school, through the army, surround them always with our aggressive, dynamic, society and these children soon have our outlook. They are not children of their parents but of Israel."

"Doesn't this cause family stress?"

"Yes, but it is unavoidable if we are to survive. The Arabs could break the old molds but they are unwilling to suffer the agony of it. The family, the clan, the village are the glue of Arab society. To disrupt this would be to endanger the entire fabric of life. Perhaps they are wise. They do not yet have the Western, European minds to lead them as we in Israel do have. So they remain, atomized, fragmented, distrustful."

"But isn't their disunity your good luck?"

"In the long run, no. If they were on our level of thought, they could stabilize their societies. We could then all learn to live in peace. A rational nation craves peace."

"But if Arabs are so unreliable why do United Nations officials always seem to prefer Arabs?"

Professor H. stirred angrily. "I don't think they prefer Arabs," he snapped. "But it is true that we have not presented our case well. For one thing we are three million people with one state. Arabs are fifty million with several states. That means U.N. votes! And they have that friendly persuader: oil. One other factor is psychological but important; Arabs radiate optimism and the Western world loves that. As you noticed this morning, our people tend to be melancholy, withdrawn, and they aren't as much fun to be with as are the Arabs. I admit it. Our nature has been tempered in the crucible of a disastrous two thousand years."

We talked of Arab anti-Semitism. Professor H. walked to a large bookcase. "Filled with anti-Semitic Arabic tracts," he said. "Hitler in his wildest days never flooded German Europe with so many vicious tracts against us. We should tell the world about this but we haven't. Consider the 'Protocols of the Elders of Zion,' a tract that Abdul Nasser's brother once published in Egypt. It has been a known forgery for fifty years. But the

Arabs use it to prove the Jews want to dominate the world, and they justify liquidating us by quoting it. It was Hitler's favorite evidence against us. Yet we do almost nothing to tell the world that Hitler's Germany lives on in the worst way in Arab lands. That is bad P.R."

"Some say that Israel's garrison state will result in a brutal, Spartan-like citizen. Is this a danger?"

"No human is immune from brutalization. But if you had heard the comments of our kibbutz soldiers about the June War, you would have the answer. They were horrified at the need to kill. They did not hate Arabs. They were angry to have been forced to fight. When killing becomes a pleasure, as for Nazis, or a religious duty as in a Muslim jihad—a holy war—then comes brutalization."

"But suppose a sustained war . . . ?"

Professor H. shrugged. "In twenty-five years of sustained war it's not happened. Why should it happen in forty? Or a hundred? Our young people love Israel. They do not hate Arabs."

"Do you consider terrorists a growing danger?"

"Yes. They will become stronger and cause us increasing casualties, perhaps go world-wide, even to America. But they cannot win. Our people must understand that the Arab, too, has dreams and grievances for which he is ready to fight and sacrifice. We must face this, perhaps all our lives.

"Arabs too should realize that these terrorist, paramilitary groups could turn and destroy existing Arab states, as they tried to do in Jordan. But we cannot talk to Arabs about this. Always, fantasy is their Achilles heel. You must understand that they do not believe we defeated them three times without outside help. They do not see Jews as soldiers. The reality of our superb soldiers evades them because they do not wish to face it."

"Do you see the end of the war any time soon?"

"I am pessimistic about that. But I am optimistic about our ability to endure. Altogether, I have great hope for our nation."

"Can Arabs go on indefinitely as they are now doing?"

"I doubt it. The rot has already set in. Nationalism has replaced religion as the ethos of young Arabs and already they are sick of it, disillusioned, fleeing to America, Canada, the West. Probably there will be collapse and chaos. Russia might then step in but Russian communism is not suitable for Arab lands. Neither is the American way of life, which the Arabs despise, because they tried it but failed. They took your television, home comforts, movies, but not your constitutional basis of political life, the altruism and dynamism of the American way."

Below us the telephone rang. Professor H. dashed off to answer it and was gone a long time. I glanced about the bookshelves. The library was that of a scholar of politics and war. Books in French, German, Italian, Hebrew, and English were intermixed. Finally I wandered downstairs. Professor H. was still at the telephone. He waved good-by.

Chapter 25

In Tel Aviv, wandering about, I stopped for coffee in a shabby small restaurant, the Café Budapest. Customers were old, seedy, preoccupied with newspapers, letters, desultory conversation, even bookkeeping. There was about these people an air of futility. Yet they appeared comfortable and settled-in, as if they were regulars.

I became aware of a carefully dressed old man in hat and overcoat sitting alone along the outer wall. He held a beautifully wrought cane in his right hand and seemed to be holding himself upright with it. He appeared sleepy, listing slightly to the right. I looked away.

Later, glancing up, I saw the old man about halfway down, not resisting, his cane held limply, an ineffectual prop. His eyes were wide open, face chalky, blue veins like wintry twigs stood out on his forehead. A very old man. Slowly he sank past his cane, like a fragile ship settling with dignity into a very big sea. People noticed but returned to their reading, writing, talk. Lower he sank, and lower until his shoulder rested on a chair. It seemed a nap. Yet his eyes were open and there was about him a helpless look. Nobody bothered. Perhaps he came here every day and rested in this way. The proprietor up front had not noticed. One short pudgy man looked up, then hunched low in his seat and buried his gloomy, unshaven face behind his newspaper.

I rushed to the manager, who quickly telephoned for an ambulance.

Four young people, three boys and a girl, happened in, passing the old man. They stopped, hesitated only a moment, then knelt to loosen his collar, remove his shoes, bathe his face, chafe his hands and cheeks, comfort him. The old man tried to talk. The girl held her ear close to his mouth but could not make out the words. Then the ambulance came and the young people followed the stretcher out to the ambulance and two of them got in beside him. No customer seemed as yet aware of the tiny tragedy.

I asked the manager why these Jews were so disengaged. He rolled up his sleeve to reveal the Nazi tattoo of the Jew. "Too much," he told me. "They have seen too much. Fathers, mothers, cell-mates all taken away to be killed, or already dead of overwork, starvation, beatings. Day after day they came to take some of us until we came not to notice. It is better for cattle not to notice the butcher who takes them away."

"But this is Israel. That was thirty and more years ago. They are safe here. After all they have been through they should help one another—"

"I beg your pardon, Mr. Englishman—"

"American," I corrected.

"Mr. Englishman, Mr. American, it is all the same. So how could I explain it to you, Mr. American, who were not there?"

I fumbled money to him and hurried out, feeling that I wanted to go home, to America. There dehumanized ghosts did not haunt coffeehouses that were really fantasies of concentration camps menaced by ineradicable recollections of Nazi jailers.

It came to me that if the Arabs lived in two worlds, as Professor H. had declared, then these thousands of rescued but dead Jews lived in no world at all, but rather in a private, imposed and sealed-off hell unspeakable and beyond even so great a descriptive genius as Dante Alighiere.

Chapter 26

Quite by chance an English friend, a journalist, introduced me to Uri, editor of the scandal sheet so much disliked by Menachem, the photographer in Eilat. We met at the Public Information Office where I frequently visited to meet Israeli and foreign journalists. Drinks were cheap there and information freely passed around. On a slow day, the P.I.O. was sure to be a source for a good story.

At first Uri seemed disinterested in talking to me. But when I told him I was doing stories for the Copley Newspapers and the *Chicago Tribune* Magazine, he quickly changed and urged me to come and visit him. "Not too many American newspapers seem to want my side of the story," he told me.

I entered his apartment above a supermarket near downtown Tel Aviv. At the door he took my camera case and rushed it to a back room. I sat wondering for at least ten minutes, alone except for droves of cats. Did he think I brought weapons? Listening devices to plant? Secret recorders? It was an uneasy feeling, and yet I knew he must be careful. He was, after all, a member of a tiny political party, dissidents in the Knesset, and had probably received many threats. And he did not at all know me.

I sat, sorry I had come to visit this strange man, really an outcast Jew respected by few but the young of Israel, and not many of them. Or so I had been told by Yosi, who had refused to come with me.

The apartment was pleasant, quiet, well-appointed with modern Danish furniture set in black and white, splashed here and there with lush, hot citrus shades. There was a sense of the Levantine about the place, with a dollop of opulent epicene sin.

Uri returned without the camera. He mixed a drink, moved with feline grace and decisiveness. He had a long face and a neat beard and was a truly distinguished-looking man of about forty. In a land of short, thick people, he was tall and lean and somewhat resembled Lincoln of the middle years.

He made martinis but did not touch his. I quickly set mine down. There was an air of tension. Be alert! Keep your head clear. Strangeness here. Several Siamese cats wandered about the room. A mother cat nursed her litter in the hallway. Two tomcats on either side of a glass partition growled at one another. Uri had two cats on his lap. Two more rubbed against my pants leg. He himself seemed feminine, suddenly too limp, too free with gestures of hand, head, shoulders as he talked about young Israelis.

And I felt as if someone had me under clandestine surveillance. I recalled Menachem in Eilat and his contempt for Uri's duplicity. Yosi detested him.

"Look, Uri," I said, "I feel I'm suspect, being watched. I'm merely a journalist come to find out about your plan for a Palestinian state."

He chuckled. "Nobody is watching you," he said. "You are my guest. Here, read this. It is my entire plan for a separate Palestinian state." He handed me a sheaf of paper.

I remained unconvinced. Still, no journalist had ever disappeared in Israel. "Just be at ease," Uri reassured. "Relax, there is no problem."

But the feeling of unease persisted.

I skimmed his three-page résumé. The prose was plain and direct, much white space. Uri obviously knew something about the psychology of composition.

He wanted two states, Israel and Palestine, boundaries to be based on the frontiers of Israel before the 1967 Six Day War. Jerusalem would serve as the capital for both Israel and Palestine, the latter composed of the West Bank and Gaza and, should she wish to join, Transjordan. There would be free movement of citizens between states and no economic barriers. But no Palestinian or Israeli could settle in either state without *mutual consent of both states.* Very neatly, Uri thus limited Arab resettlement in Israel and vice versa. There were about a dozen practical clauses explaining how the two states would function as neighbors.

"Doesn't the government of Israel want to settle the West Bank and Gaza with Jews, obviating a Palestine state?" I asked.

"Look! There are three possibilities for us. One, they wipe us out or we them. Two, a single bi-national state. Three, two separate but federated states."

"Isn't a fourth possibility the one that allows you to live with the present state of affairs?"

"This is the greedy hope of expansionists like Moshe Dayan, who has no vision, talks like a child when he thinks of the future, and lies. Look! The Arabs grow stronger and more populous every day. Today we are militarily superior. Tomorrow they will be. And already atomic weapons make a mockery of traditional warfare."

"Your program does not mention the Golan Heights."

"Who can discuss mercurial Syria? Forget them. They must first become as reasonable as, say, Egypt's leadership."

"You do find them reasonable?"

"Quite. More than ours."

"But they have consistently threatened to annihilate you?"

"Rhetoric only. They do not mean it. Arabic is so beautiful a language and they use it so beautifully. Their leaders get carried away by eloquence and say things they afterwards regret. Consider Nasser. He drew cheers with his charismatic personality and the cheers drew exaggerations from him."

"Then you do not think he meant to attack Israel in 1967?"

"He did not mean to fight. Syria forced him. Other states were demanding that he put up or shut up. He was cornered and had to attack us."

"With such a fluid condition all around, wouldn't another Arab state be simply an additional danger to Israel?"

"Terrorism is increasing. We may not be able to control it. Our best bet would be to channel all this hostility of the Palestinians into an effort to build their state. We too were once terrorists. I was a member of the underground Irgun Zvei Leumi and did my share of violence. But as soon as we got the state, all our efforts were needed to rebuild her. Terrorism ended. Just so with Palestinians."

"Then you truly believe a Jewish state can live, surrounded by Muslims?"

"Anti-Jewishness is not a critical point of view. It is merely political and our leaders use it as a weapon. We must stop being Zionists. We do not need a Jewish state, we need a secular Hebrew nation."

"You say to give up being a Jewish nation but the Muslims do not say they will give up being Muslim nations."

"They are Arab nations."

"But aren't Arabism and Muslimism so interrelated as to be indistinguishable? Don't they say that Islam is one?"

He shrugged. "You are an American and know probably less than Israelis do about Arab culture. It is our shame that we know so little. Arabic should be taught in schools, not English, as now. We are not surrounded by English-speaking peoples but by Arabic-speaking ones. Our children know nothing about the glorious Arab culture."

He was talking steadily, pacing about, picking up cats, dropping them. "We know nothing about the sweet love of the Arab for his family, his land, his clan, his village. The beauty of their poetry defies English translation. Their beautiful young men, idyllic village life, chaste girls, and modest women are not like ours. Israelis consider Arabs primitive, barbaric, simple, and they forget our own barbaric terrorism of the past; the destruction of the King David Hotel, random bombings in Arab markets, on Arab buses. The Deir Yassin village massacre. We forget all this . . ."

"Professor H. said about this—"

"You talked to him? He has read the right books and come to all the wrong conclusions."

His voice had risen. The sense of surveillance deepened. He seemed suddenly hostile. "Don't you think," I asked, needing to keep going, "that without the tradition of Judaism, Israel would become just another quietist Levantine state?"

"Who cares? Are Arab and Levantine states so undesirable? It seems so only to the ignorant and pompous who see virtue only in Western culture. Better to be a quietist Levantine state living at peace with our neighbors than this constant killing, warring, agony."

"But you might disappear as Jews, after two thousand years."

"Not a bad idea. Most Israelis do not consider themselves Jews but Israelis. We must shed Zionism and Judaism and build a Hebrew nation free of poisonous myths."

Suddenly Uri stalked out of the room and returned with my camera case. The interview was over.

"Remember! A Palestinian state is all that counts. We must give back what we took to get peace. Let Eban relish conflict so that he can create beautiful prose to justify it. Let Dayan think only of the moment. Let others romanticize foolishly about a return to biblical boundaries. We must make peace now, while we have a chance. Go talk to the young. They agree with me."

"They are not easy to talk to."

Uri nodded. "True. The Arab loves speech but our young distrust their ugly street Hebrew. They speak sparingly. But they have great hearts, if not much charm. Charm will come later."

Chapter 27

In the Public Information Office, following a briefing on a bomb explosion in a large building in Tel Aviv, I fell into conversation with Charlie and Moshe, American Jews, both journalists long in the country.

We talked about life for Americans in Israel. Charlie had lived here twenty years, felt altogether as a secular Israeli, but said, "The Israelis don't think of me as an Israeli. To them I'm still an American outsider. But my kids are accepted."

Moshe, also long in the country, was an Orthodox Jew. "I never think whether I am accepted as an Israeli or not. I feel Israeli and that is all that matters. It's enough to be here. The stones, the soil . . . for two thousand years I wanted them. Now they are mine."

Charlie was tall, lean, very handsome, and could have played quarterback for Notre Dame. Moshe was soft, pudgy, with an attractive face and way about him, but there was no mistaking his being Jewish. There was a calmness about Moshe that was unusual in an American Israeli.

I was reminded of Sheldon, near Gaza, operator of a government experimental farm. Sheldon was an American with a Ph.D. in agronomy from the University of Illinois. "It's hard to be an ex-American, an Israeli," Sheldon had said. "I developed a special kind of groundnut suitable for our desert agriculture, wrote a scientific paper on it, but when the head of our Ministry of Agriculture made the announcement of my discovery, he did not mention my name. Now you got to be a big Zionist to take that shit. And my apartment," Sheldon went on, "is too small. But I can't get another because they all go to immigrants and to people with protecksia. Sabras get rich from inflation, the housing boom, live in villas themselves, and I live in a dump. You got to be a big Zionist to take that. Too, I have the same job I had twelve years ago. No promotion. Sabras just go up and up. You got to be a big Zionist to stay here and take that."

When I told this to Charlie, he clucked in sympathy. Moshe smiled and shrugged, then said: "So our kids make it and we don't. Is that too much sacrifice to live in a Jewish country among Jews?"

"I got to get to work." Moshe stood up. "Come and visit me. I'll tell you all about American Jews living in Israel. You wouldn't believe."

Charlie called to a dark, handsome young man who at once

came to our table. He introduced me to A., an Arab journalist working for both Hebrew and English-language newspapers. He was married to a European girl, was himself a Christian-Israeli citizen. "But," he said, "the Israelis don't really trust me because I'm Arab. And the Arabs call me the 'Jewish Arab.' One day I think we must emigrate," he said.

A. had an appointment with T., a former Jordanian high official before the 1967 war had left him under Israeli rule. He invited me to go along.

We rode to a coffeehouse in the Suk, the ancient market, and there A. held a prolonged conversation in Arabic with T., who did, it seemed to me, have a kind of distant contempt for A. Later, T. invited us to his home for more coffee and discussion, for my benefit, of the present state of affairs between Arabs and Jews. But A. could not go. I was delighted to ride with T. to his beautiful house set high in the scenic hills of East Jerusalem.

T. led me through rooms that were spotless, simply furnished with good pieces that generated a sense of richness and high income, bolstered by two Mercedes-Benz cars I had seen in his garage.

We sat with our coffee for a time and had small talk, T. sizing me up, determining just who and what I was. I felt that he had me pegged even though I guarded against self-revelation. There was something about his very large, bright, penetrating eyes that seemed to strip me of neutral cover.

Suddenly T. brushed aside small talk. "There can never be peace until the Jews give back our heart, Jerusalem. We have lived here thirteen hundred years and would give Syria, Iraq, Jordan to them before Jerusalem. The Jews won three wars and may win ten more but we will eventually defeat them. The Jews cannot survive in this churning sea of Arabs."

T.'s English became garbled. Distraught, his mouth was speckled with saliva. It alarmed me to see this instant transformation. He seemed to be addressing someone beyond me, a crowd, perhaps, or a large audience of Arabs. But he was not addressing me. Incoherent as he was, I could understand only bits of his argument: the Jews had swiped a thousand acres of his own land; they had expropriated Arabic public buildings, had unconscionably blown up Arab houses. "The Jews are liars when they say they would take some Arab refugees back and compensate others. They want us to leave the country," he shouted. "To leave it all to them. They keep the Gaza Arabs poor so that they will flee Gaza. They destroy Gaza houses to force them to leave so they can settle Jews there."

I managed to work in a suggestion that the Jews claimed to do this only for security reasons.

"Untrue. A lie. They always lie too much. They want us out. Well, we won't leave our country. They will leave, not us."

Suddenly T. seemed to realize that now he was revealing *himself*. He smiled, sat back, and assumed a new role. "We know that the Jews have to have a place to go," he said, suddenly amiable. "Their homelessness is Europe's fault, not ours, but we are willing to let some of them stay here. But first they must go back to the way things were before June of 1967."

"The Jews tell me they will give lands back, but first they want a formal peace."

"They take a piece of this Arab land, a piece of that Arab land, but no peace," T. said, laughing loudly. But now that joke seemed wearyingly banal. "Realistically," he went on, "we must accept them here. World opinion is not yet ready to accept their finish."

"Can Arabs live together with Israelis after all this war?"

"We treated Jews very well before 1947. We were friends then. But now, the Jews want a peace treaty saying that the land they took from us was given by us to them. Would you make such a peace?"

"Then peace is impossible?"

"It is possible. But first they have to give back what they took."

"Land taken in 1967?"

"First that."

"What about the 1947 partition that put them here?"

"Later we will settle that. First things first."

"Is a separate Palestinian state a possible answer?"

"No, it will be weak, dominated by Jews. Our Arab economies are so interrelated that we must all be joined in a confederation of Arab states. It would not be possible with a Jewish-dominated Palestinian state."

"Won't the Arabs in time absorb the Jews here by natural superiority of birth rate?"

T. smiled happily, shrugged, but did not answer.

"The Jews say the Arabs hate them. Is it true?"

"Frankly speaking, I am hating them more and more. But only Zionist Jews. But I'll only hate them until they give back our land. If good intentions, I am prepared to be friends."

Then T. asked a strange question. He wanted to know if Americans thought all Arabs were dirty, illiterate, beggars. I told him that most Americans knew little about Arabs, probably envisioned them as romantic sheiks on horseback guarding huge harems of beautiful girls, everybody looking exactly like Americans. He thought that was funny and seemed to relax. Then, suddenly, he jumped up, saying he was late for an appointment. He offered me a ride.

On the way he explained that he was going now to settle a legal case between Arabs, to keep it out of Jewish courts. Other forms of boycott were observed, he said, such as declaring service clubs defunct until such time as East Jerusalem was returned to the Arabs.

T. dropped me off near the Suk. I walked toward the East Jerusalem business district. I could not recall that T. once used the term Israel or Israeli. He spoke only about "the Jews." The veil covering his bitter anti-Jewishness was spider-web transparent.

In the Suk coffeehouse, A. told me he had called N., another Arab, and that if I wished to see him, N. was now at home. I hurried to talk to N., who was, A. told me, a different sort of Arab, gentle, straightforward, cultivated.

N.'s house was unpretentious; the red tile roof needed repairs. It had the look of war damage about it while T.'s seemed brand new and untouched by war. T., of a certainty, had some special thing going for him. N. did not.

Inside N.'s house, his wife and sister sat in the hallway sorting vegetables in an enormous brass dish.

Dressed in pullover sweater, flannel slacks, open-collared shirt, shined brogues, he seemed the epitome of an English gentleman. He had, in fact, spent years in the diplomatic and military service of Ottoman Turkey, also during the British Mandate. Most recently he had served the Hashemite Kingdom of Jordan.

N. would not discuss a separate Palestinian state. "Call it Jordan, call it Palestine, it does not matter," he said. "First the Jews must return to pre-June 1967 boundaries and then we can work things out. But there must be no Jewish state. Arabs and Jews can live and govern together as equals. But a Jewish state among us is an insult."

"Wouldn't Islam absorb the Jews?"

"Our most assimilated minorities were always Jews. Yet while among us they remained Jews. And they created great philosophy, architecture, literature, medicine. I don't know if they are proud of that, but I am."

"If that is so, why don't you make peace and begin to absorb them?"

N. frowned. "First, the Jews must return our lands," he snapped.

"But they want you to come to the peace table first. They say: 'First give us a tiny piece of paper, that's all we ask, a paper that says you recognize our right to live, our right to have peace with you.'"

"Dramatic nonsense. Pretty propaganda. What is so special about a peace treaty? They can be, and usually are, broken. That is all talk to avoid the issue of returning what they took. They speak with a forked tongue."

The American Indians used that term, I told N., but he seemed annoyed that a primitive people had used a similar metaphor.

"Then you consider the Israelis unreconstructed expansionists?"

"Too strong. I think the Israelis do not know what they want. They'll take what they can. Let the Jews and Arabs alone and we'll somehow settle it. Each of the Big Powers, each has a special ax to grind. They use us. Left alone, we'd settle things."

"Some say Arabs are not able to negotiate with Jews on a face-to-face basis. Couldn't a Big Power act as that intermediary?"

"We are not primitives. We can sit together as cousins and talk."

"Then you believe there is still time for reconciliation?"

N. shook his head slowly. "That is a great question. It is very late. The Jews had their chance after the 1967 war. But they waited for us to come begging. Hussein did not ring them up. Nasser sent no special couriers. The Arab governments still don't beg. Jews should have moved when they had the chance. Now? I don't know."

N. suddenly seemed an old man. We talked desultorily about his fine, full life; about his family, famous in the Arab business and diplomatic world; about his days in England, Canada, the United States. He was a cultivated and charming man. But about him there was a sense of deep despair as if he himself had failed and others had not yet succeeded.

N. was thoughtfully downhearted. T. was wildly desperate. Both seemed somehow outside the mainstream of the struggle.

I wandered down the street and entered a tiny photographic studio owned by an Armenian Christian, who talked freely. He was certain the Arabs and Jews could learn to live together, would find a way, but not soon. But a woman customer interrupted, saying, "That is his opinion. I think differently. I lived in America two years and I would never talk to an American journalist like you. You twist the truth. But I'll tell you this: Between us and Jews there will never be peace. Never!" She stalked off.

The proprietor said, "She is Arab."

An Arab restaurant near Herod's Gate was nearly empty. The young waiter took my order and returned. He eyed my camera. I showed him my equipment. "Did you write about the war of 1967?" he asked. I nodded. "My sister was killed then," he said quietly; "our house was destroyed."

"How are things now?"

"Bad. I have been arrested six times, just picked up off the street and held for days. I say, 'I am no bomb thrower, so why do you hold me?' They say nothing, just hold me for days and days and then let me go and never tell me what I do wrong . . ."

"But Arabs seem to be quite free around here."

"Come back at night. They search every Arab on the street after dark. You come back. You see."

"Should the Jews be worried about terrorism?"

"One day you will see. One day there will be no more Jews. From Amman to the sea, no Jews, all Arab, and you will come here and see it."

The proprietor joined in. "We cannot live with them. You see how business is. Once I had twenty-four employees; now I have four. Taxes are twenty-five times higher. I go to Mayor Kolleck and I say I must have relief or close, and he say, 'So close!' What can I do? It must be terrible in Jewyork."

"Well, you know, the Jews don't have control of New York. Only a third of the population there is Jewish."

"They own all America. I read. I listen."

"There are only six million Jews in America and two hundred million non-Jews."

"They own. Own it all. I know. They control here, there, everywhere."

"Have you read the 'Protocols of the Elders of Zion'?" I asked.

He grinned. "Ah ha-ha! You know it too!"

"Indeed," I assured him.

He then became the suddenly confident proselytizer for the Arab cause, and he spoke intelligently of Arab complaints, hopes, disappointments. Then he sat down, leaned close and said, "I tell you something else. These Jew girls are terrible. They come here. They beg for hashish. 'Give me hash,' they say, 'and I fuck you any way.' They are so bad, those Jew women."

Nauseated by the vicious anti-Semitism that seemed somehow unredeemed by his rational pleading for the Arab cause, I stumbled out of the place and onto a bus headed for Jewish Jerusalem and Moshe, that Orthodox Jew who seemed at that moment the strongest rock in all Jerusalem.

Moshe was in his office, finishing the report on the bombing in Tel Aviv. I waited. He finally turned to me and said, "It is Sabbath eve. We need a guest, a stranger to make it truly authentic. Come home with me for dinner. You look absolutely flummoxed."

We caught a bus packed with people carrying sacks of food for Sabbath. There was no real levity about them, but facial expressions seemed softer, voices less strident. Theirs was a special air of a people suddenly elevated by Sabbath expectations.

As we rocketed along in the bus, insanely driven by a mustached Israeli who seemed as ready to come to a sudden stop as to lurch onward to a spine-wrenching start, Moshe told me that he worked for a newspaper that was decidedly secular. "And so I accommodate my orthodoxy to please them," he said.

Poor Moshe, saddled with the Law and having to loosen the cinches. I asked why he stayed with that particular paper.

"Perhaps it is slightly the American environment I grew up with. Perhaps I need that more than I know."

His was a tiny apartment, but the happiness of his wife and three kids was so patent, so fetching and contagious that I began to feel easier.

Moshe chanted the prayers with such fondness that he seemed transformed from a genial, moon-faced guy into a quite lofty and responsible pater familias.

Later, Moshe's wife declared that she had opposed coming to Israel, but now that she was here she could not conceive of living elsewhere. I was touched. The boy loved card tricks, and Moshe allowed him to show me them. The girls planned one day to join a kibbutz, "one we ourselves will help create, not just to live on, not one that others built." All this simplicity, family love, plus Moshe's noble dignity and his wife's joy at having a Sabbath guest was searingly disparate with the day's experience. The Arabs had their own family joys, kindnesses, hopes, and for most these did not encompass Moshe's family but rather, as I had found in dozens of interviews, had anticipated its annihilation. Too near tears and ashamed of it, I excused myself and stumbled into the bathroom. Two thousand years of terror was not the end of it. Over these bloodied hills and around me had raged murder, rape, destruction, treachery. *Vengeance is mine, saith the Lord,* but others borrowed it from Him from time to time.

Chapter 28

Both Charlie and Moshe had mentioned Muhammed as a typical Arab who was both a loyal Israeli and a proud Arab, and who honestly hoped for peace. Yosi thought it best that, in all encounters with Arabs, he, Yosi, be absent. Otherwise Arabs would feel constrained, less communicative. And so when I visited Muhammed, I went alone.

He was a big, thick young man who moved with grace despite his size. Charlie was lithe, a quarterback type, but Muhammed had the scale and toughness of a linebacker.

His attitude was other than that of A., who had been venomously charming, or T., who had been courtly and haughty. He seemed direct and unable to play verbal games. Perhaps it was his journalist's background, the need to cut through verbiage.

Muhammed launched at once into an elementary history of the Arab-Israel conflict. I let him talk.

"Before 1948," Muhammed began, "Jews had nothing to say. We did the talking, doing, and the British nodded. Glubb Pasha, the Englishman who trained the Jordan Legion, met with Ernest Bevin and together they decided that Palestine should be annexed to Jordan, as we wished. All set. But our Palestinian leaders were fools, did not trust the British. They put their faith in Arab armies which are not fighting armies at all. They are parade armies and the puny Jews beat all seven of them.

"Well, after 1948 we Palestinian Arabs were orphans looking

for an orphanage. We tried to get Israel to accept us, but they had few jobs for Arabs, would not let us in the army, did not trust us. We are second-class citizens here. So we put our hope in the United Arab Republic. They would rescue us, those paper governments with paper armies. They dissolved, just as all Arab plans dissolve. We hoped again in 1967 that they would help us; but no. They lost again, like fools. Now all we ask of the Israelis is that they just let us live. Here," he said, "is a letter I got for our paper from a young Arab who had attended Youth City, a kind of get-together camp for Jews and Arabs":

> You know, Michal, many Jewish girls did not come to Youth City this year because they did not like Arabs. Did our parents know there would be Jews there? They did and they did not mind us coming among you. Michal, you are my friend. You come to my house and I come to yours. But we are exceptions. Hear. I have a blond girl friend and when I walk among Jews they do not know she is Arab and they say, "Leave our Jewish girls alone! Don't you touch them." And when I walk in the street the police stop me. I must show my identification card. I hate it.
>
> Once you asked me why I work so hard. I tell you, Michal; I work hard to save money. To go to America. There will never be peace here and I don't want to stay.

Muhammed continued, "It is an honest reflection of the way our youth feel at being under Israeli rule. And yet we Palestinians stand alone. There are a million Arabs in America, but not ten percent will admit they are Arab. They are ashamed of it. But the Jews? They admit it. Pierre Mendes-France is now a Roman Catholic but his family was Jewish. When he is asked who he is, he says, 'Jew.' Ask an Arab in America and he'll say he's American, not Arab. He is ashamed.

"We Arabs are a proud people. With our mother's milk we learn how once Arabs conquered and civilized the Western world. How the Pope once came to study at the feet of Arab scholars then in Andalusia.

"Our children learn of their great past. We too, like the Israelis, are chauvinists. But the Jews do not know us, our language customs, religion. They do not know that with us religion and emotion are still dominant forces. They say we are 'primitive,' have a 'peculiar' way of thinking. Dammit, we are Arab. Not Jew. Not American. Not Russian. Arab! Different, and the world must know and accept this. Conquerors and descendants of Saladin. We cannot sit as the conquered."

"But surely you must have many great poets, warriors, philosophers, scientists in recent times to point to. Why only Saladin?"

Muhammed controlled himself with difficulty. "We have them. Have you never heard of Avicenna—a great physician and philosopher? There are thousands more."

"You make the prospects of understanding and concurrent peace seem impossible."

"There will one day be an armistice, never peace. I am an Israeli citizen, an Arab, and a Roman Catholic. I think that after twenty years I know the Jews. They are too hopeful. If we can't defeat them we shall absorb them."

"Would a separate state for you Palestinians be the best solution?"

"A separate state without Jordan would change nothing. But if Hussein moves to make peace with Israel, there will be civil war. After that, a Palestinian state to include Jordan could come into being."

"Could it live alongside Israel?"

Muhammed shrugged. "We could try."

Later, in a bookstore, I purchased three books on Arab history and culture to add to my growing library. Standing behind me, at the cash register, a man asked if I thought I could understand the Arabs from reading books. I told him that it might help. He shrugged. We walked outside together. He was E., with Israel's Foreign Ministry and had once been posted to America. He suggested coffee and I accepted.

Sitting in the restaurant, I told E. about my conversation with Muhammed and the other Arabs, and that their seeming intransigence depressed me.

He nodded. "We know that they are not happy with us."

"Wouldn't a separate Palestinian state solve it all?"

"I'm afraid not. Just as nothing would change if Israel did not exist—they'd be at each other's throats instead of ours—so a separate state for Palestinians could not resolve the inherent differences among Arabs, which are cultural, religious, deadly. If they truly want a separate state we would not seriously oppose it. But for us to openly back it would be the kiss of death."

What do you do about pro-Arab Americans? I've met plenty in and out of the State Department."

E. smiled. "What can we do? We take them around, show them progress, and the Arabs show them tragedy. The Arab offers the stronger emotion. We are realists and try not to overplay our hand. We admit things are tough. But Arabs are charming optimists and Americans like them for that. We all have a bit of the 'see no evil, speak no evil, hear no evil' in us.

"We get from pro-Arab Americans the same five stock complaints. The refugee problem comes first. They accuse us and we have our pat answers. Then comes the foreign aid part claiming Arab nations get too little, Israel too much. Their questions and our answers are a kind of a formal dance. You charge me with this and I'll defend myself with that. Ta-ta, ta-ta, ta-ta. For example, we lump all Arab states together to figure foreign aid. Your pro-Arabists counter with, 'Yes, but put it on a per capita basis and Arabs get the short end.' Then I counter by saying a tank is a tank and requires five Israelis, just as it takes five Egyptians, and has nothing to do with populations. It really gets humorous at times.

"Dorothy Thompson was here a few years ago. She hated Israel and disliked Jews. I escorted her about the country and every time I pointed to some development, she would say, 'Oh yes, I saw that in Afghanistan, or was it Syria?' For days it went on until her husband lost patience and said, 'For heaven's sake, Dorothy, these people have had only fifteen years to do all this.' "

I mentioned Muhammed's emphasis on Arab pride as a factor that Jews do not consider.

"We do consider it," E. said. "But when they cry pride we have a pat answer, too: 'That is all very well,' we say, 'but we too have our pride, and when you Arabs will not even sit at the table with us, recognize us, talk with us, *our* pride is terribly wounded.' They counter: 'Arabs have suffered humiliation for a thousand years.' We answer, 'We have suffered two thousand years and we too have honor, custom. But our custom is to settle things peaceably.

" 'We understand third-party mediators,' we tell them. With us, the fact of reconciliation is more important than the form."

I told E. that Muhammed seemed uncertain of his Arab culture heroes. He could think only of Avicenna and Saladin.

E. smiled. "Saladin was no Arab, but a Kurd. Avicenna was a Persian, born in Turkistan, but he wrote in Arabic, so they claim him. Muhammed is a good journalist but he is ignorant of Arab culture heroes."

"Then there are many?"

"Yes. Just as Christian culture had to wait for the Renaissance, Arab culture is just now emerging from five hundred centuries of Dark Ages. Still, Islam has many good poets, novelists, and philosophers. Their religious thought is superb, but since it is Muslim, Western people do not know it. Incidentally, Avicenna has been dead nearly a thousand years."

In Yosi's apartment I played the tape of Muhammed's interview, and showed the Arab youth's article. When we had finished, Ruth went to her room and got a poem clipped from the *Jerusalem Post*. "A Jewish boy wrote this," Ruth said, "after Arab terrorists bombed his house."

NO USE TALKING
I've got nothing to say to you.
No use telling you that you could have killed my
little brother, because you'd have been happy if
he was killed, and you're quite sad that you've
only killed one man—our neighbor. Seeing the blood
on his face would only have made you happy. No use
asking why. No use speaking to you about conscience,
humanity, mercy. Who said man is superior to the
animals? What tiger, what snake would have tried to kill
a baby of another tiger or snake, which he
had never even seen? Hatred! Only hatred. Millions
of "no's." Not one "yes."
It's no use talking to you.

Then Yosi added, "In the Zohar, the Book of Splendor, it is written: 'The exile under Ishmael is the hardest of all.' Don't let A. or T. or Muhammed snow you. Our life under the Muslims was tough."

Chapter 29

Yosi and Ruth loved to walk through the old part of Jerusalem. "The part denied Jews from the time of Jordan's occupation until we won it back in 1967," Yosi explained.

"And the western wall, do you visit it?" I asked.

Ruth and Yosi looked at each other. "He will tell you no," Ruth finally said. "But somehow, at each visit, we end up there. Yosi won't pray or speak or sing or dance or anything. He just stands there more quiet than at any other time. Just stands there. . ."

"There is a feeling . . . some kind . . . ridiculous, I know, but there is . . . ," Yosi said, shrugging, a bit shamefaced.

One afternoon, Yosi said he was taking me to the Old City and he asked Ruth to stay home. "The pimps," Yosi said; "we're going to talk to them and you would only inhibit them."

It was late in the afternoon and some merchants already had closed their tiny cavelike shops with the ubiquitous corrugated iron shutters. We walked far back in the Suk to a tiny restaurant, entered, passed a few Arabs at a table, moved on to another large room behind a clever partition that seemed, at first glance, to be a wall. It housed a hidden, narrow door through which we passed. The large room was dingy, redeemed by marvelous vaulting arches, parabolas soaring from corners to ceiling center.

Mostly young men sat in the room. They were passive, even languid, and had nothing to say to one another. "Hashish," Yosi said. "It was a hashish den before the Six Day war and we let it continue. We try not to excessively disrupt normal life in the Suk."

"Are pimps and whores common among Arabs?"

"So-so," he said, "but many of these are Jewish pimps working Jewish whores."

"Jewish whores! In Jerusalem? And Jewish pimps?" I exploded, shocked at the notion.

Yosi roared with laughter. "Why not? It was no different in Jesus' time. In Israel they fuck just as everywhere, and when they can't get it when or how they want it they look for girls."

"But Jewish girls. I never would have thought. . ."

"We're a modern nation now. As Jews, it would be almost unpatriotic to ask others to serve our vices. These pimps wait for their whores to bring *kessef*, money. They play cards, smoke a bit of hash, drink coffee, arrack, sweat out the time until their girls return like homing pigeons. I'll see if I can get one to come over and talk. Pretend you're a tourist. I'll say you want a girl."

It took time. Arrangements seemed Levantine. He brought back to the table a pimply young fellow, sloe-eyed and handsome in an innocent, helpless way. "This is Igal," Yosi said. "His girl is very tired. She worked all day, but if you'll be here at noon tomorrow she will go with you."

I thanked Igal. Yosi ordered coffee. The waiter brought the young man's nargile to our table, smoking and smelling of tobacco although the place reeked with the sweet, slightly irritating fumes of hashish.

"She is a very talented girl," Igal said. "You will like her. She is very young."

"How young?"

"You know how these Atlas Mountain Moroccan girls are?" Igal shrugged. "They are never sure. Perhaps she is fifteen."

"How did you get her into this?" Yosi asked.

"I did not," the youth bridled. "She was sleeping with boys and her family dismissed her. She was pregnant when I found her sleeping in a doorway in Haifa. I took her to my place, made her comfortable, let her have the baby. Too poor, no work for me, Haga started to 'supplement' our income. I hated the notion but she persisted. Once both of us had regular jobs, but together we never made more than a hundred dollars a month, so we came here. Now she makes as much as a hundred dollars a day, when the police leave her alone."

"Are they a big trouble?" Yosi asked.

"They try to reform us. Or put a sociologist onto her. The silly biddies want her to work in a laundry or as a maid or some foolish thing that pays nothing! We are used to this life. I help her in every way, give her a good home, mind the baby, advise her, manage the money. She loves me."

"Are you married?" Yosi asked.

"To her? Ridiculous!" Igal said haughtily. "Someday I'll marry, but she'll be a virgin, you can be sure of that. Not a whore like Haga. She'll marry. I'll get her a husband. It's my duty."

The girls were drifting in, and the boys took them to separate tables. Each girl passed her handbag to her pimp and ostentatiously they counted the money and compared receipts. Yosi whispered that the pimps wanted to determine the relative efficiency and integrity of their meal tickets.

Haga came in, kissed Igal lovingly, gladly sat down to talk. She was almost a child, and her short skirt enhanced her childishness. But her body was short, stocky with a look of rugged strength. Her head was small, feminine, but her features were awash with cosmetics, false eyelashes, and deep, black eye shadow. On close look, the eye shadow was not all fake. She leaned against Igal and let her arm hang limply down.

"The police again," she told him. "They would not let us alone. Finally six of us teamed up for a time, then quickly separated and they could not follow us all. After that I managed to work. A tourist. Igal, you wouldn't believe! His wife came along and watched, like his mama. What kind of wife would do such a thing?" she asked, turning to me in disgust. "I would never do such a thing. It is not Jewish."

Igal patted her hand, had her drink a huge glass of orange juice, made her lean on his shoulder, close her eyes and rest. "We will go soon, Haga." He turned again to me. "Isn't she beautiful? You will like her. She knows so many things."

"Tell him how much."

Igal coolly evaluated my worth. "Twenty dollars," he said. Haga sat up as if shocked. She looked closely at me, smiled. "I will treat you very well," she said.

"But that is a little high, Igal," Yosi said. "He is a friend of mine. Can't you do better? He is a poet and not rich like tourists."

Haga removed her hand. "Ah-h-h, a poet," she said. "How wonderful. Igal, can't we do something for him?"

He shoved her harshly away. "Haga! Shut up! If you want to go back to cheap turns, just keep on. I will tell you what to do and you will do it. The price is twenty dollars. Finish!"

Haga wept at Igal's harshness. He relented, stood, patted her shoulder, helped her up, and the two of them walked toward the door. "Noon tomorrow, mister. She is tired now. You can see."

I felt weak and a little sick. Yosi noticed it. "So we are not all military heroes, noble farmers, martyred rabbis, pious Jews. What did you expect?"

"Hardly whores and pimps, and so many of them."

"But there are not so many. That's the miracle. With so many extended Oriental families living impoverished and in crowded conditions; with the shifts in culture, the terrible parent-child stress, it is a wonder we have so little. In this great city there are only a few young whores like Haga. And they come here from all over the country, drawn here because their families won't have them or some tragedy has put them on the street. It's bad, but not so bad. They like the life, find it exciting, and they live damned well and get better husbands than they ever could have got as poor girls."

"Is venereal disease a problem?"

"Of course. But they are picked up so often and examined, that there is little spread of it. The police are on the ball."

"No payola?"

"In Israel, the police are not bought off. That is another miracle, considering their low pay."

"How do you account for it?"

"Status. We respect our police and they do great things. Many Oriental Jews love police work. It's a proud job and boosts status."

We walked through the dark alleyways toward the western

part of Jerusalem. The sky was a bruised deep red just over the broken edge of housetops. The night sky was near, black and red, reminiscent of Haga's fatigue, her flesh and bruises. Yet she did not seem unhappy. It was an ancient way of life, yet so sad. So sad. A man could go mad counting the ways of life here.

Chapter 30

I met Edith W. through Dov, Secretary of the Association of Americans and Canadians in Israel.

I needed a good typist and Dov considered Edith the best.

She lived in an attractive apartment in Rehavia, a fashionable old neighborhood that was as free of Arabs as Jordan of Jews. She was a charming woman, American, quick to smile. She was not really a typist, was more like a court reporter, she said, making records of business meetings between Hebrew-speaking Israeli businessmen and their English-speaking counterparts. She was gracious in her refusal, invited me in for coffee.

Edith had come to Israel in 1949, fallen in love, then returned to America for a time. Her sweetheart followed her to America and brought her back to Israel in 1953. He was a sabra, one Israeli born, and Edith called hers a mixed marriage. "But," she said, "I loved the land before the man."

Would she advise American Jews to settle in Israel? She considered the question, smiled wryly, and said: "Israel is not for all Jews. It takes a special kind of American to make it; one who wants very much and without reservations to live here. Here we have our own special variety of competition. We do not go around in a special state of grace having feasts of love, our mouths agape with adoration for one another. Everything is struggle."

Obviously Edith was happy. I asked her what she found to be special about Israel.

"Aside from the mystique of the land, of Jerusalem, it is just damned convenient. Kind of *heimisch*. A special Hebrew school is not necessary; Hebrew is our everyday language. And the atmosphere is easy, the feel of the place is kindly. I don't have to go looking for Jews.

"I like worrying that my Jewish maid should leave before sundown on Sabbath eve; I like it that Hanukkah is everybody's holiday and that I don't have to worry about my kids singing Christmas carols at school. I am comfortable here."

"But many Americans are not happy here and go home."

"Often it is the woman's fault. She cannot adjust, feels herself somehow diminished by Israel's old-timers. And the Jewish family back home wants its children back. And our Jewish Agency misrepresents Israel, promises too much. I know a New York taxicab driver who came here with a promise from the Jewish Agency that he could have a taxicab license as soon as he passed some easy tests. But as with Egged bus drivers, a license to drive requires special clout, you must know the right people, have *proteksia*. A taxi driver makes excellent money and the jobs are limited. This poor man has been a café waiter for a year and now knows he'll probably never drive a cab.

"And impatience plays a part. Americans become desperate over lack of housing. I am a volunteer counselor for new immigrants. One of my families, South Africans, has been here seven months living in a temporary dwelling. Jobless, kids unhappy. I can see the family deteriorating."

"Did others of your family come over?"

"I haven't the courage to tell them to come. They are lower-middle-class people with no special skills. Maybe they could eventually earn $150–$200 a month, but it takes at least $350 a month to live in Jerusalem."

"But are there other less expensive places?"

"No American is going to live in a settlement town among Oriental people. He'll insist on Jerusalem, Tel Aviv, or Haifa."

"It appears that you and your husband do well enough."

Edith swept her arm around the comfortable living room. "My

husband is a trained business administrator. Also, he's native-born and from an old family. As anywhere, it takes connections and he has them. And I work."

"What of the hundreds of thousands who had to come here, from Europe and from Arab lands around the Mediterranean, without *proteksia?*"

"*Ein brera,* as we say; they had no choice. Not all of them manage. There are terrible problems with Levantine Jews used to Arab ways and medieval Jewish customs. In Musrara, a suburb of largely Oriental Jews, twenty-five percent of the Jewish kids from Arab lands miss up to a third of each year's schooling."

"How do you solve such problems?"

"Time. The army is an enormous factor in teaching cooperation, training, Western ways. It brings an increasing sense of national purpose. A knife slits a Moroccan's throat as quickly as a Yekke's, from Germany. I would not mind it if a son of mine married such an Oriental."

"Really?"

"Well, not too much."

"Does it ever work in reverse, with Western Jews adopting the Levantine ways?"

"The Oriental Jews have many beautiful ways. Gentleness, touching religious ritual, filial respect, hospitality. Their ways include beautiful traditions, even biblical customs that would only improve our Western ways."

"I take it yours is not a religious family."

"No. But I don't cook on Sabbath—not for religious reasons, you understand, but because I need the rest. Too, I serve a special Sabbath dinner and my oldest son loves that. But we do drive on the Sabbath."

"Many feel a deep sense of mystery about Jewish victory in the Six Day War," I remarked.

"Our boys are better soldiers, that's all. Still—I have to say it —there was, I don't know what—a moment's feeling . . . faint intimations of something . . . intangible as fog . . . I never felt it before. . ." Edith started to laugh. "I begin to sound like those crazy rabbis of ours."

Chapter 31

One Monday night Edith called to invite me to the Absorption Center where she was a volunteer counselor. On the way she explained the system of absorption in Israel. From boat or airplane the immigrant families moved directly to a furnished apartment where they lived rent-free for six months. They were given all of life's necessaries including some money while they went through an intensive Hebrew language training program. It was a new program designed to ease the radical shift to a new life. Edith counseled and encouraged them.

"But it is hard," she said. "Western immigrants often expect too much. I'm not sure I should try to ease their life. Eventually, the crunch of being on their own will come and then how will they stand it? It is easier for Oriental Jews, used to very little."

"Who organizes the counseling service?"

"That is why I asked you to come. One old man, Maimon, seventy-two years old, has been doing this for twenty-two years. He organized this program. A great soul."

Edith left me with Maimon, walking, making his rounds, shy, distracted.

"Maimon! Maimon! *Shalom,* Maimon," children shouted from a balcony. They waved yellow lollipops and Maimon smiled at them. "We teach their parents," he said.

A spindly-legged but enormous female bore down on Maimon, seized him by the lapels, pulled him to her and, nose-to-nose said in Polish: "Maimon, I must have a Policher or Yiddisher to help my husband with his Hebrew. He cannot learn from these Englishers." Maimon, on tiptoe, seemed not alarmed. His long, sagged face with the drooped lower lip seemed to bobble as she held him. His battered old hat fell off. Rimless glasses slipped down, hanging slightly askew. With one hand the Amazon reclaimed the hat, put it on Maimon's head, kissed his cheek and yelled, "So? So?"

"I shall do it soon," Maimon answered quite calmly. "As soon as we have someone. I promise."

"Ah, Maimon," the huge Polish woman roared, "you are so good. I love you," kissing him full on the mouth.

"Somewhat emotional," Maiman murmured as we hurried on. Soon he stopped and turned to a little girl tugging at his wrinkled coat. "Maimon, you promised. My mother is waiting."

Maimon consulted his list. "After Purim. We shall surely have someone to teach Mother. I shall keep my promise."

The little girl backed away and then ran shyly off.

"Her mother is from Tunis," Maimon explained. "She doesn't know Hebrew and the little girl is ashamed. Every evening she stops me. The mothers are ashamed to go to school or haven't the time. They think that they cannot learn, or that people will laugh. These Oriental ones are so proud. As with Arabs, pride is a terrible barrier."

We approached a stairway and a dark little man hurried past us. "Zion!" Maimon called. "Wait!"

"I cannot," Zion said. "I am late to synagogue. I must go."

"But only a moment, Zion. I must ask some questions." But the man hurried on, driven by habit, guilt, helplessness, or the need to hold fast to familiar ways in this strange land.

People opened doors to see what the argument was about. They all offered *"shaloms"* to Maimon. Their smiles were very sweet. He seemed not to be aware of anything but the list in his hand.

On the top floor Maimon knocked and we entered the apartment of Zion, the Indian Jew who had left us. His pretty wife was dressed in a plain sari. I asked her why they had waited so long to come to Israel. "So many came here and then returned," she said.

"Why did they go back?"

"Here the rabbis are not so sure we are pure Jews. We say we are. They say 'perhaps.' We cannot exactly trace our lineage. There are breaks in it."

"But you did come. Why?"

"It is hard in India. They say all religions are free there. Yet you saw what happened between Moslems and Hindus; millions slaughtered. We Jews are between them."

"But you've lived there successfully for two thousand years, since the destruction of the Temple—"

"Some say that. Some say only since the Spanish Inquisition, only five hundred years..."

"In either case, a long time."

"It is a long time to stay a lower caste in India. So we try it here. We hope to be the same caste as everyone. If not we go back."

The apartment was sparsely furnished by the government. Their own belongings were stored awaiting permanent housing. The rooms were tiny, crowded with the six small children. No pictures. No rugs. It had the feel of a transient place. I asked what her husband worked at.

"Nothing yet. He is a very good fruit vendor."

"How long have you been here?"

"Seven months."

A high school boy was sitting near her, ready to counsel in Hebrew. Later Maimon told me the boy had come from Egypt as an infant. Now he helped train others.

"The Oriental Jews feel inferior," Maimon said. "It helps to have other Orientals talk with them, show them that they too can learn, become a part of the land."

Upstairs and downstairs, from apartment to apartment, I followed Maimon. The old man seemed tireless. He would say just a word, nod encouragingly, make notes about problems, reassure the people.

In one apartment, indistinguishable from all the others, we found Edith with her South African family. Sam, the father, had gone out on his own and found a job that paid $225 a month as manager of a men's clothing department in a cooperative. "How we can manage on that small money I can't imagine," Sam said despairingly.

"We'll manage, Sam," Doris, his wife, said. "You'll see. I'll work. We'll save. We'll make do." Her laughter bubbled but Sam did not smile.

Edith walked outside with us. She hugged Maimon and his lower lip, always pendent, bobbled as it had when the Polish woman grabbed him. "He made it, Maimon; that little nothing guy just went out and got a job for himself. Never mind faulty Hebrew, bad stomach, depressions and all. He did it." Luckily, Maimon had raised his briefcase defensively before him so that Edith's exuberance did not hurt him. He seemed quite accustomed to such treatment.

"Edith," he finally said, "why should you be so surprised? Wasn't it so in America? Wasn't it so with me? Millions of others? Somehow people get along."

"Some more than others, Maimon?" Edith suggested.

Maimon shrugged. We moved on to another charge: a Moroccan family with five children. They had fled to France where they were citizens. I asked Yair why he, a Frenchman, safe in France, had come to Israel.

"We were not comfortable in France," he said. "There is a little anti-Semitism in most Frenchmen. And when the Six Day War came, thrilling us, and De Gaulle called Jews arrogant, elitist, that was chilling. Then he embargoed all supplies that Israel needed and we said it is time to go."

"Was it the right decision?"

Yair slowly raised his shoulders and hands. "Who knows?"

Outside I mentioned Yair's despair.

"Tonight only," Maimon replied. " 'Joy cometh in the morning.' His is a valley all pass through."

Another family. Both parents born in Poland, survivors of Nazi death camps. The husband, Albert, said they went for work to Belgium after World War II. He had a Ph.D. in psychology, but taught high school mathematics.

"Was life so bad in Belgium?"

"No, it was good."

"Then why did you leave?"

Albert seemed embarrased. "We were never Zionists. We love

the European culture. Israel seemed so primitive. Fighting Jews! The idea was strange to us."

"But you came," I persisted.

"You want to know," Albert suddenly said. "I tell you. In Belgium the Jews are tired. Most are like us, old, beaten, relics from Nazi camps. We blend into the cities, don't admit we are Jews, want to live out our lives. Want to die in peace. So little to ask for. Few came here."

"But you came."

Albert made a tiny smile. "Really I cannot tell you why. The Six Day War came . . . we gradually awakened . . . our eyes opened . . . we came. I can't explain. . ."

Maimon was finished with his work, and we clambered into a canvas-covered truck and rode toward his home. He invited me in for coffee.

Inside his apartment all was neat and I supposed that, since his wife had died, neighbors looked after the frenetically busy septuagenarian.

Maimon told me of the absorption center. "They do not come," he said sorrowfully, "the volunteers do not come. Edith says it is because they are too selfish, have it too easy, the ones already established. But I know how it is. They get tired, discouraged, have no time for others. Military service is enough. Still, we are only a hundred volunteers. We need a thousand."

"It seems to me that your program works beautifully."

Maimon shrugged, poured the coffee, sat down wearily at the table. "It is hard to keep the immigrants' courage up. They look around at all the successful Israelis and they think they can never manage life here. There is a saying here that the best is the enemy of the good. These are good people, but the Israelis, the best, intimidate them, make them feel inferior."

I left Maimon sagged with fatigue. He had risen at four, visited his son in a kibbutz far north, returned to work that afternoon, then spent three hours with volunteers, two with me. Yet his eyes were keen, his step not more shuffling than earlier. Only his lower lip seemed more pendent so that his mouth gaped slightly, and his lips trembled. I recalled what Edith had said to my murmurs of admiration about Israelis helping one another: "We do not go around in a special state of grace, having love feasts, our mouths agape with adoration for one another."

Well, I had met one man who did! If his was not a state of grace, of brotherly love, then I could never hope to see one.

Chapter 32

Quite by accident we saw Teddy Kolleck, mayor of Jerusalem, in the lobby of the King David Hotel, where you are likely to see almost anyone. Yosi took me to meet him, and Kolleck invited me to visit him in his office. I remarked that official Israel was not an aspect of my work, adding that I wrote about the seventy varieties of ordinary Israelis. Quickly Kolleck replied: "Some of our best officials are ordinary as hell." He had a tight, grim, cold smile, seemed very tough, very sure of himself.

I did not really want to call on Kolleck. He was of the Establishment, a smooth and polished man who had been kibbutz-raised but later polished in the smoothing crucible of Ben-Gurion's cabinet. In fact, Kolleck had been Ben-Gurion's secretary.

Yosi kept after me to call Kolleck. "A great man. One of our best. No horse shit about him whatsoever. You must talk to him."

Eventually I did call his office for an appointment. "Anytime between six A.M. and nine P.M. he is here, working," his secretary told me. "Pick a time."

At breakfast on the appointed day I had a telephone call canceling the appointment and making another. Three times this happened. On the fourth appointment, I hurried to the Municipal Building only to meet Kolleck leaving.

Kolleck was a frighteningly busy fellow. I understood something of the vastness of the problem of physically integrating into one city, Jews from seventy lands together with seventy thousand Arabs. And it had to be done under the disapproving religious eyes of the Muslim and Christian worlds. But I, too, had a time schedule. Finally, I said to hell with it.

Yosi would not accept my decision. He was furious, insisted on making an appointment, came to get me to be sure I kept it. He left me at the door to Kolleck's office. I waited inside.

The mayor's aides and secretaries seemed almost insultingly indolent, lounging about, chatting, drinking coffee, taking their ease. It seemed like one long executive coffee break and I wondered how the fantastic work load got done.

But Kolleck was not at ease. He seemed frenetically busy, charging in and out, snapping orders, taking innumerable telephone calls. He seemed a man who must do everything for himself. And that, I knew, made for a waspish disposition.

At last I was ushered into his huge office and sat waiting as he riffled through a stack of papers three inches thick. Letters were scanned quickly, a note made on each, then passed to his relaxed secretary.

Kolleck was fat, harassed, fierce-looking, with a thick shock of wild hair. Only a tieless open collar indicated his humble origin.

A fine Oriental rug covered the office floor and in the center sat a huge brass brazier. The walls were covered with good Israeli art. Yosi would be pleased to know that not one piece of foreign art had been accorded honor on the mayor's wall. The furniture was excellent. The former son of a socialist kibbutz had come pretty far.

Finished with his work, he turned to me. "So! What can I do for you?"

"Well, you invited me to visit you. I finally managed it."

"Oh yes. You're writing a book. What's it about?"

"The people of Israel."

Long pause. Steady stare. The feeling one gets when one discovers he has attended the wrong funeral.

"Do you think an outsider capable?"

"Alexis de Tocqueville did a pretty good job on the Americans in 1835 and 1840. We still read him."

"And just how do I fit into your work?"

"Let me ask you questions, as I have done all over Israel. Let the people of America know who and what you are. Okay?"

"You can try." Very guarded. Chin in palm. Eyes fixed on me and wary. Cigar chomped tight, unlit. A man tensed for battle.

"Do you think that peace will come soon between Arabs and Jews?"

The Mayor spun back and looked away. "I think that is a damned impertinence coming from an American. It is none of their business."

Shock! Then dismay. Then anger. "Listen," I snapped—the frustrations of all those broken appointments welling up to half-choke me—"it sure as hell is my business and I'll ask what I damn well please."

"Don't get angry," he said smugly, half-smiling, delighted to have roused me.

"So answer the question."

Again the hostile, direct gaze. "We'll have peace one year before you have it in Chicago, Los Angeles, New York."

That relentless stare. I gulped. "Well, how about the possible value of a separate state for the Palestinians?"

"That's what I pay the Foreign Ministry to decide. That's their business."

"You pay?"

"The rhetorical 'I'; 'we,' if you don't understand English."

"But Israelis all over the country discuss the possibilities of a separate Palestinian entity. Israelis are everywhere concerned."

"Why should I care what Israelis are concerned with? They don't give a damn about me."

"But I never met an Israeli who did not respect you," I replied, and it was true. He seemed to soften. I changed the subject. "Tell me," I asked, "do you see any special mission for Israel? Can she be a light unto the nations in the biblical or some other sense?"

A quieter Kolleck said, "Not by trying. We will show the

world how three religions can live side by side, in Jerusalem, in peace. We will preserve the beauty of the city, its archeology, its history for all the world, and that is no slight light. Here in Jerusalem we weld Jews from all over the world into a single united group, and perhaps other nations in the world will take heart from that and with their minorities go and do likewise. America, for example."

"Then you don't think the Oriental Jews present a time bomb that will destroy Israel, as some have declared?"

"It is nearly solved now. It'll take you in America five generations to solve your Negro problem. We will solve ours in one."

"But mustn't you first learn how to live with the Arabs? Some say that will take five generations."

"We live with them. Walk anywhere in the old city and you will be safe. Go at midnight and no one will touch you. It is not that way in Central Park in New York, or in Grant Park in Chicago. And it will not take us a hundred years to live in peace with the Arabs. We will manage in forty. Fifty at most. You obviously have not studied your lesson. You must learn that there are no precedents for social equality between Jews and Arabs. Always we were second-class among them."

"Is it a religious problem?"

"No. It is a problem of adjusting to different ways of life."

"Do you propose to return to national politics?"

Kolleck reddened. "Dammit, I don't propose to waste another minute talking about anything but Jerusalem!"

"Could we discuss the housing shortage in Jerusalem? How many needed? How soon built?"

"As to the first, there are figures on that and you should have got them before you took my time. As to the second, I cannot answer it. Go ask the members of the Knesset. They appropriate funds."

"But there are a hundred and twenty of them!"

Kolleck grinned for the first time. Triumphantly.

Too much. I stood and told the mayor the interview had been a disaster.

"Oh, not so bad," Kolleck said, standing, obviously pleased at my chagrin. I walked out. "You just haven't studied your lesson," Kolleck called after me. Then, as always the clever politician, leaving the door open, inviting options, not knowing for sure what the opposition had up its sleeve, Kolleck invited me to come back sometime.

Outside, I told Yosi that I hoped never again to see the arrogant, cigar-smoking, kibbutz-deserting, conceited Kolleck.

"You had best hope that he will be fruitful of ideas and multiply good deeds for the city's Arabs and Jews," Yosi said.

We discussed Kolleck's attitude. It puzzled Yosi, who said, "First, you have got to realize that he has been passed over for big affairs of state; national and international affairs for which he is one of our most qualified and able men. Second, there is the possibility that you've found one Israeli who just plain hates your guts for no particular reason at all. *Nu?*"

But a third possibility offered itself. His honor the mayor had gone, shortly after my interview, into the hospital to submit to an operation for hemorrhoids. When Yosi and I read that in the newspaper we laughed for five minutes. "Go and see him when he is well and not in pain. You'll see then that he is a gentleman." I agreed to do so but never did. I did not want to test Yosi's second possibility. I preferred to believe the mayor's hostility due to his painful piles.

Chapter 33

Chaim was a juggler in Jerusalem. Of philanthropists. When generous Jews came to Israel to marvel at the fruit of their donated money, Chaim saw to it that they were fed, housed, escorted, impressed. In fact, like a superior traffic manager, Chaim moved these generous Jews about the land. In the process he elevated their souls.

Chaim was a very firm, smooth, suave fellow who assured me in gently acid words that American Jews did not give *all* that much money to Israel. "Between five and ten percent of our needs," he remarked. "It soothes their consciences still bruised from the little they did and gave to help save Europe's Jews from the Nazis."

"But their money is today a great help to you?"

"Ten percent is ten percent," he said with cool, crisp assurance and the manner of a Wall Street customers' man. Too, Chaim wore a white shirt and tie to back the impression.

So far, Chaim had been crisp and formal with me, distant and wary. Then I asked if the spirit of philanthropy, traditional with Jews, still was a part of their world outlook.

Chaim's eyes softened, "It is a good question. I am too hard on these foreign Jews. There is something about them, even the most assimilated of them, that is different. The spirit you mention does exist, is strong in many, and I can't explain it. In many cities, Jews who have no feeling for Judaism, belong to no synagogue, are Jews peripherally in all ways, will collectively ante up for suffering Jews, as much as ten percent of the total amount raised by their community's United Fund drive. And the Jews give to that fund too. The sense of responsibility for fellow Jews everywhere remains strong among Jews. A mystery."

We talked a long time. Chaim, it turned out, was a typical educated Israeli. He wanted to be a writer, a novelist, but had never had the time to work at it. He insisted that I meet an early Israeli novelist, now an old woman nearly forgotten by Israelis. "She writes in the spirit of the early *aliya* immigrants," he said. "She has the heart for it. Today, our novelists . . . well . . . they are Western, shallow, and have not felt the anguish of the earlier ones and so cannot know what it is to write with heart about our people."

I had not planned to give more time to inspirational living statuary but I could not shake Chaim from his demand. Very firmly, very softly, he indicated that I had best see Rivka. One did not deny Chaim, and so I nodded assent.

He made a telephone call, nodded, hung up, and declared, "It is fixed. A car and driver will pick you up on Sunday. You will talk with Rivka. Luckily, there is a *brit mila* for the son of a famous air force officer raised in Rivka's *moshav*. You know *brit mila?*"

"Circumcision ceremony?"

Chaim nodded. He made another call to Simcha of the Jewish Agency, requesting him to talk to me about the Lakhish area where Rivka lived.

I left to talk to Simcha.

Simcha was uneasy with me. Each time a jet roared overhead he would look up and say, "That's where I belong. Not here." I understood that he was a reserve pilot.

All at once, Simcha seemed to tire of me, as I of him, during his dull description of the Lakhish area, of its *moshavim* and kibbutzim, of its agriculture. "Look," he said suddenly, "why don't I take you there tomorrow. Show you the agriculture, let you talk to some of the farmers, see for yourself. That'll be worth more than a thousand talks." Simcha was suddenly up and near the door. I understood the interview was over. As I walked out, Simcha told me he would pick me up at six in the morning and we would spend two days in the Lakhish area.

The next morning there was no car, no Simcha. By midday I was angry at having wasted time, and called Simcha's office. After repeated busy signals I finally got through.

"Hello-o-o?" came the slow, sweet, sensuous female voice.

"Could I speak to Simcha?" I gave my name.

"Just one minute."

Ten minutes passed, then: "Hello-o-o? Are you still on?"

"Yep. Still here. Did you get Simcha?"

"Just one minute." Another long wait, then: "Could you again give me the name, please?" I gave my name. Another long wait. The telephone had been in use now for nearly an hour. Finally, that lovely voice: "But Simcha is not here," it purred.

"Can you tell me," I asked, "when he'll return?"

"Just one minute."

Long wait. Then, "Perhaps he'll return in half an hour."

"Well," I asked, "should I leave my name or is it better for me to call him?"

"Better you should call him," the voice said.

"Perhaps I should ask for you," I suggested hopefully. "May I know your name?"

"It is Shoshana," she said.

In exactly half an hour I started to call back. Forty-five minutes later I made connections, requested Shoshana.

"Which Shoshana?"

I requested the one in Simcha's office.

"But there are several," the girl replied. "A very big office."

"Well, get the one who took my earlier call."

"Just one minute," the voice suggested.

A long wait.

Then, "Could I have your name again?"

I gave it.

"Just one minute, please."

Ultimately she reported that Shoshana was not there. I again asked for Simcha, shouted that it was important, an American writer—very important.

"Just one minute," came back the usual calm answer.

Another long wait.

It was nearly three o'clock before she reported that Simcha was not there, that he had gone to the country. Furious, I ranted to the poor girl about Jewish Agency inefficiency. She listened to the end, and then quite calmly suggested that I write a letter to Simcha.

"But," I replied, "nobody answered letters."

"Well, you could try," she said sweetly.

I never heard from Simcha.

On Sunday, Chaim's car and driver, yet another Uri, drove me to Kfar Achim to see Rivka. On the way we stopped by an orange grove and I suggested that we pick fruit for Rivka. "It is the law of Israel," Uri said, "that all may eat of the fruit as much as they want but they may not carry any away." It was nice to know that one could, if hungry or thirsty, satisfy his needs without fear. Suddenly there were echoings of distant injunctions against harvesting the corners of one's fields. Leave some for the widow, the stranger, the orphan, the poor. Three thousand years of tradition here packaged and presented as an instant's fleeting insight . . . don't hog it all.

We squatted on our heels, stuffing ourselves. From an irrigation tap we took wash water clear and cold. "It comes from the Jordan, through the national water carrier," Uri said. "From the melting snows of Mt. Hebron it flows to Lake Galilee and on down to us here, to make the land live up to its promise."

Promises from Genesis, injunctions from Leviticus, New Testament miracles, crusades, blood, desolation after desolation. And suddenly there came a spinning revelation of the personal and world-wide group love for this land—by Jews, Muslims, Christians, Bahai. Especially Jews who can never leave it; can be put under it, perhaps, if Arabs win it back, but never out of it. Where should they go?

I was not eager to feel more unnerving experiences and so did not with joy approach Rivka's tiny house. But she was a sweet old lady, her face wrinkled but plump. Happy. She wore a long-sleeved, plain dress, obviously home-sewn. Her house was furnished simply. Just so were the cookies, coffee, and service, and I began to ease myself behind the wall of tender human contacts, Jewish mothers, and away from biblical, crucified emotion.

Rivka and Mordechai had come from Russia in 1924. Mordechai had tried to build his life as a farmer, but he was more a bookish man. His deeply creased neck, ineradicable tan, and loose skin over swollen knuckles indicated he'd tried very hard to make it at farming. No good. He soon was employed teaching new immigrants to farm!

"We thought them so primitive, at first," Rivka said. "But it is just a difference in ways of seeing life. Their women used to deliver their own babies. A friend was scandalized at the infant mortality. Once she found a Yemenite woman doing laundry one hour after giving birth. My friend made her go back to bed and my friend finished the laundry. When my friend next stopped by, she found that this Yemenite woman had enormous piles of dirty clothes in expectation of her coming. She thought that we Israelis wanted to wash clothes. She could not fathom that we were interested in her health. Why should she? She saw nothing harmful in centuries-old ways of giving birth."

"Do they later see life differently?"

"Their children do. And it is not all gain. Stable family patterns break down. Children are disrespectful. Juvenile delinquency results. Their ways are backward but beautiful. I remember a Kurdish Jew who was scornfully known as 'he-who-danced-in-the-potato-field.' I asked him how he came by the name and he told me sadly that his wife cared for his ten children, his home, and helped in the field; she had little joy. 'And so,' the man said, 'one day we finished weeding a long row of potatoes and my wife sighed and I saw her hair was wet with sweat and her eyes dull as parched earth, and I realized how little joy I had given her, and I wondered how to make her happy, and I took her hand and we danced there together at the field's end and they saw our happiness, and they did not understand.'"

"To be so tired and then to make her dance seems a curious way to give his wife joy," I suggested.

"To you it is strange," Rivka said. "To him it was all he could give her. His neighbors were fools—not he."

Uri then told of a Kurdish Jew who came running to the police saying he'd caught a Kurd thief. "'I tied a rope to his leg and left him in my village,' the Kurd said.

"'Did you tie him well?' the policeman asked.

"'Very well. I tied the other end to a stone in the road.'

"'Ah,' the police officer said, 'but suppose he picks up the stone and runs away?'

"Stunned, the Kurd had to stop and think. Suddenly his face broke into an enormous smile. 'It's all right,' the Kurdish Jew said, 'he won't run away. He is not so wise as I and, if I did not think of that, how could he?'"

Uri thought it uproariously funny but Mordechai and Rivka did not smile.

"Many Israelis think the Kurdistani Jews are unintelligent,"

Rivka said, "but it is a question of values; a way of looking at things. Once Mordechai and I had a running argument with an old Kurd, who, like Abraham, was childless. He built a separate shack for his wife and moved her from his house into it. Then he went to fetch a second, younger wife.

"We were scandalized. We could not stop the alliance. The old man paid for his bride and brought her to his home for the marriage vows. Everyone went to the celebration and there we saw that the bride was a cripple, certainly unmarriageable. And just before, in a nearby village, a thirty-year-old woman killed herself rather than continue to bear the shame of spinsterhood, a terrible disgrace among Oriental Jews. It occurred to us that this old Kurdish man was, after all, not so foolish; he needed children to say kaddish for him and also to pray his old wife to heaven. His second wife was damaged; who would want her? The old man made a respectable woman of her. His first wife understood and acquiesced. So tell me, what is wise and what is foolish?"

"But that was bigamy! Against Israeli law," Uri insisted.

"For the sake of a life, the law may be twisted," Mordechai said softly.

And I thought of Yosi's story of the Bedouin riding while his wife walked, and the contemporary Jewish notion of *chutzpah*.

"They are Torah-oriented," Rivka said. "As few of us are. When our Jewish Agency people after World War II heard there were Jews in Bugmez, far back in the Atlas Mountains of Morocco, they journeyed many days to meet them. The community had lived there long before the Arabs, perhaps since the Roman dispersion of 66 C.E. When our emissaries ended the visit they found the Bugmez Jews ready with packs on their backs. 'You tell us that Israel is reborn as it is told in Torah. The Messiah will come. We must be there to meet him.' Just so close to the Torah and its meaning were these Bugmez Jews."

We drove from Rivka's to Kfar Bilu. It appeared parklike before us. Flowers graced every house. Grass was mowed, houses painted, roads paved. There was a feel of affluence about the place, the feel of a small American village before 1950, when our agricultural revolution began. Rivka and Mordechai had helped start this *moshav*, and I remarked how great a source of pride that must be to them. "I know a poem," Rivka said. "You should record it. Nathan Alterman, a great poet wrote it."

> Today they go through the country and see
> Workshops and gardens and fruitful fields,
> Farmers, laborers, Jewish soldiers
> Villages, settlements, Jewish towns.
>
> They say: a nation of farmers and builders—
> Who would have dreamed it; how times have changed!
>
> And those who see them
> Say about them:
> What peculiar people!
> It's all so simple...
> What is there to wonder at, or marvel?
> Really, what very peculiar people!

The community center was packed with farmers from miles around. The ceremony had begun with the elders taking turns holding Zori's infant, borrowing prayer shawls for the moment of participation, grinning, clowning, clumsy, they obviously rarely prayed. The mohel, doing the praying and surgery, was in white, complete with white cap and mask although, since no one else had bothered to observe sanitation of dress, his outfit seemed more one of status than health. The mohel quickly cut the tiny foreskin. The baby gave a tiny cry. Children crowded the windows to see. Mothers turned their faces away from the infant's pain. The elders smiled with great pride and the soldier-father, Zori, looking like a small, mischievous elf, grinned at all this foolishness. A quick prayer, a bit of anesthetizing wine on the infant's lips, and he slept. The mohel pronounced that yet another Jew was rooted to the Covenant that went back unbroken to Abraham. For a moment even Zori seemed bemused at the notion.

It had been a strange ceremony with only Rivka, Mordechai, Zori's father, Nehemiah, and a few others directly involved.

Near me stood a young physicist, a Ph.D. and teacher at Hebrew University. He had grown up with Zori on the *moshav*. "It is barbaric," he said. "Medieval. My son was circumcised by a medical doctor in the hospital, properly, I can tell you that. Dirty mohel! Silly prayers!"

Mordechai introduced me to Zori's grandfather, a lean and acsetic man of seventy-four. A farmer all his life, he was now retired and looking forward to living with his daughter in Jerusalem where he would enter Hebrew University to study biblical Hebrew and Aramaic, as well as Jewish history. "All his life he forced himself to be a farmer," Mordechai remarked of him. "Now he is like a child at the prospect of going back to school."

Uri took us to Zori's father, Nehemiah, who wanted me to see his cattle and chickens. Nehemiah looked a creased red image of his son: short, thick, vigorous chest, bold blue eyes, the rough skin of a farmer. His chickens looked scabrous, lice-ridden, with feathers gone off their backs. Cloacal openings picked open and raw. Too little protein, too little something. Nehemiah's calves looked better. He bought them direct from farmers who, when their cows freshened after calving, sold the milk, thus had to sell their calves.

Nehemiah hauled garbage from the hospital at Gedera and dumped it in feed bunks for his calves. I could make out apples, oranges, bread, beans, peas, tomatoes, bandages, broken glass, bloody cotton, and several throw-away syringes. I asked if he lost cattle sickened with "hardware disease."

"We don't ever lose one that way," Nehemiah said. "The calves are too smart to eat such. Perhaps it is because they are Jewish calves." He grinned hugely and Rivka chuckled benignly.

"Is there money in growing calves?" I asked him, and he replied that he grew dollars not calves! More chuckles. I did not try again.

Nehemiah's house was lined with books. Everywhere there were well-handled hardbacks. He looked a peasant but I guessed him to be a learned man. Another son came in, a geneticist at Hebrew University. A third son was killed as a paratrooper. This dead son of Nehemiah's was one of ten from Kfar Bilu killed in three Arab-Israel wars. A goodly number in a village of eighty families.

On the way home to Rivka's I asked if in all this time of troubles she had ever regretted leaving Russia for Israel.

"A Tunisian story tells it best," she replied. "Once upon a time there lived a poor man whose family was always hungry. He could not provide for it and his wife constantly nagged. One day he climbed a mountain prepared to throw himself over its side. At the edge of the precipice he found wild peas growing and absently plucked a pod, shelled it, ate the peas, and threw the pod over the cliff. Below him he saw a man pick up the discarded pod and eat it. And that is the way it has always seemed to me. Bad, but not so bad."

Driving back to Jerusalem, Uri asked me if I knew of Rivka's sons. I did not. "All Israel knows of them," Uri said. "Rivka's *moshav*, Kfar Achim, village of the two brothers, is named for them. The *moshav* is peopled by damaged Jews rescued from concentration camps and Rivka preferred to memorialize those who had not survived. But the village insisted on naming it after her sons, both of whom were killed in the War of Liberation in 1948. One was a fine soldier, the other a gifted poet."

The ways. Oh, the ways! Suddenly I understood why some American Jews go only to Europe, or Asia, but cannot bring themselves ever to visit Israel. Radars of intuition warn of arrows of emotion that can wound forever. Life's tough enough!

Always, behind the plucky, gutsy, rocklike survival of Israel, there lurk those spectral gray and rotted six million Jewish corpses hidden in the cellar of the id, rising at the damndest times through the stabilized threshhold of each Jew's sanity, rising to jangle and threaten it when defenses are down. And a visit to Israel predisposes lowered defenses. Who needs that?

Chapter 34

Yosi one day decided that I must visit Hebrew University and talk with Avraham, a lean old man who knew more about the Bedouin than any other Israeli. He had lived among them, studied them for years. I explained to Yosi that I was not so much interested in Arabs as understanding Jews. "You must understand the Bedouin, of all our Arabs, if you are to understand the Jews." I shrugged. It was time for a rest, anyway. But we were not destined to see Avraham.

Young people swarmed over the new campus like concerned bees. Westward, a valley. To the east, the Israel museum, at home in the hills, intangibly joined to the University where we stood. "You cannot see it," Yosi said, "but the garden of sculpture donated by Billy Rose is just this side of the museum. The Orthodox Jews insisted that it be hidden from the eyes of their sons and daughters at school; no graven images! That Second Commandment, Thou shalt not. . ."

Yosi pulled out his syringe and for the first time that day sprayed his throat.

Israel Museum. Billy Rose Garden of impious sculpture. Hebrew University. All stood rooted in the intellectual, facing the esthetic, nudged by the millennial Jewish tradition that, like a thunderhead, cast its cautionary shadow over soaring secular images of art, education, modernity. Pause! Reflect! Consider! Jewish tradition thundering commandments and approbations. Jeremiads, harsh imprecations of Isaiahs.

Thou . . . shalt . . . not!

Thou shalt not refrain in any generation from dragging your past behind you, that battered tail of tradition that demands a peculiar order of priorities, way of life. Small wonder that in every generation only a few stay with it. Just enough. No crowding.

In the cafeteria we joined a table of students. Yosi tried to lead them into the question of rabbinical meddling in state affairs, that old church-state question, but they seemed surpirsingly reticent. "But Gideon," Yosi asked one boy, "I thought you had strong views on separation of church and state?"

"It's just that we've discussed it for twenty-five years and have found no answer." He shrugged. Gideon was tall, lean, blond, taciturn, unsmiling and very formidable-looking. Obviously a good soldier. Now he studied for his Ph.D. in Jewish philosophy.

"I have the answer," Avi remarked. "No religion! No religious people to tell us what to do and not do." Avi was a freshman, Latin-looking, slight, angry-eyed.

"But how will you know if you have chosen well?" retorted Eli, an Orthodox Jew wearing a yarmulka. Eli had fought fiercely at Karameh, in Jordan. He planned to spend his life in religious studies. "Avi," he went on, "you do not know what it is to be Jewish. You are like boys I knew in the army who did not know what was *tefillin,* articles of prayer. So how could they judge? God has given us in the Torah what to do and what not to do."

"But those rabbis never compromise," Gideon answered.

"If you throw them out of the government, how can they compromise? Can a man who has lost one hand bandage the other?" Eli replied.

"They are there now and do not compromise," Joel said. Joel was tall, languid, handsome. "The religious build empires for themselves. I don't trust such people. Religion in government could yet be our doom."

"You forget," Abraham said. "Our neighbors hold that Islam and nationalism and government are inseparable. Arab nations are not secular." Abraham was thickset, beetling, fat and unsmiling. He, too, wore the yarmulka of the Orthodox Jew.

The argument had gained great momentum. Other students stood or sat at the long table. An extra table was drawn up. Perhaps twenty people now joined the argument but they came and went as the need to study or attend classes drew them away. It became difficult to keep order. The needle on the tape recorder jumped insanely. Finally Yosi sprayed a long, long drink from his syringe, then sat everyone down, the religious on one side, non-religious on the other, the uncommitted at the far end.

Abraham went on: "If we are not a religious nation, the Arabs are right and we have no reason for being here. Abba Eban said in 1947 that we wanted Israel because the Torah said it was ours. Today he has other reasons. He says that was then, but now is now. Is that a policy?"

"It is a pity," Eli added, "that our religious leaders must be in government just to protect religious values. They ought to be there for the special wisdom they can bring the state."

"I have to say it," said Hannah, a young girl, red-headed, innocent, fragile. "We badly need them there, for it is religion that holds us together. . ."

"Tears us apart," Joel shot back.

". . .together," said Hannah, "as it has done since the Babylonian exile. I am not religious. But if we are not a religious country I would rather live in America or England where life is easier."

"And what about anti-Semitism there?" Joel asked her.

Hannah shrugged. "One can live with it."

"But why," Avi insisted, "should I be told what to do on Sabbath? Why must I stay in my room and not ride a bus?"

"You can stroll anywhere in Jerusalem," someone shouted. "You don't have to ride a bus."

"Every day I stroll it," Avi retorted. "So what's so special. . ."

"Then one more day is good for you."

"Foolishness, Avi," Abraham said. "You can ride with friends in their car. But I too own part of the bus company, as do all of us. And I know the driver needs a day of rest."

"But my friends are like me; without cars. Only the rich have cars. Therefore, you favor the rich. You call that religious?"

"We do not favor—"

"You do! You do—"

"Quiet," Yosi commanded. "Go ahead, Eli."

"I think Abraham is right and for still another reason. Jews all over the world look to us for religious direction. We are told to remember the Sabbath day to keep it holy. We must."

"So keep it holy in the synagogue, if you insist," Avi said, "but let me keep it holy in my own way, on the beach with my girl, or just doing what I want to do on the one day a week that I have for myself."

"You flatter yourself, Eli," Joel said. "Reform Jews don't look to you for guidance. Neither do conservative or secular Jews. Only five percent of American Jews are Orthodox."

"Numbers!" Abraham shouted. "The saving remnant has kept us going throughout the centuries."

"It is ridiculous," Avi spat out. "Stupid divorce and marriage laws used thousands of years. A brother must marry the widow of his brother. Even if he is eight years old."

"Now Avi," Eli said gently, "you know we have ways of obviating that biblical law. We keep it because we know that once a breach is made in the dam containing the sea of Torah, the trickle will grow to a flood. All Judaism could be lost."

"And civil marriage?" Avi said, unconvinced by gentle Eli. "Our people must fly to Cyprus or Europe to be married if they do not want to submit to a rabbinical marriage. To hell with that!"

"Avi, don't you understand at all?" Abraham said in his deep voice. "If we do not carefully regulate marriage and divorce we will be two nations—one that is secular, the other religious, as far apart as Arab and Jew, and we cannot survive it. Suppose Russia allows its two and a half million Jews to leave and half of them come here? How will we know they are Jews if they are not born of a Jewish mother? Remember, it has been fifty years since religion was allowed there. Intermarriage has been severe. How can we keep track of who is and who is not a Jew?"

"Who cares?" a tall boy to the rear said in a small, shy voice. "If they want to come, well, let them; and if they want to be Jews, well, let them; and if they only want to be Israelis, well, let them."

"I think," Eli said softly, "that we are a Jewish country, for all Jewish people. We must be, so that if Jews want to come here they can. Where else are Jews assured sanctuary?"

"And those precious bus drivers of yours who need the rest," Gideon asked Abraham, "are they less precious in Haifa, where buses run on Sabbath? Are the drivers there supermen?"

"There too it should not be," Hannah said in defense of Abraham. "No one wants to make an issue of it. You all know it was done in British Mandate times so that perishable cargo could be unloaded. Also you know that Haifa is like another country. Another type of people live there."

"You beg the question, Hannah," Joel replied. "Bowings, prayings, synagogues, yeshivas, shofars and all that. I was with the infantry at the western wall when we captured it. Then Rabbi Goren came and, like some foolish child, blew the shofar as if the time was two thousand years ago. Above us passed a funeral procession of Arabs carrying a child killed in the fighting. I felt nothing with Goren. But I felt like weeping, going with the mourners burying that innocent child. That silly Goren blatting away on that nonsensical ram's horn. I hated him at that moment."

"It's a good thing you are an exception," screamed Gideon. "Otherwise our soldiers would not have won and you and your family and all of us would have had our throats slit."

"You do not pity the Arab child and family?" Joel shouted.

"Yes. But I pity my own throat more," Abraham said. "You have no monopoly on sympathy. But we are not Isaacs to be sacrificed on the altar of pity, for Arabs."

"Gideon, you make too much of Arab vengeance," Joel said. "They are human as you. You do not even know the Arabs."

"And you?" Gideon shouted. "And you?"

"Easy! Easy!" Yosi tried to calm them. "But it is a good question. How well do you really know Arabs, Joel?"

"Quite well. I know many Bedouin."

"Everyone admires them," Avi shrugged. "They are the best of the Arabs but the smallest part of the Arab world."

"Perhaps that is why Joel likes them," Abraham remarked sarcastically. "They are so few, therefore pose no danger to his neck."

Joel grinned, now in control of himself. "I find the Bedouin superior. I appreciate them. If free of war, we could learn many things from them."

"I want nothing of their ways," Gideon retorted. "I appreciate certain inner qualities, such as the way they look at God. But we are a different culture, Western, and I am glad of that."

"Admit it, Gideon. You hate Arabs."

"I do not hate them!" Gideon shouted. "But I despise their customs. I go into a restaurant and eat off a dirty cloth. I despise that. Drying hands on a dirty towel. Do you admire that?"

"It is a way of looking at life," Joel said. "What you think is important they do not."

"Exactly, and so we can never be close," Gideon ended triumphantly.

"Education can change the Arabs," Hannah added. "One generation of education and we can live with them."

"Ah-h-h," breathed Eli. "And were the Germans, who were so well educated, so refined with Western culture, music, poetry, science—with all that, were we able to live with them? Education is a frail reed. It broke and six million of us died."

Yosi sprayed loud and sibilant. Gideon finally broke the silence. "We are a different people, a different culture, religion, outlook. So we have to get along as do Muslims, Hindus. Why not? Still, we can't interact."

"You see, you really do hate them," retorted Joel.

"Would you like a people who for twenty years has sworn to kill you!" Gideon answered. "I saw the hate in their faces in the Six Day War. Even the wounded, while we tried to heal them, hated us. But to say I hate is wrong. I just feel superior to them and their ways, I feel superior because I do not hate. But, I despi-i-se them! The dirt and filth. . ."

"Ah-hah! You hate but you merely use another word."

"Joel has a point," Avi said. "In many ways they are wise. If you talk war and politics they will be wild. But if you talk poetry or God or music—or friendship—they will be wise."

"The Arabs are what their leaders make them," Abraham said.

"And we? And we?" Joel demanded.

"The Arabs respond to stupid myths of Saladin and holy war and nationalism. Too much myth."

"And we? And we?" Joel bore down on Abraham. "Isn't the land a myth? Isn't the Jewish people a myth? Isn't the artificial Hebrew we speak a myth? Isn't all that we have done here, in the name of a return ordained by God, simply a shouting of myths?"

"We have them," Gideon admitted. "But the Arabs have no exile and that we have."

"I do not feel in exile," Joel said.

"But you are," Gideon said. "Your pants . . . your shirt . . . your sox. . ."

"What?" Joel asked musingly, plucking at his clothing. Everyone laughed.

"Gideon means that you are clothed in the exile of your parents and cannot escape it," Yosi offered.

Gideon nodded. "Arab custom and religion are different, and even if they weren't we could not be the same because of the exile. How can we escape the six million?"

"What you are really saying is that you hate Arabs," Joel repeated.

"Do you all agree with Gideon?" Yosi asked. None did. "Then do you agree with Joel?" None did. "Then you are all someplace in between?" They nodded.

"I tell you," Joel said, "there is cleverness and wit in them. They take a long view of things, broad *Weltanshauung* not common among us."

"Now we have to discuss if it is better to be a man or a monkey," Gideon snapped. "You like them so much. You like their wisdom? So go and live with them. Buy a tent, go to the desert, put in your refrigerator, television, radio, electric stove, and live like a Bedouin."

"They always seem to have time for things," Joel mused, "and they feel so much at home in their villages while we never have time and are unsure. . .unsure. . ."

"Even in the refugee camps of the United Nations they seem at ease," Hannah said.

"I would hate Jews, too, if I were an American Christian and saw the way refugees live in the camps," Joel said.

"They lived no better in hovels before 1948. We did not kick them out. They ran away."

"Still," Hannah said, "it was their land, their village, and we took both. You cannot argue."

"Not fair, Hannah," Abraham said. "You do not study your history. Only the peasants live today in camps. The lively ones left for Kuwait, Jordan, Lebanon. In the camps, they live better now than ever they did under the British."

"You have no pity in you," Joel said.

"Pity is easy," Abraham replied. "I have plenty. But the fault is not ours. Why has there been no population exchange? We took in a million refugees from Arab countries. So why can't they take Arab refugees from us? India and Pakistan had a population exchange of twenty million. Poland, Germany, Czechoslovakia after World War II all had huge population exchanges. But the Arab leaders use these refugees as political pawns. They do not want to admit that a Jewish state is in their midst and so they say the refugees must have only Israel. They have no pity."

"Still, you are accountable," Joel insisted. "If you won't let them return here and the Arab leaders won't take them in, then we must let them form their own state. Put the Jordan River's west bank and Gaza together in a Palestinian state."

"I don't mind," Gideon said.

"Just another state to make war against us," Avi added.

"And with so many, what does one more matter?" Joel snapped. "They are against us now."

"They now have a Palestine, only they call it Jordan," Abraham said. "Let them build a country there. We would help."

"But *this* was their country," Hannah insisted.

"For two thousand years we have claimed the land," Eli said. "Always there have been Jews here. Very few Arabs came until Jews started to come in numbers, bringing wealth with them, and this caused Arabs to come overland, undeterred by barriers, to Palestine. We had to come by ship, and the British limited and at times forbade entrance. Still we came. The Arabs took our money. We bought their land fair and square. We owe them nothing."

"That's what you say," Joel remarked. "They do not agree."

"Because of their primitive mentality," Gideon insisted. "They cannot understand that this land was never theirs."

"That is foolish, Gideon," Joel leaned forward and shook his finger at Gideon. "More garbage thinking. We know they have many fine people, educated like us, and very brave soldiers and good administrators. The Arab mind is clever and keen. I can understand and appreciate some of them more than some of our east European Jews. Only myths keep them distant."

Yosi held up his hand to stop the torrent of words. "But we Israelis too have myths," he said.

"With us it is necessary for life," Joel said. "If we did not believe in our perfect right to be here the Arabs would win because they believe in their perfect right to be here. So we are both trapped."

"Well, then," Yosi asked, "do you see our right as being based in a special mission for Israel to the world?"

"No," Joel replied at once. "We are like all other nations."

"I don't agree," Eli said, half standing in his eagerness. "We do have a special mission. We must show people how to find God through Torah. We are not innately superior to others. Only we are chosen . . . to show God to the world. But we have no genital superiority."

"You mean *genetic* superiority, Eli?" Yosi corrected gently.

"I too think we have a special mission," Abraham said. "About religion, that is sure. But we also must show the Middle East how well socialism can work. The Arab states call themselves socialist but they are dictatorships. And there is more. Judah Halevi said that 'Israel among the nations is like the heart within the body.' The heart gives life. And just so has the world learned from us and will learn."

"Are you saying," Yosi queried, "that the whole world ought to be Jewish?"

"I don't care what they call themselves," Abraham answered. "Let them be Christians, Moslems, Buddhists, whatever. If they only do what we have taught them and not just read about it, I will be happy."

"Aren't you forgetting the kibbutz concept?" Hannah asked. "We gave it. It allows men to be really equal by abolishing all private property and living communally. Very special."

"Do any of you plan to make your lives on a kibbutz?" Yosi asked.

No one did.

After a long pause while the students looked at one another and grinned, Eli spoke up. "Remember," he said, "that we gave the world the idea of one God, and the Sabbath and humane laws for man and beast. We were the first to come out strongly against war. And even today we have given the world all the leaders of the greatest movements—Karl Marx, Sigmund Freud, Albert Einstein. We are special."

"Special! Like bombing Arab villages!" Joel snapped. "More garbage thinking, Eli."

"A home for the Jewish people is our only purpose," Shoshana said.

"I don't like the words, 'a home for the Jewish people,'" Hannah said. "A home you can enter and you can leave. Like the American Jews leave. But I want Israel to be so special, so . . . so . . . noble in science, art, commerce, religion that Jews will come here willingly and because they want to and not feel they are coming to a dead place."

"I just hope," Avi said, "that in the future there will still be an Israel. That's all I hope."

Chapter 35

Off to visit Mike, an American Jew I had met on a bus in Jerusalem. Mike lived in a punctiliously Orthodox religious kibbutz. Yosi would not go, claiming, as usual, contempt for all forms of Judaism.

At the bus station I strolled into the cafeteria, put down my case beside the luggage pile in the center of the room. The food line stalled while the cashier argued with a deadbeat. "I did pay!" "You did not!' "I did." "Thief!" "Liar!" "Whore!" "Eunuch!"

Things finally quieted and the line slowly moved again. The luggage pile diminished until only my black case remained. Almost diffidently a man moved with my camera toward the door. I rushed to him and grabbed the case. "Easy Easy!" the man soothed me. "We must be careful. It had been there a long time."

"But it's only a camera case."

He nodded, looked into the case I had opened, then walked toward the special table reserved for bus drivers. They grinned at me as if to say, Well, what did you expect? Here they've exploded bombs before.

Only later did I think of the extraordinary bravery of the bus driver, who could not know if the case might explode, nor when.

The bus left. It stopped at every *moshav* and kibbutz lane. The closer we came to the sea the happier and less European seemed the people. Oriental Jews entered in native dress, lugging children or guiding their old people. They carried chickens, produce, even furniture. One old man's face could have been Arab except that on each side there fell those distinctively Jewish curling earlocks. He plopped a gunny sack beside me and from it came a minty fragrance that quickly filled the bus and pleasantly blended with the smell of sheep, goats, and the sweetly female odor of fresh cow's milk. These people greeted one another like well-loved cousins. The rich smells, colorful Oriental dress, happy people, Hebrew spoken with an Arabic, brittle accent—and some spoke only Arabic—all these transformed the bus from its Western air into something resembling a caravan. They seemed to belong here, together.

European Jews seemed otherwise dour, unfriendly, shrewd, withdrawn from one another. The Moslems seemed not to have twisted the Jewish soul. Or perhaps Oriental Jews were blessed with different, lesser expectations...?

The bus slowed, the driver nodded to me. He punched his thumb in the direction of the kibbutz. "One kilometer, maybe two. Not more," he said.

In the distance the cultivated land seemed to be patched with silvery lakes that upon closer inspection were seen to be fields covered with strips of clear polyethylene laid down between rows to restrain weeds, conserve moisture, hold heat for tender seedlings; ersatz compost.

In one field listless horses stood in their traces while groups of Oriental Jews hand-weeded a field, moved slowly, steadily, purposefully, giving off a sense of limitless time. Across the road a blue-clad kibbutznik hurriedly loaded irrigation pipes on a rack wagon, and then quickly started his tractor and noisily drove away. One modern man, soon gone. And then I could hear again the voices and laughter of the men and women who hoed rows in ways known to Abraham, Isaac, and Jacob.

I trudged into a squinting-blue sky flecked with clouds so white they seemed a new color. Offers to ride refused. Kibbutz must be near.

Rest beside a field of barley. A *moshavnik* scythed with rhythmic strokes the tall green plants whose grain was "in milk." His wife bundled stalks, then pitched bundles into a horse-drawn cart. I asked the workingman how far to the kibbutz, and he answered in cadence with the pinging scythe; "one . . . kilometer . . . may . . . be two . . . not more."

In Iran he had been a tailor. Here ten years, he now worked Israeli soil. Asked if life was better here than in Iran, he replied, "Here is . . . harder . . . but better . . . but better . . . bless . . . His name."

A truck stopped. I accepted the ride. Israeli notions of distance fall short of reality. The reality had made me footsore. The driver, a kibbutznik, told me that the Iranian *moshavnik* was a simple fellow. "Who else goes around cutting fodder with a scythe except Oriental Jews and Arabs? We use field choppers and automatic unloading wagons and fence-line feed bunks and milking parlors. The *moshav* way is too independent, too lonely. They work too hard for too little. And so they lose independence, become slaves to the soil, then move off the land to easier jobs, leaving wives to work the land. Or they rent out the land."

"But to rent the land to others is illegal!"

The kibbutznik nodded. "It is. But these people must live. If on ten acres of ground they can't live, isn't it better to rent it to another *moshavnik* so that he has twenty acres and *can* live? The renter then goes to Ashdod or Ashkelon and works in a factory. We wink at illegality that allows a man to take care of himself. But the kibbutz is the way of the future. We work eight hours. We lack for nothing. We have leisure, culture, permanency. The *moshav* people have nothing."

There was in this young, bronzed man not the tiniest shadow of doubt. I looked at him, his thick shoulders, enormous red mustache, fierce blue eyes. What was his parentage? Russian? German? Czechoslovakian? Where did he get this self-assurance, certainty? Not from his parents, those harassed people denied a full share of European life. Then where? The land, perhaps, its influence and steady pull like a tide into new paths? The kibbutz way of life? The army? How did it all happen?

The driver pointed to Mike's kibbutz in the distance—at least ten kilometers from my bus stop!

I began a walk which was sweet in the near-noon sun. A chameleon slipped around a "eugenic eucalyptus tree" to fix me with a dragon's stare. Warm sun, hard dry air, distant surf, shimmering fields, quiet . . . all these drained me of purpose and I stared, manlike, fixed by the dragon stare, conjoined to an immemorial, shared past. A truck honked; I stepped aside; the chameleon disappeared.

Johanan ben-Zakkai, that doveish rabbi, had here bowed to

Roman rulers who rewarded his subservience by allowing him to live and perpetuate his Academy of Jewish Studies. And so Judaism survived but the Jewish state died. Now, once again, Israel was surrounded by "Romans" who would, if they could, kill it. Perhaps, if their post-victory mood was benign, the victors might allow rabbis and fusty scholars to carry on their seemingly harmless recondite studies that were, in reality, time bombs set to detonate, not on time alone but time-plus-the-Jewish-condition—even if it took milennia, as it did this last time.

As I trudged onward, there came over me a peculiarly disjointed, unreasoning sense of fright at how tenuous life was for Israel. The Arabs swarmed like angry bees disturbed by a foreign body. The United Nations did not look with much favor on the cloutless state of a mere three million souls. Both Russia and China felt Israel to be unviable. And yet I walked toward a group of modern Essenes banded together hopefully, mingling piety and work in the face of all this hostility and, perhaps, imminent annihilation.

It was all crazy. And at that moment if Behemoth himself had suddenly moved out of the sea to the horizon before me I should not have felt especially astonished.

Vastly uneasy, I hurried on to enter the religious kibbutz where luckily I found Mike operating a tractor-with-endloader, moving equipment so that the weeds could be mowed. The gleeful reality of rank weeds steadied me.

There must have been $100,000 worth of machinery in that dump in which Mike industriously worked. And it lay sprawled, unshedded. No American farmer would treat machinery so carelessly. Rather would he take pride in it, protect and shed it. After all, machines are capital property, a sign of wealth, training, successful farming.

There was a reason for this difference. Yosi had told me that ninety percent of the land was owned by government agencies or quasi-government agencies holding it in trust for the Jewish people. Leases were renewable annually for forty-nine years to conform with the Levitical jubilee (fiftieth) year.

American farmers generally got a one-year lease only, subject to a landlord's wishes. Hence, renters tended to put faith only in property easily moved to another farm or sold. The Israeli farmer had more security in a lease that covered his life span. He could lavish his concern on the soil which, in any case, had special meaning for him. Machines were insensate, manufactured things only as important as, say, clothing, housing, furniture, about all of which the Israeli farmer was careless. A matter of values . . . ways of looking at things.

Mike joined me and we walked to the headquarters building. Everything sprawled like a summer camp. While Mike talked to the secretary of the kibbutz, I read the kibbutz schedule of the week's activities.

Shabbat	1. Prayers 2. Two lessons from the Talmud: 11:00–12:00 mornings
Post-Shabbat	1. Arts & Crafts—ceramics 2. Class in the Arabic language 3. Volleyball
Monday	1. Exercise for pregnant women 2. Three classes in the English language 3. Kibbutz committees

Tuesday	1. Family picnic
	2. Flower arranging
	3. Trip to Tel Aviv
	   a. *Hello Dolly*
	   b. *Waiting for Godot*

Wednesday	1. Lending library open all day 2. Movie
Thursday	1. Committee meetings 2. General membership meeting
Friday	1. Sabbath eve services

NOTE: Prayer service three times daily.

Mike rejoined me. "It's a structured life," he admitted, "but most build their lives around family, prayer, work. Most are married. The scheduled activities are for the old and unmarried, particularly the latter, who have it tough here, especially if they are under thirty. You see, the kibbutz is built around the family, and if you haven't one you can be very lonely."

Mike spoke longingly about the theater. As we walked to his bachelor's quarters, he told me that after college he had wanted to be a professional actor, had been good at it, in New York, and was encouraged to make a career of it. "Unfortunately Sabbath observance made that impossible. I had to choose between the theater and orthodoxy."

I suggested that in Israel, now, he did not have to be constrained, since theater was banned on the Sabbath.

"Acting is of no benefit to the kibbutz," Mike replied. "Only work that sustains the group is encouraged. I plan to use what theatrical talent I have in politics. I'm now working on my doctorate in political science."

"I should have thought a farm kibbutz the last place for a man with a Ph.D. in political science, or politics at all."

Mike grinned. "To look after their interests, each segment of our society elects representatives to the legislature, our Knesset. The kibbutz movements, too, have their representatives trying to get favorable legislation, financial assistance, preference for jobs. Since we have only thirteen religious kibbutzim, I should rise rapidly in politics."

Mike seemed a paradox. Certainly he was a committed, even isolated Orthodox Jew; so much so that in America he had never met a Christian until he had entered graduate school, nor until then had he sat in a mixed class, with boys and girls. Yet he had great admiration for men who could make money. "A great skill requiring high intelligence," Mike explained. "It's no easy thing. I invest a little money here and there. It's a marvelous game and one requiring much intelligence, intuition, subtle reasoning."

"But in a kibbutz can you have private funds to invest?"

"If I join, everything I own must then be given to the kibbutz."

A moment's pause! The unspoken question: Will Mike ever join the kibbutz, or has American capitalism, with its individual achievements, hooked him with unbreakable barbs?

I sat on Mike's roommate's bunk, an iron cot covered with crushed mattress, gray blanket. Cement floors. No pin-ups but piles of books, mostly paperback novels. Again I had the sense of barracks life, of Boy Scout camps and crowded troopships. Mike handed me a brochure he used to proselytize American Jews for the religious kibbutz life.

> Religious kibbutz members maintain that the authority of Torah to direct the life of the Jewish people is eternal . . . the Written and the Oral law are equally binding . . . Zionism is not solely a movement striving for the solution of the Jewish problem . . . it is rather a national effort for the solution of the problem of Judaism. Judaism is incapable of fulfillment in the *galut*. . . . The capitalistic system is responsible for the perversion of the social and ethical principles laid down in the Torah; it is incumbent upon us therefore to strive for a more moral Jewish society based upon the principles of Torah and labor. . . . The most important means of achievement is the education of the individual and the formation of well-knit cells for the realization of these ideals. This last is the most important function of the religious kibbutzim.

"And that's the idea," Mike said. "The whole megilla."

"Does it work?" I asked.

"We've been here twenty years. We're one of the richest communities around here. These people are excellent farmers as well as learned, so. . .?"

Mike could spend but a few scattered hours with me. "Here one must work or get out," he said. "Each has his job and all depend on him to do it. I hope you understand."

So I wandered about the kibbutz, unnoticed for the most part by these dedicated, religious Jews who lived lives based on centuries-old dicta but who machine-milked hundreds of dairy cattle and farmed the land using modern techniques.

Their cows were totally confined. The pasture was cut and chopped mechanically, then blown into a self-unloading wagon that delivered forage, cafeteria-style, to the cows. Milking was done in "milking parlors," six at a time, thrice daily, by skullcapped men in rubber boots and blue clothes, exercising a rigid sanitation undreamt of in the Torah. The foreman was too busy to talk to me but one of his men told me that the cows were the least profitable venture on the kibbutz and should have long ago been abandoned but for the fact that the older men had built the herd during years of careful, selective hard labor. "It is their life's work," the milker said. "Shall we tell them it's all been for nothing and sell the cows?"

The main production of the kibbutz came from cotton and an enormous flock of 100,000 laying hens producing hatchery eggs for Israel and Europe. Daniel was in charge of the operation. He had been brought from Italy as an infant, orphaned by the Nazis. He had graduated from Hebrew University, and then had learned the science of poultry production at the University of Indiana.

Recently his flock had suffered a devastating attack of Newcastle's disease and I could not get inside any of the dozens of laying houses. "You can carry the disease out of here on your shoes, your clothes," Daniel told me. "Best not enter." But he allowed me to peek in the windows to see his most modern operation, mechanized to the last detail, clean and obviously efficient. He told me that all the equipment could be electronically operated so that on the Sabbath no Jew had to work to throw a switch and thus violate the holy day's sanctity.

Hired labor? Kibbutz socialism would not allow it.

Daniel introduced me to Shlomo, a Belgian Jew who had survived the Nazis and now was the foreman in charge of a new project producing mink for fur. He saw no paradox in selling a product consumed in the affluent world of private capitalism. "Why not?" he said. "We need the income and one day, perhaps, they, too, will know the futility of private property. Meantime...."

To the south of the living area there lay a plowed field that drew me. It had a loamy look, fragrance too, and the liveliness of its color told of warmth and the nearness of planting time. The field fell away to the west and was met there by a neat grove of young olive trees, cultivated, managed, uniform in development. In Galilee the olive trees were scattered and black with aged, gnarled, heavy limbs tortured by time into grotesque shapes; each a piece of art. There, in season, entire Arab families swarmed out to pick the tiny, luscious fruit and to make a family outing of it, a joyous harvest festival ancient and celebrated before the time of the pharaohs.

But the kibbutz grove was altogether another thing. It was modern in conception and execution, with olives mechanically picked, sorted, canned as a gourmet item. No ceremonial "oil beaten for the light" came from these groves owned by religious Jews, who knew better than most the meaning of beaten oil. Here olives were merely a business arm of the kibbutz, like poultry, the dairy, cotton, mink. The Talmudic question here did not apply: "Why is Israel compared to an olive tree?" Answer: "Because the olive yields its precious oil only when pounded and Israel is at its best under oppression."

Johanon ben-Zakkai had said it but he could not have foreseen this colony of learned men, religiously observant, militarily qualified, the best of soldiers, dedicated to labor and Torah, and who refused to be "pounded."

The synagogue was merely a simple place for praying, large enough to accommodate its members. It was different from the synagogue at Arad, that tiny atavism used by only a few old people. Here the plain, high-ceilinged synagogue was lively, clothed with the dignity of need.

Like the synagogue the high school was stark. Its principal was a short, stocky, vigorous, middle-aged man with a long upper lip and a broad Slavic face. Except for the tiny yarmulka on his head he had about him no distinguishing features of the observing Jew—no curling earlocks or beard or exotic dress. There was a military precision to his speech and manner. He was yet another Mordechai, who had emigrated from White Russia in 1937. His family, strong believers in the Jewish return to Israel, Zionists, planned to follow him but were destroyed during Hitler's invasion of Russia. Mordechai told this quietly, almost unemotionally, as if it were a statistic as much a part of him as his heartbeat.

In 1942, the Jewish Brigade of the British army drew him from Palestine and the Hebrew University. He served as a medical corpsman. "I had to work on the Sabbath," Mordechai said. "But not for myself, only for the sick, and that is permitted."

After World War II, Mordechai had gone to Cyprus to teach refugee Jewish children in British detention camps. "One of those children, when a young man, left this Kibbutz to establish another, later overrun by Jordan. He was killed but his infant son was spirited out and we raised him here. That boy, himself now married, has gone back to rebuild that same kibbutz, retaken in the Six Day War of 1967."

Tide out. Tide in. The ebb and flow of Jewish life seemed perfectly refracted in that Jewish orphan's life.

"Here, the religious and the secular are taught as one thing," Mordechai told me. "We read Antigone along with Hebrew poetry of medieval times. And we read the plays of Sophocles and discuss his sense of fatalism and contrast it with Jewish hopefulness. Just so, in teaching Judaism it is necessary to teach of the larger world, to compare and contrast, and this seems to add special meaning to ancient works that in most schools seem stale. Plato and Socrates are no less real for being pitted against Maimonides, Heschel and Buber. Even in teaching English we read religious texts in that language, thus combining religion, composition, linguistics, semantics in a comparison of English and Hebrew that hurries the learning process. The holy tongue and our beliefs are maintained not by shunning comparable or contrasting cultures but by using them to enhance the meaning of Judaism."

"Do many of your kids go to college?"

"In the fifties we thought eight grades were quite enough. Later we thought twelve were sufficient for kibbutz farmers. In truth, we were afraid to expose our children to secular thought, worldly ways; and so we lost our best young people.

"Now we know we must offer our young more than the outside world does. More education; more responsibility; opportunity to innovate; quicker recognition of their talents. And we have brought in new people from abroad, to enliven life here and to provide marriage partners.

"We do send the brainy young to college. They learn while there that they can achieve as much and more, than do non-kibbutz youngsters. Now seventy-five percent of our children remain with us, a solid achievement."

"But if they leave the kibbutz they go out with nothing except the clothing on their backs. That's a powerful deterrent, isn't it?"

"Yes." Mordechai nodded gravely. "But because of that we are obligated to assure that life here is more satisfying than it is *outside*. Then if youngsters abandon us it is because it is the best course for them, and for us."

"*Outside*." Mike too had used the word as if these people were in military, or monastic, seclusion, as if they were a hierarchy, special caste, or a priesthood. Mordechai explained this.

"It is a dangerous problem," he said. "After all, we truly are a class apart, as idealists in a commune dedicated to Torah. Here the family unit is strengthened by extended family units, since everyone is uncle, aunt, cousin to the children of others. We are like a separate tribe, almost, with nearly total absence of competition and almost no loneliness. Petty jealousies we do have, and people who do not like one another. There are some shirkers. Dissatisfactions are part of human existence. But here all abrasions are muted because individualism has had its course changed from self to group interest. This group interest inevitably is separatist, and so we do tend to think only of our people. Others are 'outside,' as you say. It may be unavoidable."

"Twenty-five percent of your kids leave the kibbutz. Isn't that loss worrisome?"

"Humans cannot all be happy here. Some we do not want. Some don't want us. Still others follow abstract professions not useful to the kibbutz. For example, one former member is in experimental microbiology requiring laboratories, a certain climate of thought, fellow scientists. This man could not be happy or productive here. He left us. Yet he comes back on religious holidays to worship with us.

"A girl yearned to study sociology, an area not useful to us who use Torah to guide polity. But she was sincere and talented and so we allowed it, thinking that one day she might return, be our secretary, do us good. We are flexible about communal principles, but not with Torah. The law is the law. Immutable."

"Are you in any sense a Hassidic society expressing religious piety through joyous song and dance?"

He smiled again, suddenly appearing extraordinarily British in dark sweater, white shirt, soldierly bearing complete with military mustache. He had the air of N., that courtly Arab diplomat I had met in East Jerusalem. They could have been cousins. But N. had devoted himself to the welfare of the Ottoman Turks, then the British, then Jordan; while Mordechai had given himself to Israel and Judaism and kibbutz. That black skullcap atop Mordechai's head suddenly assumed eschatological implications. Pillar of fire. Flood of Noah. Burning bush. Manna for Moses. Shoal of quail. None of this seemed terribly fabulous, facing this quiet, pious man. Seeing him, one could believe in that special covenant made with Abraham, with Moses—made with Mordechai.

"It is striking to see religious Jews milking cows, feeding hens, planting cotton, tending fruit and olive groves. How did it come about?" I asked.

"Our life should not seem strange to you. There is nothing in Jewish tradition against farming. Rather is it the other way around. In Europe and Muslim countries, Jews were never secure and so they kept themselves in chattels, not real estate, gaining liquidity for quick flight. Many countries did not allow Jews to own land—there simply wasn't enough for their own people. We furnished a needed merchant and banking class. Still, when allowed, we were farmers."

"Do your kids serve in the army?"

Mordechai bridled. "Of course. During mobilization in 1967, a messenger came to summon six men to active duty. It was Sabbath and the messenger stood outside the synagogue uncertain of the propriety of calling us to ride on Sabbath. We noticed him and asked what he wanted. Informed, our secretary told him he had wasted valuable time in not interrupting worship. In five minutes those six men had their gear and were en route to their units. It is allowed to ride or do anything else on the Sabbath to save life."

"Since you mentioned the Six Day War, do you think there can be peace?"

"No. The Arabs want all the land they had a thousand years ago. They hate us not so much as Jews but because we are a Jewish nation among them. We damage their dream of supremacy. I doubt that we'll see peace."

"Would a separate Palestinian state help?"

"They could try. It might so crystallize the present fluid state that some kind of quiet could result. But we teach our children not to expect peace in their lifetime. To hope for it, yes, but not to expect it."

"There seems to be an increase of hatred by Jews for Arabs. Do you find it here?"

"It exists. But it is not deep-seated. Jews do not hate Arabs. I, for example, hate a type of Christian Pole far more than the Arabs who are, after all, still a primitive people not yet of the Western world."

"And Germans?"

"Another thing, that. Germany is cultivated, educated, a Christian nation that produced Beethoven, Goethe, Heine, and the like. What we forgive in the exploited Arab is not to be forgiven Germans. We do not allow Volkswagens to appear at the kibbutz. I will not buy German goods. And yet I know that Israel needs friends, especially now. And I understand my government's wish to forget. But I cannot. The kibbutz cannot.

"Still, the past fades. Our children argue that we should accept German youth here for their summer vacation, to educate them in kibbutz, Jewish ways. But we cannot allow it out of respect for older members, damaged by Nazis.

"For example, my wife nearly died in Auschwitz—is still crippled. What if, in the community dining hall, two visiting, innocent German youths were to come to our table and ask in German if they might sit? What should I say to them, my wife and I sitting there...forbid them? Call them sons of murderers?

Tell them to get out? What? No! I will not be put in that position. . .I refuse to be forced to. . ."

Mordechai's voice was very low. His eyes held a deep sadness. In him justice and love had become two adversaries at war over Germans.

"About the six million Jews murdered in Europe in the thirties and forties—how do religious Jews feel about what was dealt them under God's discerning eyes?"

"If you believe," Mordechai murmured, "there is no questioning. If you do not believe, there is no need to answer."

Outside his office I photographed Mordechai's fine, strong, forged face. The simple tones of black and white that the developed print made of him portrayed just another mustached, aging Jew with a knitted yarmulka clinging to the back of his skull like a healing poultice.

Chapter *36*

Eliezer was a Jerusalem-based writer. He had invited me to his home to discuss the "Greater Israel" movement, of which he was a principal theoretician. His ideology held that lands won in the 1967 war must be kept, settled by Jews, added to as need arose until the biblical boundaries of King David were once again realized, according to God's promise to Abraham.

Now Eliezer was palsied and full of years, forty-nine of them spent in Israel. His old face, gently smoothed, shone like polished jade. His mind and speech were precise, positive, kindly.

"You have to understand," he said, "that there is a Jewish geography and a gentile geography. The Christian and Muslim geography has always sought to expand—the impulse waxing and waning—but always present, to take new lands, new people for converts. The Jewish geography has been otherwise, always seeking a return to the old boundaries in order to fulfill within its own small nation its commanded purpose."

"And what is that purpose?"

"To establish here a renaissance of Jewish civilization; to have our state driven by the perfect engine of Torah—the oral and the written law. We shall use the Bible and its language as partners of the people. The past married to the present will generate an exemplary future for all mankind. Just think how far along we are! If today Isaiah or Amos were to go into our newest supermarket, he could order a dozen eggs, bread, meat, milk, and get them. The language is the same. Cicero could not do that in Rome. Nor Socrates in Greece."

"Do you see Israel as a 'light unto the nations?' "

"No. We must discover and practice Judaism for ourselves. We are much too modest to suppose that our way is suitable for others."

"Israel has done much work in Africa. Have there been black converts to Judaism?"

Eliezer laughed. "Most of our 'missionaries' wouldn't know how to utter one traditional prayer, let alone tell people how to practice Judaism. We just try to help Africans live a fuller life. I suppose that is one reason why they like Israeli experts above all others...We have no ideology to force on them. Actually the Arab and the African ways are different from ours and they have much to teach us.

"You must understand that our outlook is not really Western, Aristotelian. It is not so pragmatic and achievement-oriented. To illustrate: the Americans are not quite sure who or what the Israeli is, or that here he creates a unique society, a unique people with a unique history.

"I saw with my own eyes how this idea gripped both observant, atheistic, and disinterested Jews when in 1967 we finally broke through to what used to be called the Wailing Wall. All were overcome. 'I have arrived. I have arrived. After two thousand years I have arrived,' they mumbled, cried, prayed. That wall is a symbol, such as your flag, the Liberty Bell, Valley Forge, or

Gettysburg. No American remains unmoved before these shrines. Just so was it with us in 1967. Most of us were unaware that we could be touched by what was in essence a religious symbol. The fact that it was a religious symbol seems to me to be enormously important, indicating our future."

"How will you reconcile Arab hopes and aspirations with yours?"

"The Arabs now have many sovereign states, stretching from Morocco to the Persian Gulf. Five million acres. Even when we had only ten thousand acres they denied our right to it. If their destiny cannot be realized within the land mass they now hold, the little we have could not help them much."

"But there are 1,300,000 Arabs within your present boundaries."

"It is a problem. But we like problems. And Zionism is inherently bound up with a large Arab minority."

"Then you do not favor a separate Palestinian state?"

"No. It would be merely a legalized collection of terrorists. Palestine was never a separate state. And when Islam ruled the area, Palestine was merely part of an empire that stretched from Arabia to Sicily and Spain. Jerusalem was never Islam's capital, even in their most halcyon days of power. Over the centuries, Palestine has changed ownership sixteen times! The Arabs never thought of this land as their nation until after World War I when Jews began aggressively to buy land, to settle here. We say our right here is grounded in history, sanctified by tradition and sacrifice, and finalized by the law of nations."

"But the granitic fact remains that now, *today*, Arabs want to create a Palestinian nation."

Eliezer looked softly at his inquisitor. Patiently, slowly, he drummed his fingers together and replied, "Please. Let us be realistic. Even if we were destroyed there would be no Palestinian state. It could not be economically, militarily, politically viable. The other Arabs states should soon overwhelm it."

"But Israel could protect a separate Palestinian state, make it work, help it as you help the African nations," I said.

Eliezer slowly shook his head. "Better we should help them where they are," he said. "On the West Bank of the Jordan and in Gaza. We must put Jews in those areas, settle the wasteland, educate the Arabs and teach them to farm, establish industry, to hate us less. If our Israeli Arabs can become citizens why can't those others? After all, we have thousands of Jews who live here but remain citizens of America, England. So let the Arabs choose to be Israeli citizens or to just live here as do many Jews.

"Or let them emigrate, as three hundred thousand did—leave Judea and Samaria while they were under Jordanian rule. They went to the oil-rich sheikdoms on the Persian Gulf and did very well. And they were welcome. If not Arab workers, the sheiks should have had to import African blacks, and they did not want the racial problem you Americans have. Anyway, let them stay with us or leave. The choice is theirs."

"So now you have the refugees. The world watches how you treat them."

"We have not done enough. But we've only had the problem since June of 1967. Give us time."

Eliezer paused to let his wife bring coffee and several kinds of cake. The interview was going well and this break could spoil the easy rapport and frankness between us. But there was no stopping Eliezer's wife. She edged on in, clung to her beachhead, breached our privacy like a misguided missile.

The interview was almost over. Eliezer stood with some difficulty and only then did I realize his weariness. His wife had known best! He took my arm as we walked to the door. His grip was that of an old man. "You know," he murmured, "some problems cannot be solved. Time erodes them, but humans can't hurry the process. American Jews do not realize that. They want everything settled at once. We know better. This patience of ours is perhaps the chief difference between American Jews and us. We wait, hold on, allow time to work its gentle solution. We have been at a kind of war with the Arabs for a hundred years, really, since first we emerged from the old, walled city of Jerusalem. What's another hundred? Or five hundred?"

"Eliezer!" his wife called sharply. We shook hands. Even his eyes now seemed old and tired, their blueness hazed over. An old man.

Chapter 37

I had at last been forced to abandon my wonderful cicerone, Yosi. He now had really abandoned himself to drink, had taken to carrying his brandy in a paper sack, in the American way. Some days he did not show up at all. Other days he would appear and then, unaccountably, disappear. And he grew steadily more irascible.

Ruth wanted to marry him but Yosi's wife refused him a divorce. And Yosi did not protest too much. He seemed rather to enjoy his half-free, half-slave state of affairs that allowed him the freedom to keep a lover but none of the responsibility of being a husband. At any rate, he had become an insupportable drag on my work.

I left Jerusalem for Haifa without Yosi. There I moved into another *pension,* high in a district quite elegant during Mandate times but now rather frowzy and inadequate to the bustling port city built on the slopes of the Carmel range.

Haifa was the most European of Israel's cities. In most any café one heard almost as much German, English, French as Hebrew. And yet the pace was not European, was oddly and inexplicably slower, more languid, somehow Levantine, as seemed appropriate.

Perhaps the servants working in Hadar lent it that Levantine ambience—people like Yaakov, waiter in the *pension.* He had come to Israel from Morocco in 1951. "After 1948 and the coming of the state, Jews are not feeling so good under the Arabs," he explained, making a significant, swooping gesture. "We fly away."

"Was it good there for you before the state was formed?"

"Jews and Arabs never be close. Arabs master. They walk on sidewalk, we move off before and walk in street. Arabs always the master. We under them."

"Will there be peace?"

He shrugged. "Maybe. In a hundred years. Is all right. We give back Gaza and the West Bank. We keep the Golan and Jerusalem. America needs peace here. American Jews need peace here. We don't need peace."

A bit later this little, dark, rather handsome man, quite Arabic in appearance, made a startling statement. "The Arab, if he have much money, he no give it to his people. He no care for them. His family? Sure. His clan? Sure. His people? He know only family, clan. Even if he rich, we give him a few pounds to tell on his people and he tell our security people about terrorists our police want. Even if he is friend he tell on him for a few pounds. He care only for himself. But the Jew he is one people. Everywhere is Jew in trouble, other Jew give. He give one million. He give two million. But the Arab he give his brother nothing."

"How do you account for this?"

Yaakov shrugged and said: "Is a thing of looking at life. Who can say? But is so."

Peter, a guest at the hotel, was a physician from New Zealand who had settled here. He had been an Israeli for ten years and was contented. He did private practice only. The socialized medicine practiced by the state was abhorrent to him: "It's impossible to make a decent living working that way. They take home about $325 a month."

"Can't they moonlight and do private practice as well?" I asked.

"Some try it. But they work incredibly hard for the state. After long hours, a six-day week, they have little energy to manage a second, private practice. And their pay is so low as to allow no surplus to buy proper equipment for a private office. They are excellent as socialized physicians but bad at private practice."

"How did you manage?"

"I had money when I arrived."

Peter remarked off-handedly that he worked only six hours a day, six days a week, netting about fifty dollars an hour. In less than a month he earned as much money in salary as state-employed physicians earned in a year.

Peter practiced medicine in Jerusalem, but was in Haifa for a short-term consultation with Technion University. He found himself with some free mornings and accompanied me about the town.

The bus to the port was always crowded. Once two young men in yarmulkas stood to give us their seats. I protested. Peter accepted, saying: "They are religious Jews. They have been brought up this way. I am fifty-two, soft, gray, and they defer to me. It is merely an application of the Fifth Commandment. To refuse them is to deny them the mitzvah, the blessing, of doing a God-praising act."

I asked Peter if he himself was a religious man.

"I'm a heathen! The religion we have here is a European atavism, bad as an infected vermiform appendix."

"Still, you did take their seat."

Peter only shrugged.

At broad, modern, crowded Independence Street we left the bus. "Watch the faces of the young," Peter said. "I am no chauvinist but Israeli youth are a sound bunch. Youth groups, hikes, sports, early army training make them sound. They don't abuse themselves. *'Briut,'* health, is an important word to them. There is little excess, debauch. Rahamin, the hero of that El Al plane attacked by Arabs at Zurich a few years ago, surprised his jailers by asking to bathe every day. Consider France, where many homes have no bath; then consider Israel where almost every home has one.

"Watch the young! They are very beautiful, a mixture of many races and cultures. True hybrids. You know how vigorous hybrid corn can be? Two inbred strains are crossed and their progeny is superior to either inbred parent. Nature compensates in the outcrossing for the outrage of inbreeding. In genetics this is known as heterosis. The young Israelis are a genetic jump. A heterotic leap."

"But were Jews so isolated as to be all that inbred?"

"More than almost any other people. Too, Jews never proselytized. It was death to try it in Moslem countries. Many European countries killed both Jewish converts and converters. Thus, isolated millets of Jews had to marry within the group. When they did marry outside it, they disappeared into Christian or Moslem society. Rapes? Sure. But few rapes were fertile unions and not every pogrom indulged in rape. So you can say that for thousands of years the Jews inbred. Then came Israel. Indian Jews, African Jews, European Jews, Levantine Jews; Jews from seventy nations came, intermarried, brought forth a new type of young, a superior type."

"That sounds racist."

"No, that's the sound of a geneticist."

Near the port, oddly belying the modern, broad street, the shops were small, independently owned, rather tacky looking.

We walked slowly, savoring the crowd. Peter needed a comb and we entered a tiny cosmetics shop no more than six feet deep and twelve feet long. An old man of distinguished if sagged features stood behind the wood counter. Beauty supplies were strung everywhere, even hanging from the ceiling. Peter talked to the proprietor, who had come from Turkey where his family had lived since 1492. Life had been bearable, he said, but, as always in Moslem countries, Jews "did not have it so easy." Still, the man did not complain. Peter drew from him that he had three children, one son a researcher in an area of physics so esoteric that the old man could only shake his head resignedly in trying to explain it. One daughter was married to a physician whom Peter knew, and a second son was an electrical engineer.

Outside the shop, Peter insisted that I should recognize the revelation just unfolded. "You saw a shopkeeper in his tiny place. He seemed listless, dull, didn't he? Just an old Jew selling 'buttons.' A shopkeeper! But his children? Ah-hah! *They* are engineers, physicists, a doctor's wife. In one generation."

But this was no hybrid, I replied. This shopkeeper married a Turkish Jewish woman who had also lived in Turkey since Isabella and Ferdinand expelled all Jews from Spain.

"It's not solely genetics," Peter said. "Here, sudden freedom and independence created an *environment* for Jews that allowed latent, suppressed talent to explode into enormously creative forms. As in America, only more so. Besides, there is something mystical about the geography here, the Jewish return, a certain political climate, a pride in humanism . . . I don't know, there are some influences that we cannot explain."

"I must repeat that such emotionalism seems terribly close to racism; not the kind the Nazis preached but not altogether unrelated, either."

"I ought to cut you cold," Peter said. "Still, it's a logical question. Our enemies ask it." He grinned wickedly at me. "But our kids never think in such terms. If anything they are apolitical. Some of the old ideologists think of conquest but you'll look hard and long to find any of that in the young.

"Two foremost Nazi ideas were the German master race and its destiny to rule the world. Our young don't think that way. They are proud, healthy, vigorous, talented, but they are not killer-rulers. I think they have demonstrated that. We could have taken Syria, Egypt, Jordan, Lebanon . . . almost any lands we wanted after our victory in 1967. But we didn't. We could have killed our own Arabs and quite simply have thus solved the problem of having so many of them among us, but such is unthinkable! And so the suggestion that my thinking parallels Nazi thinking is obscene and in error. But I forgive you." He smiled resignedly as does a man in love with an abstract notion which he does not expect anyone to agree with.

We walked silently down a side street and stopped before a half-finished building. An old Jew was unloading cement sacks from a truck. The driver, Nissim, stood indolently nearby. He was dark, short, thickset, with a laborer's swollen fingers. "Shouldn't you, a younger man, be doing this heavy work?" Peter rudely asked.

"He's strong as an ox," Nissim replied. "And it's all he knows. Should we hire Arabs and allow Jews to be idle?"

We watched the old man, a pad of burlap saddling his shoulders. His helper in the truck bed moved the cement sacks to the rear where the old man turned to receive them on his back from the hands of his helper. Ten paces forward he moved to where he could ease the load onto a neat, growing pile.

"Is he well paid?" Peter asked.

"Sure," Nissim replied. "He gets three dollars a truckload and in a good day he can manage three truckloads. He can live on that."

"And you?"

"I'm a driver. Something special. So I make much more. But I've been here since 1948 . . . from Tripoli. He just got here. And he's all alone, lost his family in Rumania during the war. Lived there since. I've got three kids. And I spend six weeks a year with the infantry. He's too old for it. Suppose I get killed? What about my wife and kids? This old man goes home with no dependents to worry about while 350,000 soldiers, like me, protect his easy sleep."

"Still," Peter said, "you protect your family, too. Such a pay scale for him seems awfully small."

Nissim shrugged. "I worked much harder for far less when I first got here. My family lived in a tent in a quagmire for three years. We burned in summer and froze in winter. I quit school at fourteen to help support them. After all these years I live in a two-and-a-half-room apartment, earn $350 a month before taxes that take forty percent of it, and I'm damned resentful of the easy time of it that newcomers from Russia, England, and America now have. And that includes this old Rumanian Jew here who can't speak Hebrew and won't learn. My taxes support him and I don't mind. But don't needle me about his low pay. It's damned good and if anyone's pay is low it's mine, and I'm not complaining."

"Do you still speak Arabic?" Peter asked.

"Of course. My kids are bilingual."

"How do you feel about the new lands?" I asked.

"Keep them. Take more if we need to. What kind of a war did we fight in 1967? Was it a child's game that we should stare at annihilation, turn it around and go on to win? Then give back our winnings? Hah! And to those bastardly Arabs who kicked me out of Tripoli and would kill every Jew here if they could? I know the Arab very well. You have to break his arm, better two arms, then he respects you. Appreciate us he never can. Respect us he can and must. I hate them. Didn't I know them in Tripoli? Here? Three times I fought them. I—"

"Wait a minute," Peter broke in. "You'll burst something. On your pay I can't afford to treat you. So take it easy. Besides, maybe God is listening."

Nissim drew a deep breath, wriggled his mustache, nodded. "God can't hear. He's deaf. Where was He when buddies on either side of me were killed in the Golan Heights? Or when my family mourned at being kicked out of Tripoli after living there five hundred years? Or when children were gassed and burned by Germans? God is there, but old, very hard-of-hearing."

Peter grinned and clapped Nissim on the shoulder. The old man slowly unloaded the truck. He was a big man, thick-hipped, bald, covered with gray dust, moving like an automaton, effortlessly except that the sweat dripped off his nose and chin.

Peter asked him in Yiddish what he had done for a living in Rumania. The old man muttered something and Peter threw back his head and laughed.

"What did he say?" Nissim asked.

Peter looked at Nissim and said quite solemnly, "He said that it was nobody's business. What was his business, he said, was that a stupid truckdriver stands by and lets him work his heart out and doesn't lift a finger. All Oriental Jews, he said, should just go fuck themselves."

Nissim leaned against the truck and hooted with laughter. Then he went to the old man, said "Fuck you, too," and began to help him unload cement sacks.

In the center of the business district a brass sign on a building announced the Chamber of Commerce. "What did you expect," Peter said, noticing my surprise, "some kind of Levantine business arrangement with men seated on carpets, sucking on water pipes, drinking scented teas? Our modern commerce must have its representatives, just as labor has the Histradrut."

"Still," I suggested, "this capitalist American conservative organization . . . here, in this socialist Jewish progressive state . . . it seems unfitting. . . ."

"We have damned efficient private industry. You should talk to these people, find out what kind of human beings they are, how they think. Meet some of our entrepreneurs. Let's go in, I'll act as your assistant."

The Chamber's director was a tall, tweedy, quite British-looking Israeli who hadn't much enthusiasm for sending me to his clients, the manufacturers. But Peter charmed him with insouciance, his New Zealand background, and got him to make an appointment with a machine-tool manufacturer. We left the director with an invitation to come back and attend the next Rotary Club meeting.

In a rented car we started north to Nahariya. Just outside Haifa we picked up two soldiers whose transportation had stalled. One, an inordinately handsome, tall air force officer, was pleased to discuss his part in the Six Day War of June 1967. "We daily flew six, seven, eight sorties, where three would have been extraordinary," he told us. "Without sleep, no time for repairs, little time for briefings. Fly in, load up, take off, bomb, strafe, home and repeat. . . ." He shrugged. "But we are here," he said. "And if we hadn't fought so hard we would all be dead."

"Are you long in this country?" Peter asked.

"Twenty generations. We came here in 1492 from Spain."

"And is your family still religious?"

"Only my grandmother. Orthodoxy is of no use here. We no longer need circumcision, *kashrut*, to protect health. We now have antibiotics and refrigeration. We don't need religion or God or anything else except this land and the Israelis in it."

Peter suggested that the Arabs had their loyalties, their Moslem faith, peoplehood, and that Israelis could, like them, become just another Levantine grouping if without the cement of religious practice and activism inherent in a religious mission.

"Disagree!" shot back the officer. "There is a Jewish head, heart, history, and it is different from any other and will keep us apart, above Arab ways. We gave the world the kibbutz, and a truly humane state. Here we have to set an example for all small nations. Isn't that enough? Must we pray, too? And did it do Jews good to pray in the past? Where was God when the six million died?" The officer was belligerent, positive, and he was disgusted with our questions. He turned away and became silent.

"And you?" Peter asked the thickset, red-haired, Slavic-featured corporal, who up to then had said nothing. "What do you plan to do after your three years in the air force?"

"I don't think about it," the corporal said; "I just want to live, that's all. I just want to live."

We dropped the soldiers at an army camp where they could find a telephone to call for transportation.

We drove north through sooty, ugly industrial parks and towns. Peter murmured that we were in the Valley of Zebulon, and that a polluted stream we crossed was the River Kishon near where, more easterly, Deborah defeated the Canaanites. It was hard to sense the march of history through the smog, smears, and defilements put up by an industry come helter-skelter to Israel, where, as everywhere, the drive for productivity overrode the fragile regard for esthetics and environment.

Except for Jerusalem, Acco was Peter's favorite town, one of the world's oldest. He liked to wander through it and to let its millennial history nudge him out of considerations of bellies, livers, hearts, lungs, fevers, passions, despondencies, impotencies. "Pagans, Jews, Greeks, Romans, Arabs, Christians, Turks, British —they all were here," Peter said. "And now we are back. Fantastic fact. I still get a floating feeling when I wander this old city. It acts like a poultice drawing out stability and certainty. Day before yesterday we were here. Yesterday we were gone. Today we are back. Tomorrow. . .?"

"Do you often think such foreboding thoughts?"

"It's that corporal and his mother-wit; the solid sense of his Slavic parents. 'I just want to live,' he said. Remember that? Well, it's that way with me, too. That kid's is the ultimate wisdom."

Abruptly Peter turned off the road and into an agricultural settlement founded by German Jews who had all come from the same town. He wanted to show me their synagogue, an exact replica of one the Nazis burned. Peter saw in this act of replication an analogy to burnt-over forests in whose ashes are new seeds for regeneration, and viable roots.

I was suddenly unable to talk, speechless with the endurance of such a people, their recurrent death at the hands of men and their dogged resurrection. Christ came from them. And they still suffered as did that famous rabbi of two thousand years ago. And that rabbi had lived and died and his people had lived and died and there seemed no end to it.

"You know," Peter said, "there is a variety of conifer in New Zealand that cannot sprout until its tough waxy coating is melted by forest fire. Only then can the seed begin new life, renascence. I shudder to think that we Jews are like that but, in Israel, we do seem to offer a human parallel."

I did not comment. Peter could say that; I could not. For Peter there were still banked fires all around his state and they periodically flared to a fire fight, always controlled . . . so far. There had been parallels enough, in other lands. No more fires needed to prove his point.

The factory north of Nahariya manufactured hard-edged cutting tools for the metals industries. There was about the place a neat, uncluttered, coordinated feel that fitted well with the symmetrical, shapely sea just a few feet beyond its western wall. The owner, Stefan, a German Jew in Israel since 1937, was expecting us. He was tall, dark, lean, handsome as a satyr, but humorless. His four children were symmetrically spaced with the same Teutonic planning he gave his factory operation. With only eight years of schooling, he had learned his trade by doing it, first in optics, then as an instrument repairman with the R.A.F. in Bahrein in World War II. In Bahrein, he had seen bloody pogroms committed by Arabs against Jews and he had not forgotten.

After the war, he had surreptitiously trained as a pilot for the early Jewish forces, the Hagannah, but the British discovered the kibbutz where the school was hidden, captured him and put him in Rafiah prison. There he studied English and physics—"Best time I ever had in all my life," he recalled. "In prison I grew certain that the Jews were capable of the physical and mental skills needed to run a modern state."

Stefan described his early days easily, talking as if it were all quite normal for people to escape Hitler, learn to use and then to employ explosives, become a pilot, then an ordnance expert, then move up to establish their own machine-tool business.

Stefan apprenticed as a government defense worker. "The pace was too slow. All our best people went into agriculture or the army. Third-raters went into industry and we are only now, in the seventies, recovering from that error. I started my own business with a shop in the kitchen, gradually expanding it until I outgrew the house. Then I bought a small plant, then another and another. But the great brake on growth was a lack of trained machinists. So I started my own school."

"Did the government help you?"

"No. I knew that anything they could do, or anybody could do, I could do better."

He said with quiet pride that the annual tool production per man was about $7000–$10,000, but his plans looked to quadruple that by 1976.

"How can you figure that way when your existence is constantly threatened by hostile neighbors?"

"Peace will come. In my lifetime. I have shown how Arabs and Jews can work together. I have an Arab foreman and the Jews work well under him. I believe Arabs look for peace just as we do. When it comes I'll build a factory in an Arab village. They can work there or here. They must first learn management, skills, production techniques. That lack is why a separate Palestinian state won't work; they haven't the training for it."

"Do you think education will change the outlook of the Arabs?"

"Certainly. If every Arab were educated, owned a Volkswagen, he would stop hating us."

"Then you trust the Arabs?"

Stefan drew a deep breath, shrugged, said, "We are here.

They are here. We have to work together and we will. Yes. I trust them."

As we talked, workers with problems flowed steadily in and out of Stefan's office, a tiny cubicle that seemed more like a military command post. Stefan gave decisive replies to their questions. His manner was kind, paternal, superior. He seemed to know exactly what to do and say behind that rude, unpainted desk, himself dressed in an open-collared shirt with no jacket. But he rarely smiled. Only when an Arab foreman, a Christian, entered did he seem to grow expansive, almost jovial. His manner changed in some marvelously adaptive fashion from that shown his Jewish workers. He had curiously become like a salesman: bland, courteous, and just short of obsequious. "Ah, the German Jews," Peter whispered to me, "they have such respect for strong enemies."

Stefan left and we chatted with his sales manager, Raphael, a big, hearty, outgoing man who laughed easily, showing broad, widely spaced teeth. He was a character straight out of Brueghel. There was no falseness about him. He told of his early life, the wise move by his father of his immediate family to Israel. All the others had remained in western Russia and perished under the Nazi occupation.

"Tonight I fly to Germany to a trade fair. This will be the first time in many business trips there that I have allowed myself to stay overnight in that country. I force myself because I do not any longer wish to think of the atrocities of an older generation. Nor do I wish my children to dwell on them. We need sympathy, even from our former enemies. Germany is prepared to give this to us. They want us to think of the past as unalterably past. I am prepared to do that. I cannot live with the memory of a hundred and twenty members of my family destroyed by Germans and Russians. I cannot . . . I cannot . . . I . . ."

Raphael could not go on. Peter changed the subject and brought Raphael around to discussing himself. He was born in Haifa forty years ago. He came with the army to Hanita, a kibbutz on the Lebanese border, in 1948. He lost most of his friends in that War of Independence. Depressed and lonely, he accepted the kibbutz offer to join. "I would be there yet," Raphael said, "except that my wife did not like to have her life determined by committee. It is lonely away from the kibbutz. At Pesach we sit at home over the seder and say how lonely we are. How pleasant it would be to celebrate the Passover with kibbutz members. Still, I have my work. I like it."

"Is private enterprise generally successful in Israel?"

"Considering how new we are at it, I think so. One big hurdle for us is 'vitamin P,' *proteksia,* protection for our infant industries which then perpetuate their inefficiencies behind high tariffs and other government subsidies. Yet we grow stronger. And there are other problems. Even though our quality is better than the European, buyers don't think of Jews as workers, machinists. A Bible they think of . . . oranges . . . maybe diamond-cutters, but not heavy industry. So we must prove ourselves to be steel just to pass for brass.

"Another problem. The old-timers believe in socialism, to each according to his need, mutual help. But as industrialists, we must adopt and adapt what seems sometimes a heartless technology, a capitalism that produces a better product, cheaper, thus benefiting humanity. We *do* what socialists only *preach.* We must become a capitalist state. I believe we are becoming one."

"You mentioned Pesach. Are you religious?"

"No! My grandparents were. I use the kibbutz haggada, one they wrote. No prayers, just the Passover story, without God."

Peter mentioned Stefan's belief that peace would come in his lifetime.

Raphael shrugged. "He believes Arabs trustworthy. He cares about them. A good man. He tries hard to recruit them. And yet you know how many we have? Ten out of more than two hundred workers."

"Why so few?"

Raphael shrugged. "They don't trust us any more than we trust them. Suppose the terrorists attack near here. Would our

Jewish workers in a rage turn on their Arab fellow workers? Probably not, but the Arabs don't know that."

"Do you trust them?"

"I can't forget that while I was a soldier in 1956 the Arabs ambushed my buddies. I was called to identify the mutilated bodies. Penises cut off and shoved in mouths. Fingers cut off and forced up asses. Testicles draped obscenely over ears. . ." He could not go on.

Finally, self-composed, he said softly, "No one wants to discuss why Arab hate for us is so deep. I can think of no other reason—except that we are Jews . . . they are Arab Moslems . . . with them it is a holy war and all is permitted. Few will say it but I must. The root of their hatred is religious."

Raphael left us for Tel Aviv and his flight. He would travel in Germany, selling there and in Poland. Peter wondered how Raphael might feel, sleeping near Auschwitz, Bergen-Belsen, Theresienstadt, among the people who zapped 150 of his relatives by merely scribbling a penciled directive to destroy them. Peter wondered about this affable, intelligent man who wanted neither himself nor his children to recall the searing atrocities of the German people but who remembered and recounted unforgettably the awful experience of a single Arab atrocity.

"Perhaps," Peter said, "it is because the Nazi thing, though worse, is ended. The Arab thing . . . continues."

Chapter *38*

In Haifa that night Peter took me to visit a Polish-German Jewish woman who he thought might interest me. She was very old, very beautiful, very calm as she told us that in 1935 her husband had been taken by storm troopers and killed. She had managed to get a forged Aryan passport for herself for $5,000 and then had further bribed German guards into letting her and her two children escape to Czechoslovakia. She must have had premonitions of Munich and the casual sell-out of Europe's Jews for a "peace in our time," for she took work as a cook in a Christian household and posed as a life-long Catholic.

Her children were educated in Catholic boarding schools. She herself regularly observed mass, at first as a disguise but, slowly she came to realize the beauty of the Church, its purpose, ritual, and strength, and she then truly became a believer. Thus was she saved.

"Did you tell your children of their Jewish background?" Peter asked her.

"When my Peter was thirteen I told him. Much later I told his sister. But we rarely spoke of it. Why expose ourselves to the anguish? The evil? Death? Better to be finished with suffering," the beautiful old lady said. "My son is now a physician in Germany, married to a wonderful German girl of a fine old Catholic family. I go often to visit them. I am always welcome."

"And your daughter?"

The beautiful old lady smiled warmly. "A nun. In Germany. At first I did not like the idea of the world losing her . . . she is so beautiful and kind. Then I came to realize that the world gained so much more from her as a nun than it could possibly gain any other way. I see her often. All of us love Germany, now that it has quit all that foolish business."

"But you live in Israel. Why?"

"I came here after the war. I feel safe here. My friends are all here."

"Are there so many Catholics in Haifa?"

"But my friends are all Jews," she said smiling. "As I am a Jew. I go to Catholic church, love my faith, but I am a Jew. I understand Jews. I will be buried in Eretz Israel. As a Catholic. You understand?"

That evening Peter became quite drunk but remained lucid. I had not previously seen him drink.

I asked if the beautiful German woman had been too t/ a confrontation.

"German? Jew? What is she, really?" Peter asked, then saiu, "It is a strange thing that I who hate everything German cannot blame this woman or her children who have embraced the nation that actively, the church that passively murdered her people.

"She was clever, farsighted, and so she made it. Six million did not make it. *L'chaim*, 'To life,' the Hebrew toast has it." He drank half a glass of Scotch. "Well, she lives. Her children live. Better a live Christian than a dead Jew? Right? What? The heat from Hitler's furnaces killed a third of us and then reached out and caused distortion in the souls of the rest. Like those snakes you light on Fourth of July. It requires a Sigmund Freud to understand the paradox of that adaptable-and-so-alive apostate of a German-Czechoslovakian-Jewish woman."

Peter tried to stand but could not. He fumbled inside his coat and took out a pen. Then he acted as if he were writing a letter, speaking the words. "Dear Doctor Freud: I wish to confer with you about this fellow Jew, a woman whose millions of relatives—yours too, if you remember—were lost when touched by those who ate of poisoned, forbidden fruit. The others ate it but this woman I speak of was entirely covered by their excreta, absorbing as in osmosis the lethal toxin within that forbidden fruit. Thus she became part of the Second Fall of Man, accomplice to it, a card-carrying member. And her children settled in that Garden where the Fall took place. And they flew to the tree of that fruit. And on the bough of that very tree they built nests, one of them mated and hatched young, and all continued life as if the tree were not and never had produced forbidden fruit in a forbidden garden.

"And so, Doctor Sigmund Freud, my learned colleague, now comes the question: why did she do it? Why did her son? Her daughter? Why? Send me your answer and I'll pay you your fee when next I see you in Jerusalem. Better yet, I'll mail you a check!"

Peter put the pen to his paper napkin and wrote: "Y'r Ob't

serv't. Peter." Then he managed swayingly to stand, seeking equilibrium, somehow finding enough of it to walk crabwise but determinedly toward the door.

Chapter 39

The coastal road led north from Haifa through dismayingly polluted, industrial wasteland. The bus made a routine stop for passengers at the kibbutz of the Warsaw Ghetto Fighters. Several buses and trucks with seats lining the beds—the standard way of moving kids around the country—were parked in a small lot outside a huge, yellow, ugly building. My seat mate explained that it was a museum dedicated to the memory of those who died at Nazi hands in that rat's trap, the Warsaw ghetto. On impulse I got off the bus and joined a group of school children making their way toward the museum. An old man sold tickets near the entrance. His underarm held the blue-black numbers of some Nazi camp. He had survived, and that lifted my soul. I asked if I might later visit his kibbutz, and the old man said that visitors were not allowed but that farther north was a kibbutz that took guests. He gave me its name.

The kids did not seem constrained at all, chatted and laughed happily as they passed into the museum. But I hesitated, filled with dread at what I was certain to see inside. I stopped for one last look through windows, at fields, the road, greenery, springtime . . . life. Natural things without aberration. Then I joined the kids for their tour.

We were halted at a large-scale model of the Warsaw ghetto. Yet another ghetto survivor, a dour kibbutznik, related the history of the place. Tiny lights came on to reveal houses, blocks, streets, as he talked, describing this action and that one. He was articulate, spoke directly, unemotionally, quietly, and so lent his talk the dramatic quality of understatement.

And yet the kids seemed only vaguely attentive. What did they have to do with such old stories?—these kids who could not understand Nazi deceit played against traditional Jewish trust and optimism.

We moved past other exhibits and the faces of the kids reflected no horror, despair, anger, anguish. It was all just part of an old museum in an Israel filled with such museums, itself a banal if vast museum to these kids who lived for the future and to hell with a past their parents had been foolish enough to endure . . . meekly.

But the adult visitors looked at all the exhibits, their faces blank, their eyes somehow haunted by their personal near-miss.

There was a photograph of an old Jew on his knees, his ritual beard sawed at with a knife wielded by laughing S.S. troopers who were as young, happy, innocent as boys who tie tin cans to puppy dogs' tails and delight in the animals' terror.

A display case held original orders, in precise German, ordering the liquidation, on a certain day, at a certain time and place, of 132 Jews.

Nearby was a banjo made from the parchment of Holy Writ, Torah, the holy Hebrew words faded but still evident. Then there were displays of armbands worn by Jews not otherwise distinguishable from their Dutch, French, or Belgium countrymen; *"Jude," "Jood," "Juif,"* and so on. Striped concentration-camp clothing hung limply from nails.

All of it seemed unreal, as if the artifacts were props for a bad play that had folded after an unbelievably long run, that had been sustained only by the wealth and audacity of its backers; and uncritical, supine audiences.

Photograph: a well-knit soldier with the broken face of a Roman gladiator herding a flock of Jews down some street, using his automatic rifle like a baton to direct them on. In front is a small boy, perhaps six years old, in knee britches, Eton cap, and matching coat, stylishly dressed by a mother certain that such a dear, cute child could bring only pleasure or softness, at least pity (therefore redemption) to any human heart. But the gesturing Nazi does not see the small boy as piteous, confused, plaintive, silently pleading his right to live. The uniformed animal sees only incurably diseased meat, infectious, therefore by order of headquarters to be destroyed. Like cattle. A pagan sacrifice. The little boy seems so hopeful, as if the bad silly moment must pass and his mama and his papa must surely take him home to a good supper, a bedtime story, the comforting bed . . . a sweet dream. . . .

There is the impulse to scream at them. Wake up! Jump that goddam Nazi! Die fighting. Fight. Do anything but continue that placid, sheeplike march to eternity.

But no. They march on. Such a hopeful people. So trusting. So sure that all must turn out right. All doomed. Even the little child who leads them.

Photograph: a young man, a Jew, kneeling at the edge of a pit where his Nazi destroyer holds a pistol to the back of his head. Fascinated, a large group of boyish Nazis, neophytes engaged in steely on-the-job training, watch. The pit below the martyr-to-be is filled with bodies. The kneeling man looks outward in absolute astonishment, disbelief, even with a kind of curious interest. *Can this be me?* he seems to be thinking. *Is it really happening? Where is God? He'll surely come. He'll surely be with me.* . . .

The Israelis wandered here and there with faces masked, concealing care. They had all been there . . . been there. But the spirit has its defenses, callouses, its point beyond which it may not go and remain part of a sound mind in a sound body.

I watched those human souls look at the most formidable aspect of their quite personal and millennial history. They were witnessing the Fall of Man and, as always, they themselves were the victims whose numbers marked in this particular museum, part of the scoreboard, duration and depth of the Fall.

Chapter 40

Facing the Sea, its rump toward Galilee, within sight of Lebanon, sat the kibbutz to which I had been directed by the old ticket-seller at the museum.

There, walking toward my tiny cabin, I passed an ancient olive tree, its main trunk cut off at the base which was two feet in diameter. An old tree, perhaps a thousand years old, it was not yet dead. Its base shot forth new growth that held pale young leaves luxuriantly silvered by sunlight.

I stopped to marvel at its failure to die, its will to live, the new shoots issuing from old. Obviously, the kibbutz had consciously left it as a kind of symbol.

It was a quiet afternoon and the sun was low. Children laughed in the distance and some screamed and cried. Two old men oddly dressed in suits, with shirts and ties, raked at a flower garden, desultorily smoothing things. Kibbutzniks in blue and khaki moved purposefully about the place and the distant surf sounded like a whisper.

The preserved tree-with-shoots came to seem too obvious a symbolism, pathetic and rather sentimentally mawkish, as I stood there, listening, watching. Because the hard-core truth was that the redeemed olive tree was less a symbol for valor than were these Jews, here, living examples of mankind's heroic urge to survive.

I wished for Peter. All this would somehow have reassured him that life as lived by that so-beautiful old lady in Haifa was a circumscribed affair and that the heart, target and center of things, was here, where Jews said to hell with it. We'll live.

Later, seated at the bar in the dining room, chatting with the Polish bartender, Micah, and an English kibbutznik, Tommy, a visitor from another kibbutz, the subject turned to Americans.

"I do not like the American Jews," Tommy said. "They give and then make a big hoo-hah about it. Let them be more modest and quiet. Their gifts are a kind of desecration of charity."

"And how would we manage without them?" asked Micah. "Without such 'generous desecrations'? Tommy, you are too self-righteous. And so are your comrades. You should expose people to our kibbutz way of life and yet you will not establish a guest house."

"I should hope not," said Tommy. "When we have to build a guest house, I'm heading for a cave in the Judean desert."

"Tommy, you must realize," Micah said heatedly, "that the coarseness of some American Jews is a condition forced upon them by the environment they have had to claw their way through, not only as Americans who must all do it, but as Jews, who bear the heavy pack of Jewishness. Nobody taught them manners. British Jews may be more mannerly, French Jews more decorous; but who is the more generous? The American Jew gives of himself, his money, his skills. And the young Americans? What do you think of them?"

"Their young are different. I like them very much."

"And are they generous? Do great numbers of them visit here? Are not many of them members of the New Left that sees justice only with the Arabs?"

"No and no and yes, unfortunately."

Micah said nothing further, but turned to polish the rows of glasses lining the shelves behind the bar.

Slowly the bar filled with kibbutz personnel getting ready for two busloads of tourists expected for a toilet stop and refreshments. At about four o'clock the buses arrived and discharged their elderly passengers. All wore huge buttons describing them as members of a German nature league. They ordered orange juice or beer.

We watched their old faces, paunchy bodies, dowdy women. Tommy murmured that they seemed incredibly innocent, even *gemütlich*. One elderly man came up to us and told us in difficult English that they were all nature lovers, interested in the flora and fauna of Israel, only that. He was quite insistent, seemed to want to reassure us. Or himself.

The dining hall was phlegmy with the language of Hitler, and of Heinrich Heine, himself a kind of Jew.

The Jews behind the bar served the tourists quickly, efficiently, never saying, thank you or looking at their guests. The Germans did not look at them. The Germans always said thank you. The atmosphere seemed suddenly oppressive, unreal, strained. Micah dropped a glass and it shattered. A helper too quickly swept up the pieces, cutting her hand. Glasses were regularly overfilled, overflowing onto the hands of both bartenders and Germans—a kind of shared, symbiotic baptism. The beginning of penitence and forgiveness?

The well-fed, aging Germans asked no questions, stayed in isolated clusters, seemed indefinably uneasy. Outside, plainly visible through the wide windows, a lovely swale fell west to orange groves and wheat fields and, finally, the sea. But the German nature lovers did not even glance at it.

It was strange to feel the withdrawn, self-protectiveness of the Germans and the silent, wondering, lets-get-it-over attitude of the Jews of the kibbutz. High drama by lowly people. "I wouldn't submit to this indignity for all the money in Germany," Tommy murmured in disgust.

One burly German sat by himself and Tommy wondered whether he excluded himself or was ostracized. The man seemed uncomfortably hot and sweaty. His red, meaty face was not evil but reflected only coarse old age and fatigue. And yet there was something threatening, real or impugned, about that face. It recalled the photograph seen in the museum of that Warsaw Ghetto Fighters' kibbutz, the one of the barbaric Nazi herding a column of doomed Jews. The broken Nazi face in the photo was blurred, not sharp, as too were faces, figures of Jews, all but that first one, the little boy in very clear focus: the tiny, threatened, frightened and hopeful face of the child. It came back to me clearly etched in all its fright, like a baby rabbit lost from the nest. The tricky mind's-eye easily turned that brutish old German tourist's face, so tired and sagged now, into that pictured, battered Nazi's. Could it be?

Then they filed out, quite orderly, serviceable boots tramping the floor, alpine hats rakishly set, some even in *Lederhosen*. The familiar clothing must have been for them a kind of reassurance that there *was* a Germany, that they *were* a good nation, that they *had* a solid reality beyond this ephemeral Middle East that held a remnant of Jews washed backward into it after two thousand years of living among Moslems and Christians. And lately, Nazis.

"Those *shtunks* knew nothing," Tommy declared, "absolutely nothing. Why else would they have come to this land of ours where everywhere are souls branded by their own hot iron?"

Micah shrugged, continued to wash and dry their glasses.

We walked outside. "Isn't it odd," Tommy said, "that these sons of the murdered accept money from the murderers?"

"But you yourself just said these nature lovers knew nothing . . ."

"I said it. But I have to be wrong. They must have known. How could they not know? Now their hearts are open, penitent. They mean the apology implicit in their presence here. Don't hearts always open after the evil is defeated? Micah takes their forty pieces of silver but it's dirty business."

"But you have taken hundreds of millions in war reparations. You cannot avoid their silver. Not even you. You fight with it, eat with it, dress with it, build, plow, irrigate with it."

Tommy stopped dead in his tracks. "That was Jewish money. It is not evil to take the money returned to us, from thieves who stole it. We got only a fraction of what Nazis took from Jews. But this tourist business, playing servant to them . . . I want to puke it all up! Thank God my kibbutz forbids us the choice."

A terrible choice! Mordechai of the religious kibbutz had hinted at it. "What if," he had said, "two pleasant German youths come to our table and ask to sit beside us? What shall I say to them? Forbid them? Tell them they are sons of murderers? Tell them to get out? What? What? I will not be put in that position . . ."

That evening Amnon, one of several from America in the kibbutz, invited me for coffee—the kibbutz equivalent of brandy-and-cigars. Certain people had been invited, others pointedly rejected. Clearly, among the 250 members, cliques existed. Amnon explained that there were members who shirked work, who were unpleasant, and some who did not truly like the life but were too old, or damaged to leave it. Such formed a pariah group and were excluded from social groups, such as Amnon's.

"We are really a religious communion," Amnon declared in his bachelor's quarters, he having been recently divorced. "Only we will not admit it. We share a communal meal, the family is protected by the group and is fully sacrosanct. Adultery is unthinkable. So as not to handle cash, we use bookkeepers to debit and credit our members. Each here gets what he needs and no more. Nowhere in the world does any group come as close to approaching the Mosaic code, the Ten Commandments, as does the successful kibbutz."

His friends with their wives began to gather. They were quiet, thoughtful people about whom hung a sense of controlled sadness. Ephraim, an older man, much experienced in the world, explained that one of their members, a soldier, had been killed while on border patrol that afternoon. "He was like my own son," Ephraim said. "They are all of them our sons," said David, another of Amnon's guests.

"And yet," Amnon remarked, hustling about his tiny kitchen, making coffee, readying cookies, "and yet we have many Israelis who are uncaring, do not know a war is on."

"Not so many," said the scholarly David, a tall man with tiny mustache. He seemed frail, and yet Amnon had described him as one of the strong fighters in Israel's early War of Independence. "It is just that some of us have not become accustomed to constant war," David went on, "to hold onto sanity, such people have to build Maginot Lines of the soul, then retreat behind them. Never mind it's not safe in such static fortresses. Never mind that our tensions penetrate to them. Still, the act of withdrawal is necessary for them—a kind of psychic survival-move. There is," David said, "an eleventh commandment, unwritten but binding: Thou shalt survive."

"Kibbutz people," someone added, "have a more direct view of things, maybe because they work with nature, see death and birth every day, see both as part of life. Maybe we fear the terror in life less because it is so much a part of us."

I asked David if he saw any possibility for peace.

"The Arabs must first be free of their verbal prisons," he said, "walls of words. But words are so intimately a part of their lives, they speak them so beautifully—are so overcome by them as westerners rarely are, that the words become finished art itself while with us words are merely the tools to direct, to *make* the product, the art. I doubt that they can change this ingrained, cultural quality very soon. But peace can't come until they do."

"We don't need peace," Ephraim's wife said. "It is terrible to lose sons but I must say it, the war knits us together, both Oriental and European Jews. The agony of war is not wasted. And war brings us ever closer to our true boundaries."

"True boundaries?" I asked.

"She is right," Ephraim went on. "Either we are here because this land is ours, promised and contracted for, paid for with millions of lives, over many years—or we are imperialists. Inevitably we must stand at the Euphrates and the Nile."

"Ah, Ephraim, too strong, too strong," David murmured. "Just let us live, that's all."

"God-given boundaries?" Amnon needled Ephraim, wanting me to thoroughly understand this point of view.

"No!" Ephraim said. "God has nothing to do with it. It is simply that Jewish history and the Jewish people have a mission for this area."

"Mission?" Amnon continued, gently urging him on.

"To be a light to small nations everywhere. To show them how to exist in a voracious world of huge imperialist power. They can learn from the way we have done it."

David smiled. It was a tiny smile but absolutely tender. "I'm glad you said that," he said. "I thought you'd gone crazy at first with that foolish imperialist talk. Now I understand. Do your children agree with you about a special mission for Israel?"

Ephraim's wife said they did not. "And it's our fault. We were brought up on socialism, Russian socialism at that! We passed on the hope in the Russian messiah to our kids and they discovered the Russians have water for feet! And now that they have shown their intense anti-Semitism our kids are shocked, disillusioned, finally and forever, in their hopes—our hopes, too, for a rebirth for mankind through Russia. The question now is, can Israel be the idol to substitute for the fallen Russian idol? I doubt it. We are too young, have too little tradition, and so our young are without foundations."

"Thank God I was trained as a boy in Holland to be an informed traditional Jew," Ephraim said. "Nothing can substitute for our history, ethics, prophets. But we have not taught our young, as my wife says. We have not given them a tradition to cling to."

"Are your young people aware of the lack?" I asked.

"They reach out," Amnon offered. "I teach high school, hear my kids talk. They ask something, identification with the Jewish people, something outside these tiny borders. They want more than to be simply Israelis."

"Identification with a divine being?"

"We don't need God," David said. "To identify with the Jewish people is enough. That identification exists in some mysterious way and always has."

"But the Nazis talked of a *Herrenvolk*, don't forget that," Amnon protested. "Must we fall into the same stupid trap?"

"An obscene comparison," David said mildly, nodding like a philosopher to an erring disciple. "We are no master race with notions of inferior and superior peoples. We wish only to be a separate people so useful to the world, so exemplary that others will emulate us. We are only three million, Amnon."

"Don't be angry, David," Amnon mollified him. "But we are not altogether immune to vicious racism. We have our exponents of racial superiority, chosenness, genetic superiority."

"During World War II," Ephraim abruptly changed the subject, "I was a British Intelligence officer assigned to the French to work with Jews in Algeria, to urge them to be allies. Besides that, and unknown to the British and French, I had instructions from Ben-Gurion to bring Jews to Israel. 'Any kind of Jews,' he told me, 'white Jews, black ones, purple ones, yellow ones but bring Jews to Israel.'

"I found that these Jews, separated from their people for five hundred years, still had a sense of kinship with all Jews. I found Jews so naïve they believed that there existed a secret grotto whose outlet was in Israel and they had only to find the Algerian entrance. They thought that I knew its whereabouts! The point is that the ancient wish, the dream to return to the land and its people, was strong, even in fantasy."

"It's not strong in the United States," Amnon said. "As you know, I once proselytized there for our kibbutz movement. I can tell you, Ephraim, that American Jews will never come here in large numbers. They support us, most of them, but America is their homeland, not Israel."

"Amnon is correct," David said. "I have talked to hundreds. They do not want to stay here. The urge to Zion is softened in the stew of their melting pot."

"For them it is another thing," Ephraim said, his soft brown eyes suddenly hard, his speech authoritative, commanding, official, as it must have been when he served three masters in World War II. "They will come because they will have to. No choice. They cannot relate to themselves that which happened to Jews in Hitler's Europe; and that which is now happening to Jews in Russia and the Moslem lands. Even in the United States, black and white Christian Americans, nominal or not, are rejecting them. It is almost a categorical, historical imperative. And so if it is there, as some say, that anti-Semitism is the glue that holds American Jews together, then why not come here, to Israel, where anti-Semitism really means something?"

David laughed, then became serious. "Wishful thinking, Ephraim. Jean-Paul Sartre once told me that the world's intellectuals would not permit Israel to live. Certainly the Western power structure abandoned us in 1967. Maybe it is good that all Jews do not come here—if we should go under . . . some would be left . . . alive . . . somewhere. . . . It is a bad, hard thing to say, yet. . .?"

Ephraim stood. He drained his cup, then moved with his wife to the door. "That is unthinkable" he said. "After two thousand years you are not allowed to think such things nor say them."

David sighed.

Amnon accompanied me to my cabin. "Do you remember," he asked, "what I said about the kibbutz being a religious community but that its members do not admit it? Well, you have seen two Jews, modern prophets, and their way of thinking can only be called religious. Ephraim is a first generation, tough-talking, wire-hard kibbutz administrator. David is a ninth-generation Jerusalemite, a gentle teacher and a dreaming idealist. Neither believes in God. Or do they? In strange, arcane, twentieth-century ways do they instinctively observe His ways, believe in Him without knowing it?"

"And you, Amnon?"

"Not in two thousand years," Amnon answered, grinning impishly in the light before the door to my room. "Or do I?"

Chapter *41*

The car in which I had bummed a ride drove eastward toward Nazareth, then split abruptly southward to skirt the Jezreel Valley, passing Har-Megiddo, that pre-biblical site whose name in English transliteration—Armageddon—has gathered such awful significance. From there it led toward Tanach. Ancient names, places, paths.

A *moshav*, Midrach Oz, set off to one side almost hidden in barley, olive and fruit trees. It was undistinguished, had the usual forlorn *moshav* look, and yet the name Midrach Oz, seemed vaguely familiar.

" 'Oh my soul, tread them down with strength,' you remember the words?" my driver asked.

"Only vaguely," I replied.

"When Deborah and Barak were concealed high on Mt. Tabor with Israelite foot soldiers, they faced Canaanites who had chariots. Chariots then were like tanks today and the Israelites had none. But the chariots got stuck in mud like this sticky stuff on either side of us. Once stuck they couldn't match the tough Israelites, who were excellent foot soldiers. From rout to catastrophe it went, and the swollen waters of the River Kishon blocked the Canaanite escape."

I asked the driver to stop, let me off. He held me there, telling the story of Sisera and Jael. "She was the wife of Heber the Kenite and Sisera commander of Canaanites, fleeing from the Israelites, begged sanctuary in her tent. She let him sleep there. While asleep, she pinned his skull to the floor with a tent peg. So you remember to be careful about sleeping with Israeli women," the driver said, grinning.

"I have no chariot, only a typewriter," I told him. "And no army."

"You'll probably be safe then," he said and drove on.

I walked down the lane toward the *moshav* thinking of Midrach Oz. It meant strength. And it was still surrounded by a sea of mud.

Slender, short people walked about. In the village store I asked for the main office and found in it the secretary, who was having a council meeting. Jobi and his councilmen were all short and slight with caramel eyes, very lively and smiling. They looked like Arabs, and I recalled that Yemenite Jews were once pagan nomads, later converting to Judaism. After Mohammed's powerful vision captured the Fertile Crescent, most Jews left Judaism, attracted by force and Islam's easier ways. Only a few remained Jews and all of these, thirteen hundred years after the Moslem take-over, were ingathered to Israel in 1947. Only fifty thousand of them were in Yemen and they came on "silver eagles" wings, just the way these Yemenite Jews had always in fable known they would ultimately return to the Promised Land.

Jobi explained that the members of the *moshav* had come from the same village where they had been artisans and craftsmen, not farmers. For two years after their arrival they had lived in crude, makeshift camps and worked as road builders and tree planters. Some had worked in various kibbutzim learning agriculture and these now formed the nucleus for the moshav. Jewish Agency specialists had helped and still helped manage the vegetable farming operation. Yet the first years had been heartbreaking failures. "Artisans, shopkeepers, and craftsmen do not easily make farmers," Jobi said. "Things are now better."

Most members had switched to dairy cattle and a special breed of sheep for milking. Vegetables had been a disaster. "Too long between paychecks!" With milk the check came weekly. All the councilmen smiled and nodded.

An old man of beautiful face entered. He was Jobi's uncle, and all deferred to him. Unlike Jobi, the uncle was tall, had long, curling earlocks, and wore a typical European suitcoat against the damp. He accepted no coffee, explaining in his clipped, Arabic-flavored Hebrew that he had had a deadly, evil dream that night and was fasting against it, to counter it. He had been in the synagogue since early morning and would return there to remain all day. He would not reveal the dream; he touched his lips. Sealed! All was at once clear. A prophet, a seer, as Deborah had been a seer, did not reveal a vision's threat until he himself had personally intervened with God to avert it.

The old man returned to the synagogue and Jobi invited me to see it. We left shoes and boots outside and entered the small, austere building. The floor and the altar were covered with gorgeous Persian carpeting. Against the south wall, facing Jerusalem, was a row of a dozen Torahs; the old man passed by, kissing each Torah cover. Nine men remained behind to pray with Jobi's uncle, to help him in his effort to avert whatever evil he had envisioned.

"He talks to God," Jobi said quietly. "And sometimes God replies. I have never known my uncle to be needlessly worried by God nor to be given a false solution by Him."

"But you did not stay to pray with him!" I said.

"No, I am not so religious as the old ones. My prayers are ineffective. My generation goes to synagogue on Sabbath but not every day as do my uncle and the old ones."

"And your children, are they observant?"

"Less than I. The exile in Yemen was one thing and it led to strong religious feelings. But now we are home and our religious needs must change."

"The army has changed you?"

"The army created a new life for us. I spend forty to sixty days a year in the infantry, a lieutenant, and yes, that has changed me. And it will greatly change my children."

"But suppose there is peace?"

Jobi shook his head. "There will be no peace. I know the Arabs. Our fathers spent all their lives among them. We were friendly in Yemen with our Arab neighbors. When we left they wept. My uncle was so happy to leave that he went around and gave all his money away to the Arabs." Jobi roared with laughter. "He thought we wouldn't need it in Israel, what with the Messiah's coming and all that."

"But if you were friends with Arabs in Yemen, why not here?"

"We were under *them*, there. They are under *us*, here. To an Arab, pride is life. I do not believe they will ever accept Jews as equals. Still, they can live with us, live better than among themselves. They hate us but they hate each other more. So we will manage." Jobi smiled. "A husband and wife can build a satisfactory home even though they distrust and dislike each other. I have seen it done. For it is sometimes better that way than for both of them to face separately a hostile world." Jobi shrugged.

Jobi's wife squealed in anguish as we walked into her home. She had just come from feeding and bedding the cattle and she was manure-spattered. "Are your American women so vain?"

Jobi asked, laughing as his wife disappeared to change clothes. "We are told that Americans make the best husbands and Yemenites the worst. We make our women work, bear many children, care for the family. And so on. Yemenite men have almost no heart disease. But you Americans work your hearts out for your wives so that you can die early and leave rich widows." Jobi's eyes twinkled.

"But when intermarriage comes and you marry westernized Israelis, then you'll have to change, to give women equal rights," I said.

"We like to marry cousins," Jobi said. "In all we have sixty families here, and there is among us only one who is not a relative. She is from Tunis and used to similar ways. So you see we keep our ancient traditional ways . . . and live longer." He laughed.

Jobi's wife came back dressed in an attractive flowered dress, her head arranged in a bright scarf. She was a beautiful woman with broad cheekbones, more sturdily built than Jobi, so that one had the feeling that Jobi had picked her as he would a good brood cow. She had already borne seven children for him.

Neighbors crowded in from everywhere in the village. "We like a chance to have a party," Jobi told me. "We're glad you came." It was not yet noon.

Women stayed in the background, served the men, were decorous, drank little.

A middle-aged man of commanding presence came in and asked to speak with Jobi about a marketing problem. "Shlomo is our best farmer," someone said of him. "We depend on his judgment and skill."

When Jobi and Shlomo had finished their discussion, in Arabic, Jobi introduced his friend and at once he asked me a question: "Why don't you of the West let us alone? We can settle things with the Arabs if you allow it."

Thinking to test the worldly knowledge of Shlomo, I asked if he had any idea how many Americans there were. He knew. Russians? He knew. "I also know about oil and that we are the land bridge to Africa, to those hundred million customers you want. But you disturb things here, you and Russia. If you leave us alone, we'll make peace. Peace brings you good business, oil. Only peace."

"But left alone, you two do not seem to be able to make a peace of any sort," I said.

"You give us no chance to make peace."

We walked outside. Shlomo had come on his tractor, the only vehicle that could move on the quaggy road. His farmhand sat on the fender while Shlomo took the seat.

"Would peace be advanced if you took more land? From the Nile to the Euphrates, the Greater Israel Movement's philosophy?"

"No." Shlomo said quietly. "We have too much now, too many Arabs. We need only borders we can defend."

"I don't agree," his young helper said. "We could use Jordan. Maybe Syria. Lebanon. It is ours. The Torah tells us so. Why don't the Arabs understand that? They read our Torah. They know how it must be."

"You are a young fool," Shlomo snapped. "We need safe borders and to be left alone by the outside big powers. Only that!" He started the tractor, backed out, shifted, and started down the sodden road, mud flying off the huge wheels.

The party dispersed. Nobody seemed tipsy, all were now ready for work.

I glanced at Jobi's library. *God's Little Acre; An American Tragedy; The Official Six Day War; Confessions of a Woman.* Six volumes of the Mishnah (well-used) and five volumes of the Tanach, with-commentary (also well-used). Jobi told me that nobody at the *moshav* had ever attended a university. Only a few had finished high school. But two had gone to a teachers' seminary, he proudly told me.

The pure herd of humans at Midrach Oz maintained its genetic purity by marrying cousins. Why cousins? "We like each other," Jobi replied. Thus was there a unique, inbred genetic pool to be used by future Israelis. A genetic jump was possible, perhaps already underway.

We walked outside to watch Jobi's wife scythe a swath of

Atlas sorgo. Then she pitchforked the tall, heavy grass into a horse-drawn wagon, and later forked it into feed bunks for the cows. In a separate bunk she fed a concentrate mixture of fortified grain and cottonseed meal. She was very quick, coordinated, experienced. Jobi leaned on a hay bunk and watched her work and his eyes shone with approval and great love. "A good woman," he said. "None better. After school you shall see my seven fine children."

Chapter 42

Israel was a Jewish Agency field representative, an agricultural adviser for the Tanach area. I met him on the road outside Midrach Oz and he allowed me to ride along with him as he made his rounds. He was a short, balding man who himself was a farmer.

We drove past Megiddo, a fortified hill already a strong city in 1478 B.C.E., when Thutmose III besieged it. War after war swirled about and over it from then on. Israel remarked that the forty years of peace that came to Israel after Barak's victory over Sisera was, really, a very long span.

The names of the Tanach settlements, *moshavs*, were all biblical and Israel loved to say them: Deborah, Barak, Heber, Jael, Omen, Ram On. And more. They sat in three clutches of four villages, built for defense before the Six Day War. They hugged the ground like solid rock, yet were on the same mucky land that buried Sisera's Canaanites. Again the Jews used this mud, this time to produce food. Rich, quaggy mud. A strange change of affairs. A strange people, these Jews.

"It is odd," Israel remarked, "but we cannot mix ethnic groups within a village. If we do, the *moshav* fails. So each *moshav* is nearly pure for origin, as Midrach Oz was. You see, they do not think or work on the same levels and the problems of settling them are great without fighting cultural differences. Israelis call the Arabs primitive and yet we have people here who are as primitive as Arab fellahin. They cannot get along with educated Israelis any better than Israelis get along with fellahin.

"But it will remain that way only one generation, two at most. Even now they use a common store, recreation hall, schools. In this way they get to know one another socially and slowly, slowly, slowly, they get used to one another's ways. The parents may have different cultures but their kids won't.

"When American black kids in integrated schools must return from the homogeneity of middle-class schools to the reality of lower-class black homes, it's hard for them. We are not Negroes and Caucasians. We are all refugees. We are all Jews. These two conditions make us unique."

"They, white and black, are all Christians—" I said.

"Not really. They move easily in and out of the church, a possibility not granted to us even if we wanted to pass. As Jews we are stuck here. And it is our single most important common denominator. These kids go to school, share army experience. Their parents shop in the same store, serve on committees together. Tomorrow the kids will intermarry and we will then have a new, better, more useful generation than that of either parent."

"Do you find one ethnic group more successful at farming than another?"

"In general, they all start off being pretty clumsy at it. Only the so-called stupid Kurdistani Jews succeed at once, because they were farmers and shepherds in their homeland. Too, they had such terribly harsh treatment as Kurdish Jews that once here they understood how relatively good things were. If you've had no favors, tiny ones, suddenly come upon, seem a fortune."

Israel took me to another *moshav* and we talked to another Shlomo, a Moroccan. He showed us his tin huts each holding a thousand to fifteen hundred broilers. He hoped to market 950 a month. He also kept five hundred laying hens and raised sugar beets on his twelve acres of land. His wife, a nurse, was away working and Shlomo told us that between the two of them they managed to earn $350 a month, before taxes that took about forty percent of his gross earnings. "And we don't mind," Shlomo told us. "It is a small payment for what we have here."

"Was life then so harsh for you in Morocco?"

"Not so bad. We had a kind of relationship with Arabs. Sure, we had periodic pogroms but only a few were killed. But after 1956 matters grew worse. For example, we lived high in the Atlas Mountains and the Arabs below us got sick, one time, and accused us of poisoning the waters that flowed past us on down to them. Then, one time, a merchant was accused of raping and then murdering Arab girls in his shop. Oh, what trouble that caused!" Shlomo flicked his hand in the French fashion. "But we knew who was behind it all—the French officials starting rumors to divide and conquer. They were the anti-Semites, not the Arabs."

"Shlomo uses Arab labor to weed his beets," Israel informed me. "He hires them through contractors, just as you hire Mexican grape pickers."

"And do you get along well with them?" I asked.

"No trouble," Shlomo said. "But they do not look me in the eye. They are sullen. I feel their hatred."

"A growing thing?"

"Yes. The more we have to do with them, the less they like us. After all, we are the bosses now, not them. In the end we must defeat them so thoroughly that they will recognize once and for all time that we are here to stay. Only then can we have peace."

We drove away to visit a mixed Iranian and Moroccan village that was limping along under the guidance of Yosef and his wife Haya, two Polish Jews who, Israel told me, tried to keep peace between the two ethnic groups. The *moshav* had not prospered.

We sat in the spare room of Yosef and Haya. No pictures adorned the wall. It was like a temporary barracks. The two farmers were middle-aged, relaxed, at peace. They seemed like two people who had made their final deal with death, signed all the contracts, and were satisfied to wait with God for the end of the transaction.

Yosef was the last survivor of his family in Poland. He had fled east in 1939, and posed as a Russian. When he returned to Poland, after the war, he found no trace of his family. His family's flour mill had been confiscated by the state. Yosef had grown a beard, had aged with the terrible times, and none recognized him as he sought for and got a job in his own mill.

For thirteen years Yosef had worked there as a common laborer, hoping that something fortuitous would turn up for him so that he could reveal himself and not be penalized for his defection from Poland. Nothing had. And the statute of limitations for war reparations came and passed, yet he did not dare reveal himself to collect his due. In the end he got nothing for damages suffered in the war.

"Who cares?" Yosef said blandly. "I am here. I have Haya. Who needs their money!" His grin widened, ending in a deeply happy chuckle. Israel roared with laughter. Several curious neighbors crowded in and joined in the laughter. It was contagious. But Yosef and Haya merely chuckled, smiled, seeming incapable of full laughter.

Haya had the look of an intellectual turned farmer. Graying, body lean and brown, simply dressed, without makeup, she looked at us out of curiously kindly eyes. She had escaped from the Warsaw ghetto only to be captured by Germans and sent to the concentration camp of Maidenek, where she lost her parents. Later, at Auschwitz, she lost two sisters. Moved again, she watched while one sister and brother-in-law stripped and marched to the gas chamber. There was another brother, but Haya had never learned of his fate.

In 1945 as the Russians moved west toward victory, Haya was evacuated to Ravensbruck, in Germany. Soon the survivors discovered their jailers had fled and Haya simply walked barefooted out the gate and on to Malkov and then Leipzig. She had no plan, no hope, no purpose. She had only a compulsion to keep moving, to be free in the open, on her own. At the Elbe, the Russians found her and gave her sanctuary.

Haya told all this with a quiet smile on her face, as if she were rehearsing a play, a fiction, perhaps a vignette of horror so distant in time that relating it seemed almost naïve. In fact, she grew embarrassed at her words and said, "Oh, why do you want to hear of such things? They were so common. There are thousands with such stories."

But there were those vivid numbers on her arm. And two fingers were gone from her left hand, cut off by a machine she had tended in a concentration camp factory. The Germans killed sick or useless people, so Haya dared not take the rest her injury warranted. Friends staunched the blood and bound the wound, and Haya hid her hand when supervisors passed. The Germans never knew.

"Is it not unbearable for you to know that German tourists come here, travel about, are at ease on vacation in Israel?" I asked them.

"Not at all," Yosef said. "The Nazis were many years ago. It is not healthy to hate, it is vain and self-destructive. And one does not blame an entire people for the evil of a few. At first it was not so with me. I have killed many Germans. But now I am purged of hate. I know myself. I too have killed."

"And the young Germans?" Haya asked sweetly. "Are they to be blamed for the fathers' evil ways? I cannot. . ."

Israel stared hard at his shoes, gulping, and I too felt the near overpowering urge to weep, to protect myself from the searing saintliness manifest in these two simple, orphaned farmers.

"Our Polish children do not understand how Jews could have been led unresisting to slaughter," Israel continued. "They do not accept that Nazis duped Russians, Poles, Hungarians into unawareness just as they duped Jews. A Polish Christian is as helpless before butchers as a Polish Jew. But the young do not understand this. They think they are too clever, too wise, to be duped. . ."

"And they are. They will not trust Arab promises," Yosef said.

"If your young are so certain, so intractable, can there ever be peace?" I asked.

"No peace," Yosef said slowly. "With the Arabs there can never be peace."

"Suppose you gave back the lands captured in 1967. Would there be peace?"

"Arabs do not play for fun. We cannot play for fun. We were attacked, we died, we won. Now we are *safe*. Give up our security? Children's talk! Diplomat's talk!" Yosef said.

"Then there must be wars, and wars. . ."

Yosef shrugged. "In 1967 when the sirens sounded we did not even bother to go to the shelters. Why should we, who have heard German sirens, Polish sirens, Russian sirens, now worry about what Arabs can do to us? Let them come. Now or anytime. We shall lose, or we shall win, but now and anytime hereafter we shall fight. That much we have learned."

A young Iranian girl burst through the door and interrupted Yosef's statement. She was sobbing and wracked with a deep unhappiness. She flung herself before the feet of Israel and begged him to find a house for her husband so that she would not have to live with her father-in-law.

"Let your father-in-law build you a house," Israel said gently.

"He hasn't the money," the girl sobbed. "Please. Please help us."

Then the father-in-law burst into the house and he too took his place at the feet of Israel. Only he kissed Israel's shoes, much to Israel's embarrassment, so that he gently raised them both up and took them to the door. He returned to tell me that the girl, raised in Israel, wanted to leave the patriarchal home and the old man, from Iran, wanted her to stay. "She is modern, wants out." Israel said. "The father knows only the Oriental ways and wishes to keep his family close, for pleasure and profit. You recall the years Jacob worked for Laban to finally get his wives? Laban used his son-in-law exactly as this Persian patriarch uses his daughter-in-law. But she won't stand for it. So we'll find a place for her."

Yosef and Haya, the young bride, her ancient father-in-law,

Israel himself, neighbors . . . they all came together in a quaint tableau that floated dreamlike across the mind. But they *were* real, with real problems and a real will to solve them, to make secure the State of Israel for its people.

"One day," Israel said, "We will have a physical and mental type of human different from anything the world has yet seen. Not better but more useful, more humane. More decent. You will see."

Chapter *43*

The day before returning to the United States, I went to Jerusalem to see Yosi, to ask his pardon for dumping him, to say good-bye because he really was a wonderful man, although afflicted.

I had no chance to apologize, for Yosi grinned when he saw me and took me in a bear hug so tight I saw visions of the saintly Maimon crushed by that exuberant Polish Amazon.

We spent the day together, drinking brandy, coffee, buying gifts for home, generally easing me back into the Western world.

We wandered through Mea Shearim, that transplanted Polish ghetto where Orthodox Jews observe the punctilios of the Law— and are supported in their studies by Jews all over the world.

Yosi did not like Mea Shearim. But he knew a rabbi, head of a yeshiva, with whom his father had grown up. Yosi's father had turned printer but his friend had turned scholar.

Rabbi T. was pleased to see Yosi but he seemed to see at once Yosi's sickness and showed unusual compassion for him, finally leaving his desk to come and sit next to him, linking arms.

"I must tell you of an American who came in to see me yesterday," Rabbi T. remarked in excellent English, learned during frequent tours to America to raise money for his yeshiva. "He is a very shrewd man, very successful in business, very wealthy and our most generous patron. He told me of his unease for having devoted his life to business and not Torah. Now he wants to shelve all those things and return here to me and a life of Torah study. He was very earnest, sincere, a man not given to impulse or frivolity. He had thought long about it. . ."

"Marvelous," Yosi interrupted. "You who are always short of funds can now have a live-in philanthropist. I'm happy for you."

The rabbi smiled. "I told him not to do it. To stay there."

"You what!" Yosi half-yelled.

"Yosi, a crow cannot sing like a canary. This man has spent his life tuning his mind to business, money, schemes. He cannot suddenly turn off these years of training and suddenly convert his mind to the discipline of Torah. He would be filled with self-contempt at his failure."

"How did you tell him?" Yosi asked in a very tiny voice.

"I said, 'If God had wanted you to be a scholar, He would have made you one. But He made you the clever businessman you are. Return to your family, business, life in New York, as God intended.'"

"Oh ho!" Yosi chortled. "I get it now. You want him back there earning dollars for you here. Clever."

"No, Yosi. You think me cynical. But I meant it. He did not take it well and left in anger. I am certain he will search until he finds a yeshiva that will take him. Then, both the yeshiva and my friend will be unhappy."

"Rabbi, permit me—you were wrong . . . you needed him."

"If God had wanted me to have a well-endowed yeshiva, He would have sent me a wiser rich American."

"Rabbi," I asked, "let me pose a terrible question. If you think it blasphemous, don't answer and I'll understand."

"Questions are never blasphemous. Answers, sometimes."

"You speak of God's will. Let me ask a question of you, the same one I asked of a teacher in a religious kibbutz near Ashkelon: how can you justify God's willingness that six million Jews be murdered in Europe?"

"The teacher's reply?" Rabbi T. asked, his eyes deep pools of sorrow. "He said, 'If you believe, there is no questioning. If you do not believe, there is no need to answer.'"

Rabbi T. stared at me a long time. Meanwhile he patted Yosi's arm as if in consolation, encouragement. Finally he said, "You did right to ask the question. I think the kibbutz teacher wrong because that question is the most significant one for generations now alive and to come, it is *the* question. I think that we have learned from those murders, those times, that hell has come above ground, is no longer below, is among us and stalks the earth. We now know that. And it is through the Jews that we have been made aware, they were the instruments to announce it, to warn mankind that Satan is abroad and that if man does not follow God, now, not later, he will perish from the earth as His emissaries did, all six million of them. An early warning.

"Translate Job to read Jew and you begin to see it. Job, too, was restored. And the remnant of Jews has been restored to Israel. The Jews are the evidence of God's hope for mankind. The six million martyrs warn of the absolute scandal of Satan's seeming victory over men.

"Some say we are witness to mankind's second Fall. But there have been many Falls. Still, in our time we have seen the most terrifying Fall God has ever visited upon mankind. And His greatest miracle: three million Jews living in their own land, Israel."

"A harsh God. Too harsh. Terrible," Yosi said. "I will not tolerate Him."

"A harsh God, Yosi. Harsh. Terrible," Rabbi T. replied gently, "but he is our God and there is no other." Rabbi T. shrugged and nodded. "A timeless question-answer for us who are Jews. You are here. I am here . . . is that not the miracle of miracles?"

Chapter 44

A friend, an old man reared in Little Rock, Arkansas, drove me to the airport outside Tel Aviv, "that modern Nineveh," as Ben-Gurion once had labeled it. Morris had been in Israel fifty-five years, owned a fleet of seven trucks, and made a fair living from them. Now eighty, he planned to return to the United States after his retirement. "But only for a visit," he said. "I have never been back and I'd like to see all my people."

"When do you plan to retire?"

"At eighty-two."

I asked him about the changes that he must have seen in his long sojourn in the land of Israel.

"Strange things have happened here," Morris replied. "Odd things that I can't explain. The Jews here are different, and I can't tell you just how. But an old Arab friend of mine, from Nablus, whom I had not seen for twenty years—until the 1967 war made it possible for us to meet in East Jerusalem—he walked with me and talked about the changes. We spent the entire day together in fellowship. He is a fine, honorable man. But we could not quite catch the intimate, easy air we once shared. He was slightly diffident, withdrawn. Just before we parted he asked a strange question. 'Tell me, Moshe,' he asked, 'what has happened to these Jews? Our boys used to walk along the streets and sometimes throw stones through the windows of Jewish homes in the Jewish quarter. Quickly the Jews would douse their lights, close their shutters, become quiet. Nothing more. Our Arab youth meant no harm. It was only a joke. After all, Jews and Arabs, as you and I are cousins and friends. We got along very well together. But now the Jews rush out to fight us. Tell me, Moshe. What happened to them?'"

"He was a very old man," Moshe went on, "and I could not offend him. How to explain? So I just told him that we had changed, that's all, just changed. Actually, had I been pressed to explain, truly explain, I don't think I could have."